# Justice Douglas and Freedom of Speech

*compiled and with an introduction by*

HAIG BOSMAJIAN

The Scarecrow Press, Inc.
Metuchen, N.J., & London 1980

Excerpts from Go East, Young Man: The Early Years, by William O. Douglas, copyright © 1974 by William O. Douglas, are printed by permission of Random House, Inc.

The opinions reproduced in this volume were taken from the United States Reports.

**Library of Congress Cataloging in Publication Data**

Douglas, William Orville, 1898-
Justice Douglas and freedom of speech.

Includes index.
1. Liberty of speech--United States--Cases.
2. Freedom of information--United States--Cases.
3. Douglas, William Orville, 1898- I. Bosmajian, Haig A. II. Title.
KF4772.A7D68 342'.73'0850264 79-26635
ISBN 0-8108-1276-2



Manufactured in the United States of America

TABLE OF CONTENTS

# INTRODUCTION

By September 1922, when William Orville Douglas had taken a freight train out of Yakima, Washington, to go east to study law at Columbia University, he had witnessed as a youth the mistreatment of the poor, the injustices heaped upon the migrant workers, and the violence against the Wobblies in the Yakima Valley. As a child not yet in his teens, he had fought a bout with infantile paralysis, strengthening his spindly legs by hiking in the Cascade foothills and mountains.

After his father, a minister, died in 1904, when the future Supreme Court Justice was only six years old, the Douglas family moved to Yakima. There the young William developed a dislike of the clergy, except for a Dr. William Robinson, whose appeal, declared Douglas in <u>Go East, Young Man</u>, "was in his application of the teachings of Christ to the problems of life--and in particular to those of the Yakima Valley." The other preachers, said Douglas,

> seemed to be defenders of the status quo and against the rabble. The rabble were the hundreds of itinerant workers who came north with the sun, picked Yakima's fruit, and moved on to Canada's wheat harvest. Some were IWW's (Industrial Workers of the World); others were families traveling by jitney from valley to valley in pursuit of a livelihood. Dr. Robinson pricked the conscience of Yakima when he talked to them. The other local ministers treated them as scum. Vagrancy was a crime--how much of a crime, I was to discover years later.

A brief boyhood experience as a "stool pigeon" for a minister "bent on ridding Yakima of prostitutes and bootleggers" eventually led Douglas "to feel a warmth for all these miserable people, something I never felt for the high churchman who hired me. They were scum that society had produced--misfits, maladjusted, disturbed, and really sick." This experience resulted in Douglas's "resentment against hypocrites in church clothes who raise their denunciations against the petty criminals, while their own sins mount high. This feeling somehow aligned me emotionally with the miserable people who make up the chaff of society."

While Douglas spent the summer months working in the orchards and packing houses, the winter found him rummaging in the alleys and garbage cans of Yakima for burlap sacks which he sold to the produce house or searching for "scrap iron for which a junk dealer might pay a pittance." This all left a strong impression on Douglas: "Years later, in Washington, D. C., I saw the junk collectors with their two-wheel carts slowly making their rounds in the early morning hours. They were usually Black men and I felt sorry for them recalling my own experience."

After discussing the discrimination against blacks and Indians in Yakima, Douglas goes on to write: "By the time my teen-age years ended, I had met a different group of outcasts, who made a very deep impression on me. They were the Wobblies, or IWW's, of the Far West.... Though Yakima denounced them as criminals, I came to know the Wobblies as people who deserved more than our society had meted out to them."

The mistreatment of the Wobblies was made especially clear to Douglas in 1917, when at the age of nineteen he witnessed a trainload of workers rounded up by the government. Douglas describes his reaction: "The train that passed through Yakima was not carrying men on display. These were sealed boxcars carrying human beings, thirty or forty in each car. The authorities were taking outcasts through our city. There were no toilets, no food, no water, just sealed boxcars with these poor bastards inside. I walked home with tears in my eyes."

As for the police, young Douglas saw them as representing "the ultimate personality of the Establishment that owned and ran the Yakima Valley. They were harsh and relentless and bore down heavily on the nonconformist.... I knew their victims too intimately to align myself with the police. My heart was with the impoverished, restless underdogs who were IWW's."

After graduating from high school, Douglas continued

his education on a scholarship at Whitman College in Walla Walla, Washington. The impact of young Douglas's education and work on his later tolerance and encouragement of unorthodox speech is alluded to by Vern Countryman in Douglas of the Supreme Court:

> He arrived there [Whitman College] in the fall of 1916 with little else but the bicycle he rode. Varying jobs as store clerk, waiter, and janitor provided food and a tent provided shelter during the school terms. During summer vacations there was employment in the wheat fields and an opportunity to debate with other laborers the revolutionary doctrines of the Industrial Workers of the World. This experience may have built up some immunity against alarm over extravagant political discussion, but it did not produce a revolutionary.

By the time Douglas left for his studies at the Columbia Law School in 1922, his spirit of independence, tolerance, and self-reliance had been developed in the agricultural fields of Washington, the streets of Yakima, and the mountains of the Cascades. "I learned early," Douglas wrote in the autobiographical Of Men and Mountains, "that the richness of life is found in adventure. Adventure calls on all the faculties of mind and spirit. It develops self-reliance and independence. Life then teems with excitement. But man is not ready for adventure unless he is rid of fear. For fear confines him and limits his scope. He stays tethered by strings of doubt and indecisions and has only a small and narrow world to explore."

Again and again one finds in Go East, Young Man a concern for conquering a variety of fears; Douglas concluded the chapter entitled "Fear" with: "Once I wrote: When man knows how to live dangerously, he is not afraid to die. When he is not afraid to die, he is, strangely, free to live. With the passage of time, I would state the basic idea a bit differently. Death is inevitable, but the thought of it usually breeds fear. Yet the fear that is truly debilitating is the fear of the unknown in the environment around us. When we rid ourselves of that fear, we are free to live and can become bold, courageous, and reliant."

The fear that the young Douglas experienced at his father's funeral in August 1904 was somewhat overcome by the presence of the nearby towering mountains: "As I stood by the edge of the grave a wave of lonesomeness swept over me. Then I became afraid--afraid of being left alone, afraid because the grave held my defender and protector. These feelings were deepened by the realization that Mother was afraid and lonely too. My throat choked up and I started to cry. I remembered the words of the minister, who had said to me, 'You must now be a man, sonny.' I tried to steel myself and control my emotions." Then Douglas looked toward the mountains and saw Mt. Adams "towering over us on the west. It was dark purple and white in the August day and its shoulders of basalt were heavy with glacial snow. It was a giant whose head touched the sky." The six-year-old Douglas stopped crying: "My eyes dried. Adams stood cool and calm, unperturbed by the event that had stirred us so deeply. Suddenly the mountain seemed to be a friend, a force for me to tie to, a symbol of stability and strength."

The transitory nature of the lives of humans and their inventions and the permanence of nature and the universe were "facts" that made a deep impression on Douglas and influenced his outlook toward people. His Physics and Geology professor at Whitman College, Dr. Benjamin Brown, wrote Douglas,

> lived at the cosmic level, not the ideological one. Russia had gone Red in the revolution of 1917, but Daddy Brown knew that come spring, the fields of Russia would be alive with the brilliance of wildflowers. Creeds and dogma come and go, but planetary life goes on undisturbed. He taught us man's small role in the universe, the immensity of the Glacial age, the magnitude of the Pleistocene, and so on. He taught us to observe the winds and the rocks. Rocks become round by rolling, and that was all we needed to know to find old watercourses. Wind carried dust. Who loses the dust? Who gets it? Solve that, and you know what lands are becoming poorer, what lands richer. That lesson was useful to me years later in North Africa.

Douglas shared Professor Brown's concept of life after death: "The loveliest image Daddy Brown could draw was illustrated by a skull he had unearthed near an apple tree. The root of the tree had grown through the eyes of the skull, sucking up into the tree the entire brain of the deceased. 'How wonderful to become an apple tree!' he exclaimed. 'Can anyone think of anything more choice for an afterlife?'" Concludes Douglas: "Father would have been shocked, but I shared Daddy Brown's feelings."

This view of life and death, coupled with his attitude toward fear, came to be reflected in Douglas's tolerance for diversity, for new ideas, for "foreign" ideologies; with such a cosmic conception of life, seemingly immediate dangers, physical and ideological, come to be perceived as less perilous to society, dangerous only to those who are afraid. Douglas clearly agreed with Justice Brandeis, whom he greatly admired; in his 1951 Dennis dissent he quoted at length from Brandeis's famous Whitney concurring opinion. "Fear of serious injury cannot alone justify suppression of free speech and assembly. Men fear witches and burnt women. It is the function of speech to free men from the bondage of irrational fears." "Those who won our independence by revolution," Brandeis wrote, "were not cowards. They did not fear political change. They did not exalt order at the cost of liberty." These were sentiments Douglas could easily accept.

The independence, tolerance, and self-reliance developed by the youthful Douglas was to be reflected years later in his First Amendment decisions related to the civil liberties of "dangerous" political propagandists, unpopular religious groups, outspoken street-corner agitators, nonconformist professors, protesting students, annoying distributors of obscene materials, and minorities demonstrating to get civil rights long denied them.

But Douglas's encouragement of tolerance of differing political and religious views, his criticism of Yakima's political and religious leaders, and his spirit of independence did not set well with all the citizens of his hometown. When Franklin Roosevelt named Douglas to the Supreme Court, the Yakima Daily Republic published an editorial alluding to Douglas's "strange isms that are not compatible with Americanism," concluding with, "We want to go on record that Yakima is not to blame." "This editorial," Douglas says in Go East, Young Man, "was written by N. K. Buck, one-time police judge and later mayor.... The piece delighted me no end, and I foolishly carried it in my wallet for so long that it finally crumbled away. Unfortunately, someone destroyed that entire edition of the paper after a few hundred copies were run off, and apparently no copies are extant."

The Daily Republic, however, did make some positive editorial comments in other issues. The March 21, 1939, issue ran an editorial beginning with the following paragraph: "By appointing William O. Douglas to the supreme court, President Roosevelt put on the high bench a young man worthy to follow in the tradition of Justice Louis D. Brandeis. Douglas is a leading New Dealer, but he is no weak-kneed sycophant, no mealy-mouthed yes-man. He is a man long since arrived at his liberal conclusions through independent judgment and hard mental application. His knowledge of social and economic organization was tempered by struggle against adversity. Even those persons who cannot agree with Douglas' outlook on life still respect his views because they are honest views." An editorial on the following day, March 22, 1939, stated: "It is not alone because William Orville Douglas has a Yakima background that his nomination is highly satisfactory to the residents of this community. The consensus is that he is qualified to fill the high position to which he has been named.... Douglas has ability of the first rank. He has made his own way. He stands as a refutation of the complaint that there is no longer opportunity for a young man."

On April 4, 1939 the United States Senate confirmed Douglas's nomination to the Supreme Court. But the story was given short shrift by the Daily Republic, which had as its April 4 headline: "MOB SLAYS ENGLISH CONSUL AT MOSUL." In smaller type the paper reported: "Douglas Gains Vote of 62 to 4 on Court Post." The other local paper, the Yakima Morning Herald, on its April 4, 1939 front page carried stories related to an emergency defense bill and the freeing of some New York kidnap suspects. Nowhere was there any mention of the Senate confirmation of Douglas. Nor did the April 5 issue contain any news item related to the appointment of Yakima's most famous resident to the Supreme Court. Meanwhile, 150 miles away, the April 4 Seattle Times carried the headline "SENATE CONFIRMS DOUGLAS."

When Douglas took his seat on the Court several days later, the Daily Republic on April 17 ran a headline dealing with the Court's decision that former membership in the Communist Party did not subject an alien to deportation. Below this story there appeared in smaller type a story about Douglas taking the oath: "An oath to support the constitution and to administer justice impartially today made 40-year-old William O. Douglas the youngest member of the supreme court in 127 years." This was followed with mention of Douglas's Yakima background: "The former chairman of the Securities Commission, who rose in life from a Yakima newsboy and janitor, took his seat on the nation's highest tribunal before a packed courtroom." The Morning Herald did not even bother to mention that Douglas had taken the oath and was now officially seated on the Supreme Court. (Its April 18 issue did, however, have on its front page a large picture of Adolf Hitler, who was celebrating his fiftieth birthday on April 20.)

While Douglas was being disowned by some local residents, his early education, his formative experiences in Yakima, his working associations with the migrant workers and the Wobblies, his reaction to the police, preachers, and propertied class, his hiking in the Cascades--all of these had too great an influence for Yakima to disassociate itself from Douglas. As Fred Rodell has said in Nine Men, "Douglas, despite his Minnesota birth (he was still an infant when his family left the state), was a product of the Pacific Northwest, the last American frontier." Douglas himself observed in Go East, Young Man that the conclusion of the Yakima newspaper that asserted "We want to go on record as saying that Yakima is not to blame" was "humorous, but wrong." Said Douglas: "The Yakima system was in large measure responsible for the kind of person that I became, in the sense that its teachers were quickening influences that helped me see the dimensions of the world of that day."

Fifty-three years after Douglas left Yakima to enter the Columbia Law School and thirty-six years after he was appointed to the Supreme Court, the members of the Court said in their November 14, 1975 message to retiring Justice Douglas: "So much has been said and will be said on other occasions about your remarkable career that no more need be noted now than to recall that it is far more than a record of longevity, for it spanned a period in American history comparable to that of the formative period early in nineteenth century when Marshall and then Taney were here." For thirty-six years the remarkable Justice from Yakima sat on the Court defending especially our First Amendment freedoms against private and governmental censors. Right up to the time of his retirement he took his consistent stand defending freedom of speech.

One month before he left the Court, Douglas was

dissenting in some obscenity cases, when the majority (including all the Nixon appointees) was denying certiorari and in effect upholding the convictions of persons convicted of exhibiting and mailing "obscene" materials. For example, October 14, 1975: 'No. 74-1282. RATNER V. UNITED STATES. C.A. 5th Cir. Certiorari denied. MR. JUSTICE DOUGLAS, being of the view, stated in his previous opinions and those of Mr. Justice Black, that any state or federal ban on, or regulation of, obscenity abridges freedom of speech and of the press contrary to the First and Fourteenth Amendments, would grant certiorari and summarily reverse the judgment. Reported below: 502 F. 2d 1300."

In June 1975, five months before his retirement, Douglas declared in his concurring opinion in Erznoznik v. City of Jacksonville, a case dealing with nudity being shown on a drive-in movie screen visible from a highway: "Any ordinance which regulates movies on the basis of content, whether by an obscenity standard or by some other criterion, impermissibly intrudes upon the free speech rights guaranteed by the First and Fourteenth Amendments." In a footnote to his opinion Douglas reasserted: 'I adhere to my view that any state or federal regulation of obscenity is prohibited by the Constitution." For almost two decades since his Roth dissent in 1957 Douglas had consistently taken the position that obscenity was speech protected by the First Amendment.

Amongst all the Justices who have sat on the United States Supreme Court only one has given his full support to the First Amendment's guarantee of freedom of speech as applied to obscenity and symbolic speech and loyalty oaths and group libel and offensive speech and controversial religious and political speech. While other Justices have given First Amendment protection to obscene materials they have not given the same protection to symbolic speech. Other Justices have found offensive speech unprotected; still others have decided loyalty oaths constitute a legitimate governmental inquiry into a person's beliefs and associations. But only Justice Douglas has had the wisdom to see, for over the longest period of time, the value and necessity of giving constitutional protection to a diversity of kinds of speech to maintain and perpetuate the free society. So important is the need to maintain free and open discussion, to be watchful that the State does not get into the business of thought control, to recognize that different people use different means of communication, that Douglas has given freedom of speech a preferred position in the hierarchy of our constitutional rights. No other Supreme Court Justice has argued at such length for the protection of so many different kinds of expression and means of communication.

After Douglas's appointment to the Court in 1939 very few other Justices came close to his consistent protection of the First Amendment rights, especially freedom of speech. Such Justices as Felix Frankfurter, Robert Jackson, Fred Vinson, Tom Clark, Earl Warren, John Harlan, William Brennan, Potter Stewart, Warren Burger, and others did on occasion find themselves lining up with Douglas on various freedom of speech cases, some agreeing with him more often than others, depending on whether the cases dealt with picketing, obscenity, loyalty oaths, investigating committees, symbolic speech, or distribution of literature on the streets or in shopping centers.

Of the Supreme Court Justices, Hugo Black, who was appointed to the Court two years before Douglas, is the one with whom Douglas has been most often identified on First Amendment issues. But absolutist that he may have been, Black's record on freedom of speech is not the same as Douglas's. In his February 1956 Yale Law Journal article, "Mr. Justice Black: A Biographical Appreciation," John P. Frank said of Black: "His opinions on the subject dearest to him, freedom of speech, are oddly fragmentary; most of the powerful free speech dissents have been by Justice Douglas, and yet the views of the two are not quite the same."

On the freedom of speech issue it was not Hugo Black but Thurgood Marshall with whom Douglas had most in common, Marshall, the great-grandson of a slave, who had been appointed to the Court in 1967, almost thirty years after Douglas had taken his seat on the Court. While Marshall and Black lined up with Douglas on cases related to obscenity, loyalty oaths, and investigating committees, it was Marshall, not Black, who joined Douglas on the several symbolic speech cases, such as Tinker, Logan Valley, and Street.

## Symbolic Speech

Before Marshall joined the Court, Douglas and Black had been at odds on whether First Amendment protection should be given to such forms of communication as picketing, sit-ins, and demonstrations. While Douglas gave the civil rights demonstrators sitting-in to desegregate a Louisiana public library First Amendment protection in Brown v. Louisiana (1966), Black dissented, declaring: "The First Amendment, I think, protects speech, writings, and expression of view in any manner in which they can be legitimately and validly communicated. But I have never believed that it gives any person or group of persons the constitutional right to go wherever they want, whenever they please, without regard to the rights of private or public property or to state law.... Though the First Amendment guarantees the rights of speech, press, and religion, it does not guarantee to any person the right to use someone else's property, even that owned by government and dedicated to other purposes, as a stage to express dissident ideas."

Again, in Adderley v. Florida (1966), Black argued against finding for the civil rights demonstrators who had assembled in front of a county jail to protest racial segregation, including segregation in the jail. Douglas, with whom Warren, Brennan, and Fortas concurred, disagreed with Black and stated in his dissenting opinion:

> The jailhouse, like an executive mansion, a legislative chamber, a courthouse, or the statehouse itself ... is one of the seats of government, whether it be the Tower of London, the Bastille, or a small county jail. And when it houses political prisoners or those who many think are unjustly held, it is an obvious center for protest. The right to petition for the redress of grievances has an ancient history and is not limited to writing a letter or sending a telegram to a congressman; it is not confined to appearing before the local city council, or writing letters to the President or Governor or Mayor.... Conventional methods of petitioning may be, and often have been, shut off to large groups of our citizens. Legislators turn deaf ears; formal complaints may be routed endlessly through a bureaucratic maze; courts may let the wheels of justice grind very slowly. Those who do not control television and radio, those who cannot afford to advertise in newspapers or circulate pamphlets may have only a more limited type of access to public officials. Their methods should not be condemned as tactics

> of obstruction and harassment as long as the assembly and petition are peaceable, as these were.

Black disagreed and speaking for the Court concluded that "the State, no less than a private owner of property, has power to preserve the property under its control for the use to which it is lawfully dedicated. For this reason there is no merit to the petitioners' argument that they had a constitutional right to stay on the property, over the jail custodian's objections, because this 'area chosen for the peaceful civil rights demonstration was not only "reasonable" but also particularly appropriate....'"

In still another 1966 Supreme Court decision, Cox v. Louisiana, in which the majority found for the civil rights demonstrators involved in courthouse picketing, Black dissented in one of the judgments in that case. "Picketing," said Black, "though it may be utilized to communicate ideas, is not speech and therefore is not of itself protected by the First Amendment."

One year later, Black joined the majority in Walker v. City of Birmingham upholding the convictions of the Southern Christian Leadership Conference Leaders--Wyatt Walker, Martin Luther King, Ralph Abernathy, Fred Shuttlesworth, Andrew Young, and others--who had violated an injunction against parading and demonstrating in Birmingham, Alabama, in April 1963. Douglas did not join Black but instead argued that the injunction abridged the petitioners' First Amendment rights "peaceably to assemble, and to petition the Government for a redress of grievances."

While Black was no ally of Douglas's in these cases dealing with symbolic speech, the Justice from Yakima found an ally in Thurgood Marshall, the Justice from Baltimore. One year after his appointment in 1967 Marshall delivered the opinion of the Court in Amalgamated Food Employees Union v. Logan Valley Plaza, a case involving picketing at a shopping center. The majority, Douglas included, decided, for the picketing members of the union. Marshall flatly stated: "We start from the premise that peaceful picketing carried on in a location open generally to the public is, absent other factors involving the purpose or manner of the picketing, protected by the First Amendment." Black dissented, asserting that "petitioners cannot, under the guise of First Amendment rights, trespass on respondent Weis' private property for the purpose of picketing."

In 1972 (two years after Black had left the Court), the majority of five, four of them Nixon appointees, decided in Lloyd Corp. v. Tanner that the Lloyd Shopping Center in Portland, Oregon, could prohibit the distribution of antiwar handbills in its malls, that "the handbilling by respondents in the malls of the Lloyd Center had no relation to any purpose for which the center was built, and being used." The majority, composed of Powell, Burger, Rehnquist, Blackmun, and White, contended that the handbillers could have passed out their materials on the public sidewalks and streets and that "it would be an unwarranted infringement of property rights to require them to yield to the exercise of First Amendment rights under circumstances where adequate alternative avenues of communication exist." The shopping center's prohibition, the Court decided, was warranted and constitutional.

Marshall filed a dissenting opinion in which Douglas, Brennan and Stewart joined. In his dissent Marshall gave freedom of speech a preferred position: "We must remember that it is a balance that we are striking--a balance between the freedom to speak, a freedom that is given a preferred place in our hierarchy of values, and the freedom of a private property owner to control his property. When the competing interests are fairly weighed, the balance can only be struck in favor of speech." Marshall observed, as Douglas had six years earlier in Adderley, that some people do not have available to them the more traditional forms of communication: "For many persons who do not have easy access to television, radio, the major newspapers, and other forms of mass media, the only way they can express themselves to a broad range of citizens on issues of general public concern is to picket, or to handbill, or to utilize other free or relatively inexpensive means of communication. The only hope that these people have to be able to communicate effectively is to be permitted to speak in those areas in which most of their fellow citizens can be found. One such area is the business district of a city or town or its functional equivalent." Marshall concluded that "when there are no effective means of communication, free speech is a mere shibboleth."

Three decisions in 1968, Tinker v. Des Moines Independent Community School District, Street v. New York, and Gregory v. Chicago again demonstrated the different perspectives Douglas and Black had on the "speech" elements involved in symbolic communication. In Tinker the majority, including Douglas and Marshall, decided for the Tinker children, who had been suspended from their schools for wearing black armbands to protest the war in Vietnam. In giving First Amendment protection to the children the Court declared: "...the wearing of armbands in the circumstances of this case was entirely divorced from actually or potentially disruptive conduct by those participating in it. It was closely akin to 'pure speech' which, we have repeatedly held, is entitled to comprehensive protection under the First Amendment." The Court then said in its now classic statement: "It can hardly be argued that either students or teachers shed their constitutional rights to freedom of speech at the schoolhouse gate."

Justice Black dissented in a strongly worded opinion in which he spoke of the immaturity of students and warned of disasters in the schoolhouse. Public school children, said Black, are not "sent to school at public expense to broadcast political or any other views to educate and inform the public.... It may be that the Nation has outworn the old-fashioned slogan that 'children are to be seen not heard,' but one may, I hope, be permitted to harbor the thought that taxpayers send children to school on the premise that at their age they need to learn, not teach." Concerned about discipline in the schools, Black then went on to say: "Here a very small number of students have crisply and summarily refused to obey a school order designed to give pupils who want to learn the opportunity to do so. One does not need to be a prophet or the son of a prophet to know that after the Court's holding today some students in Iowa schools and indeed in all schools will be ready, able, and willing to defy their teachers on practically all orders. This is the more unfortunate for the schools since groups of students all over the land are already running loose, conducting break-ins, sit-ins, lie-ins, and smash-ins."

The extent of Black's perturbation is hard to explain. The quiet wearing of the armbands which led to no disruption of school activities--which Tinker was all about--is something quite different from "break-ins" and "smash-ins"--which this case was not about.

In Street v. New York the majority, including Douglas, found for Street, who had been convicted of violating a New York statute that made it a crime to publicly "mutilate, deface, defile, or defy, trample upon, or cast contempt upon either by words or act [any flag of the United States]."

Justice Harlan, speaking for the majority, said: "We have no doubt that the constitutionally guaranteed 'freedom to be intellectually ... diverse or even contrary, and the 'right to differ as to things that touch the heart of the existing order,' encompass the freedom to express publicly one's opinions about our flag, including those opinions which are defiant or contemptuous." Street had taken his American flag and burned it on a street corner in Brooklyn, New York, in June 1966 after hearing of the shooting of civil rights leader James Meredith by a sniper in Mississippi. At the time of the burning Street was heard to say: "We don't need no damn flag.... Yes, that is my flag; I burned it. If they let that happen to Meredith we don't need an American flag." The Court concluded that "disrespect for our flag is to be deplored no less in these vexed times than in calmer periods of our history.... Nevertheless, we are unable to sustain a conviction that may have rested on a form of expression, however distasteful, which the Constitution tolerates and protects."

Black dissented, asserting that "the conviction does not and could not have rested merely on the spoken words but that it rested entirely on the fact that the defendant had publicly burned the American flag--against the law of the State of New York." Black concluded: "It is immaterial to me that words are spoken in connection with the burning. It is the burning of the flag that the State has set its face against.... The talking that was done took place 'as an integral part of conduct in violation of a valid criminal statute' against burning the American flag in public. I would therefore affirm this conviction."

What we have then, is that no other Supreme Court Justice has given so much First Amendment protection to symbolic speech as has Justice Douglas, with Marshall more than any other Justice carrying on the Douglas tradition in giving this form of communication constitutional protection.

## Obscenity

The applicability of the First Amendment to obscenity was never in doubt as far as Douglas was concerned. For almost two decades--from 1957, when the Warren Court gave us the *Roth* definition of obscenity, to 1973, when the Burger Court gave us the *Miller* definition--Douglas consistently asserted that obscenity was protected by the First Amendment. Douglas, with whom Black concurred, concluded his dissenting opinion in Roth with: 'I would give the broad sweep of the First Amendment full support. I have the same confidence in the ability of our people to reject noxious literature as I have in their capacity to sort out the true from the false in theology, economics, politics, or any other field."

When the Court gave First Amendment protection to Fanny Hill in 1966, Douglas wrote a concurring opinion in Memoirs v. Massachusetts attacking the causal relationship argument that obscenity leads to antisocial behavior:

> Perhaps the most frequently assigned justification for censorship is the belief that erotica produce antisocial sexual conduct. But that relationship has yet to be proven. Indeed, if one were to make judgments on the basis of speculation, one might guess that literature of the most pornographic sort would, in many cases, provide a substitute--not a stimulus--for antisocial sexual conduct.... As I read the First Amendment, judges cannot gear the literary diet of an entire nation to whatever tepid stuff is incapable of triggering the most demented mind. The First Amendment demands more than a horrible example or two of the perpetrator of a crime of sexual violence, in whose pocket is found a pornographic book, before it allows the Nation to be saddled with a regime of censorship.

In 1974 the Court decided in California v. LaRue that the California Department of Alcoholic Beverage Control could prohibit the presentation of explicitly sexual live entertainment and films in bars and taverns that were licensed by the state to sell liquor. Rehnquist, speaking for the Court, wrote:

> The substance of the regulations struck down prohibits licensed bars and nightclubs from displaying, either in the form of movies or live entertainment, 'performances' that partake more of gross sexuality than of communication. While we agree that at least some of the performances to which these regulations address themselves are within the limits of the constitutional protection of freedom of expression, the critical fact is that California has not forbidden

> these performances across the board. It has merely proscribed such performances in establishments that it licenses to sell liquor by the drink.

What the majority had decided was that plays or films which might not be legally "obscene" by the tests and standards established by the Court could be prohibited in state licensed bars and nightclubs. Justice Stewart wrote a concurring opinion but Douglas, Brennan and Marshall dissented.

Marshall was concerned that the prohibited entertainment did not have to be determined legally "obscene":

> Roth held fifteen years ago that the suppression of serious communication was too high a price to pay in order to vindicate the State's interest in controlling obscenity, and I see no reason to modify that judgment today. Indeed, even the appellants do not seriously contend that these regulations can be justified under the Roth-Memoirs test. Instead, appellants argue that California's regulations do not concern the control of pornography at all. These rules, they argue, deal with conduct rather than with speech and as such are not subject to the strict limitations of the First Amendment.

Part of Marshall's dissent was devoted to the state's argument that the rules were necessary "to prevent sex crimes, drug abuse, prostitution, and a wide variety of other evils." Marshall answered:

> These are precisely the same interests that have been asserted time and again before this Court as justification for laws banning frank discussion of sex and that we have consistently rejected. In fact, the empirical link between sex-related entertainment and the criminal activity popularly associated with it has never been proven and, indeed, has now been largely discredited. Yet even if one were to concede that such a link existed, it would hardly justify a broadscale attack on First Amendment Freedoms.

Douglas, in his dissent, clearly stated that "certainly a play which passes muster under the First Amendment is not made illegal because it is performed in a beer garden."

A year before he retired, Douglas dissented in Hamling v. United States, a case involving the mailing of an illustrated version of the 1970 Presidential Commission on Obscenity and Pornography Report. Brennan, Marshall, Stewart, and Douglas dissented, the latter declaring in his own short opinion:

> In 1970 the President's Commission on Obscenity and Pornography issued its report. Dean William D. Lockhart was chairman. Eighteen others were members. It was as a 646-page report. One member, Charles H. Keating, Jr., filed a dissenting report of some 60 pages with at least as many pages of exhibits. The report contains many references to many facets of sex: e.g., petting, coitus, oral sexuality, masturbation, and homosexual activities.
>
> What petitioners did was to supply the report with a glossary--not in dictionary terms but visually. Every item in the glossary depicted explicit sexual material within the meaning of that term as used in the report. Perhaps we should have no reports on obscenity. But imbedded in the First Amendment is the philosophy that the people have the right to know. Sex is more important to some than to others but it is of some importance to all. If officials may constitutionally report on obscenity, I see nothing in the First Amendment that allows us to bar the use of a glossary factually to illustrate what the report discusses.

While Justices Black and Marshall, like Douglas, consistently gave First Amendment protection to obscenity, Black retired in 1970 and Marshall has been on the Court a decade; other Justices, such as Brennan, Stewart, and Warren, at times have given obscenity First Amendment protection, but at other times they have not; still others like Rehnquist and Burger have seen obscenity as not meriting constitutional protection. Hence, it has been Douglas who more than any other Supreme Court Justice has decided on more occasions that regulation and censorship of obscenity, under our system, "abridges freedom of speech and of the press contrary to the First and Fourteenth Amendments."

Offensive Speech

Douglas also accorded constitutional protection to a variety of types of "offensive" speech to which other Justices refused to give First Amendment protection. While he did join the majority in 1942 to deny protection to the "fighting words" involved in Chaplinsky v. New Hampshire, he dissented in 1951 in Feiner v. New York, a case involving the conviction of a university student who had delivered a speech on a Syracuse, New York, street corner, calling that city's mayor "a champagne sipping bum," referring to President Truman as "a bum," calling the American Legion "a Nazi Gestapo," and telling his audience that "the Negroes don't have equal rights; they should rise up in arms and fight for their rights." Some of Feiner's listeners found his speech offensive and became angry; one man threatened to silence Feiner forcibly. The Court majority upheld Feiner's conviction, contending that

> the findings of the New York courts as to the condition of the crowd and the refusal of petitioner to obey the police requests [that he stop speaking], supported as they are by the record in this case, are persuasive that the conviction of petitioner for violation of public peace, order and authority does not exceed the bounds of proper state police action. This Court respects, as it must, the interest of the community in maintaining peace and order on its streets.

Douglas declared in his dissenting opinion that

> public assemblies and public speech occupy an important role in American life. One high function of the police is to protect these lawful gatherings so that the speakers may exercise their constitutional rights. When unpopular causes are sponsored from the public platform, there will commonly be mutterings and unrest and heckling from the crowd. When a speaker mounts a platform it is not unusual to find him resorting to exaggeration, to vilification of ideas and men, to the making of false charges.... But those extravagances ... do not justify penalizing the speaker by depriving him of the platform or by punishing him for his conduct.

Justice Minton concurred with Douglas, and Black wrote a

separate dissenting opinion. Feiner began serving his prison sentence in February 1951.

Two years earlier, Douglas, speaking for the Court in Terminiello v. Chicago, found for a speaker who had delivered a speech containing racial and ethnic slurs and whose speech was greeted with hostility and stone-throwing, the disturbance leading to the conviction of the speaker for breach of the peace. Douglas wrote some statements in the Terminiello opinion that were to be quoted again and again in years to come in later court opinions. The trial court had defined "breach of the peace" as "misbehavior which violates the public peace and decorum" and that the "misbehavior may constitute a breach of the peace if it stirs the public to anger, invites dispute, brings about a condition of unrest, or creates a disturbance...." Douglas retorted: "... a function of free speech under our system is to invite dispute. It may indeed best serve its high purpose when it induces a condition of unrest, creates dissatisfaction with conditions as they are, or even stirs people to anger. Speech is often provocative and challenging. It may strike at prejudices and preconceptions and have profound unsettling effects as it presses for acceptance of an idea."

One year later, in Beauharnais v. Illinois (1952) the majority found against Beauharnais, who had written and distributed racist leaflets attacking Negroes and as a result was convicted for violating Illinois's "group libel" statute. Offensive as the leaflets were, Douglas was prepared to give the material constitutional protection. He stated in his dissenting opinion:

> Hotheads blow off and release destructive energy in the process. They shout and rave, exaggerating weaknesses, magnifying error, viewing with alarm. So it has been from the beginning; and so it will be throughout time. The Framers of the Constitution knew human nature as well as we do. They too had lived in dangerous days; they too knew the suffocating influence of orthodoxy and standarized thought. They weighed the complusions for restrained speech and thought against the abuses of liberty. They chose liberty. That should be our choice today no matter how distasteful to us the pamphlet of Beauharnais may be.

In all three cases, Feiner, Terminiello, and Beauharnais, only Douglas and Black consistently found for the "speakers."

The offensiveness of the name-calling, and racial and ethnic slurs found in the speech of Feiner, Terminiello, and Beauharnais differed from the offensiveness of the "obscene" speech involved in several later cases in which Douglas again decided for the "speakers."

In 1969 Douglas and Black went their different ways in Cohen v. California, a case that involved Cohen's conviction for wearing in the Los Angeles County Courthouse a jacket on the back of which were inscribed the words "Fuck the Draft." The majority of the Supreme Court decided for Cohen; Justices Black, Burger, and Blackmun dissented.

The Court pointed out, among other things, that this was not an obscenity case: "Whatever else may be necessary to give rise to the States' broader power to prohibit obscene expression, such expression must be, in some significant way, erotic.... It cannot plausibly be maintained that this vulgar allusion to the Selective Service System would conjure up such psychic stimulation in anyone likely to be confronted with Cohen's crudely defaced jacket."

Nor did the Court see Cohen's message as "fighting words": "No individual actually or likely to be present could reasonably have regarded the words on appellant's jacket as a direct personal insult.... There is, as noted above, no showing that anyone who saw Cohen was in fact violently aroused or that appellant intended such a result."

As to whether the State must protect the public from such "offensive" speech, the majority said: "Surely the State has no right to cleanse public debate to the point where it is grammatically palatable to the most squeamish among us. Yet no readily ascertainable general principle exists for stopping short of that result were we to affirm the judgment below. For, while the particular four letter word being litigated here is perhaps more distasteful than most others of its genre, it is nevertheless often true that one man's vulgarity is another's lyric."

The dissenters, Black, Burger, and Blackmun, contended that "Cohen's absurd and immature antic ... was mainly conduct and little speech." The three dissenters also contended that the case appeared to be "well within the sphere of Chaplinsky v. New Hampshire," that is, Cohen's message constituted "fighting words." But if Cohen's "immature antic" was "mainly conduct and little speech," the applicability of Chaplinsky becomes questionable, since Chaplinsky's conviction was upheld in 1942 on the basis of his speech, the fighting words, not his "conduct." The dissenters appeared to want it both ways: Cohen's "antic" was conduct, which does not get First Amendment protection, and the "antic" was also "little speech" which also does not get protection.

The majority recognized what the dissenters did not, and that is that a prohibition of the words we choose to express ourselves may affect, in the end, the ideas we want to communicate. The majority, including Douglas, contended that "we cannot indulge the facile assumption that one can forbid particular words without also running a substantial risk of suppressing ideas in the process. Indeed, governments might soon seize upon the censorship of particular words as a convenient guise for banning the expression of unpopular views. We have been able, as noted above, to discern little social benefit that might result from running the risk of opening the door to such grave results."

In 1972, while the Nixon appointees Burger, Blackmun, and Rehnquist were arguing to suppress "offensive" speech, Douglas and the remaining members of the Warren Court were deciding to give constitutional protection to speakers who had referred in public discourse to policemen as "motherfucking fascist pig cops" and "Goddamn motherfucking police" (Lewis v. City of New Orleans and Brown v. Oklahoma).

In 1973 Douglas joined the majority in Papish v. Board of Curators of the University of Missouri to give constitutional protection to a graduate student who had been expelled for distributing on the University of Missouri campus a publication that had on its cover a political cartoon "depicting policemen raping the Statue of Liberty and the Goddess of Justice. The caption under the cartoon read: '... with Liberty and Justice for All.' Secondly, the issue contained an article entitled 'M-----f----- Acquitted.'"

The Court declared that "the mere dissemination of ideas--no matter how offensive to good taste--on a state university campus may not be shut off in the name of 'conventions of decency.' Other recent precedents of this Court make it equally clear that neither the political cartoon nor the headline story involved in this case can be labeled as constitutionally obscene or otherwise unprotected."

Burger, Blackmun, and Rehnquist dissented in Papish, contending that "the public use of the word 'M-----f-----' is 'lewd and obscene' as those terms were used by the Court in Chaplinsky v. New Hampshire...." The Papish case, they said, "is indeed a case where the observation of a unanimous Court in Chaplinsky that 'such utterances are no essential part of any exposition of ideas, and are of such slight social value as a step to truth that any benefit that may be derived from them is clearly outweighed by the social interest in order and morality' applies with compelling force." But the Nixon appointees presented neither evidence nor argument to demonstrate that Papish's distribution of the publication led in any way to disturbances or disorder or immorality.

What the Nixon appointees did not recognize about the functions of "offensive" language, the Cohen majority, including Douglas, was sensitive to when it stated:

> ... we cannot overlook the fact, because it is well illustrated by the episode involved here, that much linguistic expression serves a dual communicative function: it conveys not only ideas capable of relatively precise, detached explication, but otherwise inexpressible emotions as well. In fact, words are often chosen as much for their emotive as their cognitive force. We cannot sanction the view that the Constitution, while solicitous of the cognitive content of individual speech, has little or no regard for that emotive function which, practically speaking, may often be the more important element of the overall message sought to be communicated.

## Governmental Loyalty Oaths and Investigations

In his efforts to protect freedom of speech from governmental encroachments Douglas found himself at odds with the Nixon appointees, this being evident not only in the obscenity and offensive-language cases, but also in those involving loyalty oaths and disclaimer affidavits. Douglas joined the majority in Baird v. State Bar of Arizona (1971), finding for an attorney who had refused to answer the Arizona Bar Committee's question about whether "she had ever been a member of the Communist Party or any organization 'that advocates overthrow of the United States Government by force or violence.' When she refused to answer this question, the Committee declined to process her application further or recommend her admission to the bar." Justices Burger, Blackmun, and Harlan dissented.

Black, announcing the judgment in Baird, stated:

> The First Amendment's protection of association prohibits a State from excluding a person from a profession or punishing him solely because he is a member of a particular political organization or because he holds certain beliefs.... Similarly, when a State attempts to make inquiries about a person's beliefs or associations, its power is limited by the First Amendment. Broad and sweeping state inquiries into these protected areas, as Arizona has engaged in here, discourage citizens from exercising rights protected by the Constitution.

In another oath case, In re Stolar, decided the same day as Baird, the Court again divided along the same lines: Black, Douglas, Brennan, Marshall, and Stewart deciding for Stolar, who had been a member of the New York Bar and was asked by the Ohio Bar Committee, when he applied for admission to Ohio's Bar, questions related to all the organizations to which he had been a member. He refused to answer the questions, and the Ohio Bar Investigating Committee recommended that his application to take the Ohio Bar exam be denied. Referring to Baird the Court said:

> Without attempting in that case to bring about a complete reconciliation of all that this Court has previously said about this particular phase of First Amendment protection, we held that under the circumstances present there, Mrs. Baird could not, consistently with the First Amendment, be denied a state license to practice law because she refused to state whether she had belonged to the Communist Party or any organization that advocated overthrow of the United States Government by force. Here we hold that Stolar's refusals to answer certain questions asked him by the Ohio Bar Committee were also protected by the First Amendment.

The dissenters were Burger, Blackmun, White, and Harlan.

The Court decided still another oath case on February 23, 1971, Law Students Research Council v. Wadmond, this time Justice Stewart delivering the opinion, in which Burger, Blackmun, White, and Harlan joined. Marshall filed a dissenting opinion, in which Brennan joined. Douglas joined Black in a dissent in which the latter wrote:

> Here the Court upholds a New York law which requires that a Bar applicant not be admitted 'unless he shall furnish satisfactory proof' that he 'believes in the form of the government of the United States and is loyal to such government.' Rules 9406, New York Civil Practice Law and Rules. It also approves certain questions about political associations and beliefs which New York requires all applicants to answer. From these holdings I dissent.

The First Amendment, declared Black,

> was intended to make speech free from government control, even speech which is dangerous and unpopular. And included within the protection of the First Amendment is the right of association; the right to join organizations which themselves advocate ideas.... It therefore follows for me that governments should not be able to ask questions designed to identify persons who have belonged to certain political organizations and then exclude them from the practice of law.

For over two decades Douglas had come out squarely against governmental investigations of the associational ties of citizens, governmental inquiries into citizens' beliefs and expression of those beliefs, and a variety of loyalty-security programs. When in 1951 the majority of the Court upheld the convictions of the leaders of the Communist Party in this country for violating the Smith Act, only Douglas and Black dissented. Douglas's dedication to freedom and open discussion of even "dangerous" ideas was presented forcefully in his Dennis v. United States dissent, which warrants extended quotation as a reminder of how much more correct Douglas was in 1951 than were those who upheld the convictions:

> The opinion of the Court does not outlaw these texts [books by Marx, Engels, Lenin, and Stalin] nor condemn them to the fire, as the com-

munists do literature offensive to their creed. But if the books themselves are not outlawed, if they can lawfully remain on library shelves, by what reasoning does their use in a classroom become a crime? It would not be a crime under the Act to introduce these books to a class, though that would be teaching what the creed of violent overthrow of the Government is. The Act, as construed, requires the element of intent--that those who teach the creed believe in it. The crime then depends not on what is taught but on who the teacher is. That is to make freedom of speech turn not on what is said, but on the intent with which it is said. Once we start down that road we enter territory dangerous to the liberties of every citizen.

* * *

Free speech has occupied an exalted position because of the high service it has given our society. Its protection is essential to the very existence of a democracy. The airing of ideas releases pressures which otherwise might become destructive. When ideas compete in the market for acceptance, full and free discussion exposes the false and they gain few adherents. Full and free discussion even of ideas we hate encourages the testing of our own prejudices and preconceptions. Full and free discussion keeps a society from becoming stagnant and unprepared for the stresses and strains that work to tear all civilizations apart.

* * *

The First Amendment makes confidence in the common sense of our people and in their maturity of judgment the great postulate of our democracy. Its philosophy is that violence is rarely, if ever, stopped by denying civil liberties to those advocating resort to force. The First Amendment reflects the philosophy of Jefferson 'that it is time enough for the rightful purposes of civil government, for its officers to interfere when principles break out into overt acts against peace and good order.' The political censor has no place in our public debates. Unless and until

> extreme and necessitous circumstances are shown, our aim should be to keep speech unfettered and to allow the processes of law to be invoked only when the provocateurs among us move from speech to action.

Douglas's defense of freedom of speech in his Dennis dissent was a practical application of the philosophies of John Milton and John Stuart Mill as reflected in their works Areopagitica and On Liberty.

In 1959, in Barenblatt v. United States, the majority of the Court upheld the conviction of a professor who had been convicted for refusing to answer questions about his past political affiliations put to him by the Subcommittee of the House of Representatives Committee on Un-American Activities; Douglas, along with Black, Warren, and Brennan, dissented.

In 1961 the majority upheld the conviction of Frank Wilkinson, a longtime opponent of the House Committee on Un-American Activities, who was asked by the Committee several questions that he refused to answer. "He was then asked the question which was to become the subject of the present indictment and conviction: 'Mr. Wilkinson, are you now a member of the Communist Party?' He declined to answer the question...." In his dissenting opinion Douglas said: "The First Amendment rights involved here are more than freedom of speech and press. Bringing people together in peaceable assemblies is in the same category.... 'The right of peaceable assembly is a right cognate to those of free speech and free press and is equally fundamental.'" Douglas, with whom Black and Warren concurred, concluded his Wilkinson dissent by saying: "We cannot allow this man to go to prison for 12 months unless we hold that an investigation of those who criticize the Un-American Activities Committee was both authorized and constitutional. I cannot read the Resolution [House Resolution defining the Committee's purposes and powers] as authorizing that kind of investigation without assuming that the Congress intended to flout the First Amendment."

In 1967 Douglas delivered the opinion of the Court in Whitehill v. Elkins, a case dealing with a professor who had been offered a teaching position at the University of Maryland but who refused to take the following oath, which he challenged as being unconstitutional:

> I, ____________, do hereby (Print Name---including middle initial) certify that I am not engaged in one way or another in the attempt to overthrow the Government of the United States, or the State of Maryland, or any political subdivision of either of them, by force or violence.

In deciding for Whitehall, Douglas said:

> The prescribed oath requires, under threat of perjury, a statement that the applicant is not engaged 'in one way or another' in an attempt to overthrow the Government by force or violence. Though we assume <u>arguendo</u> that the Attorney General and the Board of Regents were authorized so to construe the Act as to prescribe a narrow oath (1) that excluded 'alteration' of the Government by peaceful 'revolution' and (2) that excluded all specific reference to membership in subversive groups, we still are beset with difficulties. Would a member of a group that was out to overthrow the Government by force or violence be engaged in that attempt 'in one way or another' within the meaning of the oath, even though he was ignorant of the real aims of the group and wholly innocent of any illicit purpose? We do not know; nor could a prospective employee know, save as he risked a prosecution for perjury.

'We are in the First Amendment field," said Douglas, and "the continuing surveillance which this type of law places on teachers is hostile to academic freedom."

In 1972 the Court found against some citizens who had brought a class action "in the District Court seeking declaratory and injunctive relief on their claim that their rights were being invaded by the Department of the Army's alleged 'surveillance of lawful and peaceful civilian political activity.'" Douglas, with whom Marshall concurred, dissented in <u>Laird v. Tatum</u>, concluding his strongly worded opinion with the following paragraph:

> This case involves a cancer in our body politic. It is a measure of the disease which afflicts us. Army surveillance, like Army regimentation, is at war with the principles of the First Amendment. Those who already walk submissively

> will say there is no cause for alarm. But submissiveness is not our heritage. The First Amendment was designed to allow rebellion to remain as our heritage. The Constitution was designed to keep government off the backs of the people. The Bill of Rights was added to keep the precincts of belief and expression, of the press, of political and social activities free from surveillance. The Bill of Rights was designed to keep agents of government and official eavesdroppers away from assemblies of people. The aim was to allow men to be free and independent and to assert their rights against government. There can be no influence more paralyzing of that objective than Army surveillance. When an intelligence officer looks over every nonconformist's shoulder in the library, or infiltrates his club, the America once extolled as the voice of liberty heard around the world no longer is cast in the image which Jefferson and Madison designed, but more in the Russian image....

Government surveillance, especially by the Army, was no more acceptable to Douglas than were the loyalty oaths and investigating committees, all in one way or another intruding on our First Amendment rights, an intrusion Douglas would not tolerate.

## Douglas as the Sole Dissenter

On a few occasions Douglas found himself the sole dissenter in cases involving freedom of expression. In 1969, he was the sole dissenter in Byrne v. Karalexis, a case dealing with an injunction related to an obscenity prosecution. While the other Justices spoke more directly to the injunction question, Douglas's dissent dealt primarily with the question of censorship and the threat of censorship of unorthodox ideas:

> Prior to the Bill of Rights, state law, when it spoke of freedom of the press, meant only freedom from prior restraint. But an author or publisher could be held accountable for publishing what the statehouse thought was against 'the public good.' In other words, the First Amendment did not build on existing law; it broke with tradition, set a new standard, and exalted freedom of expression. There

> is no trace of a suggestion that 'obscenity,' however defined, was excepted.
>
> That does not mean that 'obscenity' is good or that it should be encouraged. It only means that we cannot be faithful to our constitutional mandate and allow any form or shadow of censorship over speech and press.
>
> When our rewards go to people for thinking alike, it is no surprise that we become frightened at those who take exception to the current consensus. Then the hue and cry goes up for censors; and that is the start of an ominous trend. What can be done to literature under the banner of 'obscenity' can be done to other parts of the spectrum of ideas when party or majoritarian demands mount and propagandists start declaiming the law.
>
> The 'obscenity' issue raises large questions. To what extent may government watch over one's shoulder as he reads?

Douglas concluded his dissent with the observation that our commitment to freedom of expression is what makes us different from other societies: "We forget today that under our constitutional system neither Congress nor the States have any power to pass on the value, the propriety, the Americanism, the soundness of any idea or expression. It is that insulation from party or majoritarian control provided by the First Amendment--not our gross national product or mass production or pesticides or space ships or nuclear arsenal--that distinguishes our society from other planetary regimes."

This same view was stated by Douglas four years later in his Paris Adult Theatre I v. Slaton dissent, one of the several dissents coming from the Court in the five obscenity cases decided in June 1973 along with the now-famous Miller decision. Said Douglas: "When man was first in the jungle he took care of himself. When he entered a societal group, controls were necessarily imposed. But our society--unlike most in the world--presupposes that freedom and liberty are in a frame of reference that make the individual, not the government, the keeper of his tastes, beliefs, and ideas. That is the philosophy of the First Amendment; and it is the article of faith that sets us apart from most nations of the world."

In United States v. O'Brien, a 1968 draft-card-burning case in which the Court upheld the conviction of O'Brien, who had publicly burned his draft card to communicate his protest against the military draft and the war in Vietnam, Douglas was the sole dissenter.

The majority in O'Brien argued: "...even on the assumption that the alleged communicative element in O'Brien's conduct is sufficient to bring into play the First Amendment, it does not necessarily follow that the destruction of a registration certificate is constitutionally protected activity. This Court has held that when 'speech' and 'nonspeech' elements are combined in the same course of conduct, a sufficiently important governmental interest in regulating the nonspeech element can justify incidental limitations on First Amendment freedoms."

Douglas spoke in his dissent more directly to the question of conscription in a time when there was no formal declaration of war than to the First Amendment question:

> The Court states that the constitutional power of Congress to raise and support armies is 'broad and sweeping' and that Congress' power to 'classify and conscript manpower for military service is beyond question.' This is undoubtedly true in time when, by declaration of Congress, the Nation is in a state of war. The underlying and basic problem in this case, however, is whether conscription is permissible in the absence of a declaration of war. That question has not been briefed nor was it presented in oral argument; but it is, I submit, a question upon which the litigants and the country are entitled to a ruling.

While Douglas did not speak in his O'Brien dissent to the freedom of speech issue, he did suggest one year later in his concurring opinion in Brandenburg v. Ohio that O'Brien's "speech" was protected: "...O'Brien was not prosecuted for not having his draft card available when asked for by a federal agent. He was indicted, tried, and convicted for burning the card. And this Court's affirmance of that conviction was not, with all respect, consistent with the First Amendment."

In 1971 Douglas was the sole dissenter (Brennan concurred and dissented) in Younger v. Harris, a case dealing with an indictment charging Harris with violating California's Syndicalism Act. Harris

> filed a complaint in the Federal District Court, asking that court to enjoin appellant, Younger, the District Attorney of Los Angeles County, from prosecuting him, and alleging that the prosecution and even the presence of the Act inhibited him in the exercise of his rights of free speech and press, rights guaranteed him by the First and Fourteenth Amendments. Appellees Jim Dan and Diana Hirsch intervened as plaintiffs in the suit, claiming that the prosecution of Harris would inhibit them as members of the Progressive Labor Party from peacefully advocating the program of their party, which was to replace capitalism with socialism and to abolish the profit system of production in this country.

The majority answered: "Although Dan and Hirsch have alleged that they desire to advocate doctrines of the Progressive Labor Party, they have not asserted that their advocacy will be of the same genre as that which brought on the prosecution of Harris. In short, there is no reason to think that California has any ripe controversy with them."

Douglas dissented, stating that

> Harris' 'crime' was distributing leaflets advocating change in industrial ownership through political action.... If the 'advocacy' which Harris used was an attempt at persuasion through the use of bullets, bombs, and arson, we would have a different case. But Harris is charged only with distributing leaflets advocating political action toward his objective. He tried unsuccessfully to have the state court dismiss the indictment on constitutional grounds. He resorted to the state appellate court for writs of prohibition to prevent the trial, but to no avail. He went to the federal court as a matter of last resort in an effort to keep this unconstitutional trial from being saddled on him.

Douglas concluded his dissent with the declaration that "the eternal temptation, of course, has been to arrest the speaker rather than to correct the conditions about which he complains. I see no reason why these appellees should be made to walk the treacherous ground of these statutes. They, like other citizens, need the umbrella of the First Amendment as they study, analyze, discuss, and debate the troubles of these days. When criminal prosecutions can be leveled against them because they express unpopular views, the society of the dialogue is in danger."

As the lone dissenter in Public Utilities Commission v. Pollak Douglas vigorously argued for the prohibition of "speech" forced upon a "captive audience" traveling on a streetcar into which was transmitted by radio music, news, weather reports, and commercial advertising. Douglas refers to Pollak in Go East, Young Man:

> The question was whether the government was entitled to drill into the heads of those people--truly a 'captive' audience--its particular brand of news, propaganda, politics, and the like. I thought it violated due process and went against the grain of our constitutional philosophy, and I voted against the company. Felix Frankfurter would doubtless have joined me had he sat, but he was so terribly offended by the lower court's decision that he felt he could not be objective and stated as much publicly. The Court, speaking through Justice Burton, held otherwise. The sole letter I received applauding my dissent was from Groucho Marx.

## Conclusion

Unlike those Justices who have had the view that the people, being too weak, too uninformed, too prudish, too naive, and too unreliable, have to be protected from certain types of speech, Justice Douglas has held the position that the people could be trusted to deal with "dangerous" speech, "obscene" speech, and "offensive" speech. As he stated in the conclusion of his Roth dissent in 1957, "the First Amendment puts free speech in a preferred position."

> Freedom of expression can be suppressed if, and to the extent that, it is so closely brigaded with illegal action as to be an inseparable part of it.... As a people, we cannot afford to relax that standard. For the test that suppresses a cheap tract today can suppress a literary gem tomorrow. All it need do is to incite a lascivious thought or arouse a lustful desire. The list of books that judges or juries

> can place in that category is endless.
>
> I would give the broad sweep of the First Amendment full support. I have the same confidence in the ability of our people to reject noxious literature as I have in their capacity to sort out the true from the false in theology, economics, politics, or any other field.

It was that confidence that made it possible for Douglas to give First Amendment protection to so many diverse types of speech and speakers while so many of his colleagues on the Court turned to censorship as a means of protecting "our people," in whom they did not share Douglas's confidence.

The Douglas record in the area of freedom of speech has been one which history will record as constitutionally correct and as protective of our society's need for free and open speech through a variety of means of communication. Brennan, who had written the Court's 1957 Roth opinion upholding an obscenity conviction, dissented in 1973 in Miller and the four other obscenity cases decided the same day, rejecting what Douglas had rejected all along. Brennan, with whom Stewart and Marshall joined, said in his Paris Adult Theatre dissent: "I am convinced that the approach initiated 16 years ago in Roth v. United States, 354 U.S. 476 (1957), and culminating in the Court's decision today, cannot bring stability to this area of the law without jeopardizing fundamental First Amendment values, and I have concluded that the time has come to make a significant departure from that approach." Later in his dissent, Brennan wrote:

> Our experience since Roth requires us not only to abandon the effort to pick out obscene materials on a case-by-case basis, but also to reconsider a fundamental postulate of Roth: that there exists a definable class of sexually oriented expression that may be totally suppressed by the Federal and State Governments. Assuming that such a class of expression does in fact exist, I am forced to conclude that the concept of 'obscenity' cannot be defined with sufficient specificity and clarity to provide fair notice to persons who create and distribute sexually oriented materials, to prevent substantial erosion of protected speech as a byproduct of the attempt to suppress unprotected speech, and to avoid very costly institutional harms.

In his own Paris Adult Theatre dissent Douglas acknowledged Brennan's change of mind: "I applaud the effort of my Brother BRENNAN to forsake the low road which the Court has followed in this field. The new regime he would inaugurate is much closer than the old to the policy of abstention which the First Amendment proclaims."

Douglas's attacks on loyalty oaths, security programs requiring citizens to divulge their political beliefs and associations, and "un-American" investigating committees were, from our historical perspective, warranted and wise. The intrusions upon our First Amendment rights during the McCarthy and "Un-American Activities Committee" period in our history will no doubt be compared in years to come to the "Red Scare" of the previous decades and to the Alien and Sedition Acts of 1798. It will be Douglas's dissent in Dennis, not the plurality opinion, to which we will turn for guidance and perspective.

There is no question that Douglas is also right on the "symbolic" speech issue. We know that human beings communicate through the use of verbal symbols and symbolic conduct. As James Leahy put it in his 1970 Brooklyn Law Review article: "...legitimate expressive-conduct should not be cut off simply by classifying it as conduct and allowing government to punish it as such. The Court should accept the view that an apparently limitless variety of conduct can be labelled 'speech' when the 'speaker' in good faith intends to express an idea by his conduct."

The 1968 Columbia Law Review article "Symbolic Conduct" begins with the assertion that "symbolic conduct is an exceptionally vivid means of communication"; and the article concludes with the argument that "symbolic speech ... must be recognized by the courts, for there can be no doubt that nonverbal expression is speech, both in fact and in law. Our treatment of this increasingly popular mode of communication must accord it equal protection under the first amendment." The functions and importance of symbolic speech were recognized earlier by Douglas, and he argued, more than any other Justice on the Supreme Court, that such speech warranted First Amendment protection.

While some other Justices would have us saddled with loyalty oaths and disclaimer affidavits, investigated by governmental agencies and committees, spied upon by military personnel, denied access to "obscene" books and films, limited to the means of communication we could use to express ourselves, Douglas had eschewed all these inquiries and controls that restrict and put a chill on our First Amendment freedoms. During his thirty-six years on the Court Douglas has left a record defending the right of the people to speak out, to listen, to remain silent, a record that will not be matched, considering the composition of the present Court, for at least the next half-century.

Haig Bosmajian
University of Washington
Seattle

# PERMITS

# AND

# LICENSES

Murdock v. Pennsylvania, 319 U.S. 105 (1943)

A city ordinance requiring a license tax to distribute door-to-door religious tracts is declared unconstitutional by the Supreme Court. Douglas, delivering the opinion of the Court, states: "Considerable emphasis is placed on the kind of literature which petitioners were distributing--its provocative, abusive, and ill-mannered character and the assault which it makes on our established churches and the cherished faiths of many of us.... But those considerations are no justification for the license tax which the ordinance imposes. Plainly a community may not suppress, or the state tax, the dissemination of views because they are unpopular, annoying or distasteful. If that device were ever sanctioned, there would have been forged a ready instrument for the suppression of the faith which any minority cherishes but which does not happen to be in favor. That would be a complete repudiation of the philosophy of the Bill of Rights."

* * *

MR. JUSTICE DOUGLAS delivered the opinion of the Court.

The City of Jeannette, Pennsylvania, has an ordinance, some forty years old, which provides in part:

"That all persons canvassing for or soliciting within said Borough, orders for goods, paintings, pictures, wares, or merchandise of any kind, or persons delivering such articles under orders so obtained or solicited, shall be required to procure from the Burgess a license to transact said business and shall pay to the Treasurer of said Borough therefore the following sums according to the time for which said license shall be granted.

"For one day $1.50, for one week seven dollars ($7.00), for two weeks twelve dollars ($12.00), for three weeks twenty dollars ($20.00), provided that the provisions of this ordinance shall not apply to persons selling by sample to manufacturers or licensed merchants or dealers doing business in said Borough of Jeannette."

Petitioners are "Jehovah's Witnesses." They went about from door to door in the City of Jeannette distributing literature and soliciting people to "purchase" certain religious books and pamphlets, all published by the Watch Tower Bible & Tract Society.[1] The "price" of the books was twenty-five cents each, the "price" of the pamphlets five cents each.[2] In connection with these activities, petitioners used a phonograph[3] on which they played a record expounding certain of their views on religion. None of them obtained a license under the ordinance. Before they were arrested each had made "sales" of books. There was evidence that it was their practice in making these solicitations to request a "contribution" of twenty-five cents each for the books and five cents each for the pamphlets, but to accept lesser sums or even to donate the volumes in case an interested person was without funds. In the present case, some donations of pamphlets were made when books were purchased. Petitioners were convicted and fined for violation of the ordinance. Their judgments of conviction were sustained by the Superior Court of Pennsylvania, 149 Pa. Super. Ct. 175, 27 A. 2d 666, against their contention that the ordinance deprived them of the freedom of speech, press, and religion guaranteed by the First Amendment. Petitions for leave to appeal to the Supreme Court of Pennsylvania were denied. The cases are here on petitions for writs of certiorari which we granted along with the petitions for rehearing of Jones v. Opelika, 316 U.S. 584, and its companion cases.

The First Amendment, which the Fourteenth makes applicable to the states, declares that "Congress shall make no law respecting an establishment of religion, or prohibiting the free exercise thereof; or abridging the freedom of speech, or of the press...." It could hardly be denied that a tax laid specifically on the exercise of those freedoms would be unconstitutional. Yet the license tax imposed by this ordinance is, in substance, just that.

Petitioners spread their interpretations of the Bible and their religious beliefs largely through the hand distribution of literature by full or part time workers.[4] They claim to follow the example of Paul, teaching "publickly, and from house to house." Acts 20:20. They take literally the mandate of the Scriptures, "Go ye into all the world, and preach the gospel to every creature." Mark 16:15. In doing so they believe that they are obeying a commandment of God.

The hand distribution of religious tracts is an age-old form of missionary evangelism--as old as the history of printing presses.[5] It has been a potent force in various religious movements down through the years.[6] This form of evangelism is utilized today on a large scale by various religious sects whose colporteurs carry the Gospel to thousands upon thousands of homes and seek through personal visitations to win adherents to their faith.[7] It is more than preaching; it is more than distribution of religious literature. It is a combination of both. Its purpose is as evangelical as the revival meeting. This form of religious activity occupies the same high estate under the First Amendment as do worship in the churches and preaching from the pulpits. It has the same claim to protection as the more orthodox and conventional exercises of religion. It also has the same claim as the others to the guarantees of freedom of speech and freedom of the press.

The integrity of this conduct or behavior as a religious practice has not been challenged. Nor do we have presented any question as to the sincerity of petitioners in their religious beliefs and practices, however misguided they may be thought to be. Moreover, we do not intimate or suggest in respecting their sincerity that any conduct can be made a religious rite and by the zeal of the practitioners swept into the First Amendment. Reynolds v. United States, 98 U.S. 145, 161-167, and David v. Beason, 133 U.S. 333 denied any such claim to the practice of polygamy and bigamy. Other claims may well arise which deserve the same fate. We only hold that spreading one's religious beliefs or preaching the Gospel through distribution of religious literature and through personal visitations is an age-old type of evangelism with as high a claim to constitutional protection as the more orthodox types. The manner in which it is practiced at times gives rise to special problems with which the police power of the states is competent to deal. See for example Cox v. New Hampshire, 312 U.S. 569, and Chaplinsky v. New Hampshire, 315 U.S. 568. But that merely illustrates that the rights with which we are dealing are not absolutes. Schneider v. State, 308 U.S. 147, 160-161. We are concerned, however, in these cases merely with one narrow issue. There is presented for decision no question whatsoever concerning punishment for any alleged unlawful acts during the solicitation. Nor is there involved here any question as to the validity of a registration system for colporteurs and other solicitors. The cases present a single issue--the constitutionality of an ordinance which as construed and applied requires religious colporteurs to pay a license tax as a condition to the pursuit of their activities.

The alleged justification for the exaction of this license tax is the fact that the religious literature is distributed with a solicitation of funds. Thus it was stated, in Jones v. Opelika, supra, p. 597, that when a religious sect uses "ordinary commercial methods of sales of articles to raise propaganda funds," it is proper for the state to charge "reasonable fees for the privilege of canvassing." Situations will arise where it will be difficult to determine whether a particular activity is religious or purely commercial. The distinction at times is vital. As we stated only the other day, in Jamison v. Texas, 318 U.S. 413, 417, "The states can prohibit the use of the streets for the distribution of purely commercial leaflets, even though such leaflets may have 'a civic appeal, or a moral platitude' appended. Valentine v. Chrestensen, 316 U.S. 52, 55. They may not prohibit the distribution of handbills in the pursuit of a clearly religious activity merely because the handbills invite the purchase of books for the improved understanding of the religion or because the handbills seek in a lawful fashion to promote the raising of funds for religious purposes." But the mere fact that the religious literature is "sold" by itinerant preachers rather than "donated" does not transform evangelism into a commercial enterprise. If it did, then the passing of the collection plate in church would make the church service a commercial project. The constitutional rights of those spreading their religious beliefs through the spoken and printed word are not to be gauged by standards governing retailers or wholesalers of books. The right to use the press for expressing one's views is not to be measured by the protection afforded commercial handbills. It should be remembered that the pamphlets of Thomas Paine were not distributed free of charge. It is plain that a religious organization needs funds to remain a going concern. But an itinerant evangelist, however misguided or intolerant he may be, does not become a mere book agent by selling the Bible or religious tracts to help defray his expenses or to sustain him. Freedom of speech, freedom of the press, freedom of religion are available to all, not merely to those who can pay their own way. As we have said, the problem of drawing the line between a purely commercial activity and a religious one will at times be difficult. On this record it plainly cannot be said that petitioners were engaged in a commercial rather than a religious venture. It is a distortion of the facts of record to describe their activities as the occupation of selling books and pamphlets. And the Pennsylvania court did not rest the judgments of conviction on that basis, though it did find that petitioners "sold" the literature. The Supreme Court of Iowa in State v. Mead, 230 Iowa 1217, 300 N. W. 523, 524, described the selling activities of members of this same sect as "merely incidental and collateral" to their "main object which was to preach and publicize the doctrines of their order." And see State v. Meredith, 197 S.C. 351, 15 S. E. 2d 678; People v. Barber, 289 N.Y. 378 385-386, 46 N. E. 2d 329. That accurately summarizes the present record.

We do not mean to say that religious groups and the press are free from all financial burdens of government. See Grosjean v. American Press Co., 297 U. S. 233, 250. We have here something quite different, for example, from a tax on property used or employed in connection with those activities. It is one thing to impose a tax on the income or property of a preacher. It is quite another thing to exact a tax from him for the privilege of delivering a sermon. The tax imposed by the City of Jeannette is a flat license tax, the payment of which is a condition of the exercise of these constitutional privileges. The power to tax the exercise of a privilege is the power to control or suppress its enjoyment. Magnano Co. v. Hamilton, 292 U. S. 40, 44-45, and cases cited. Those who can tax the exercise of this religious practice can make its exercise so costly as to deprive it of the resources necessary for its maintenance. Those who can tax the privilege of engaging in this form of missionary evangelism can close its doors to all those who do not have a full purse. Spreading religious beliefs in this ancient and honorable manner would thus be denied the needy. Those who can deprive religious groups of their colporteurs can take from them a part of the vital power of the press which has survived from the Reformation.

It is contended, however, that the fact that the license tax can suppress or control this activity is unimportant if it does not do so. But that is to disregard the nature of this tax. It is a license tax--a flat tax imposed on the exercise of a privilege granted by the Bill of Rights. A state may not impose a charge for the enjoyment of a right granted by the Federal Constitution. Thus, it may not exact a license tax for the privilege of carrying on interstate commerce (McGoldrick v. Berwind-White Co., 309 U. S. 33, 56-58), although it may tax the property used in, or the income derived from, that commerce, so long as those taxes are not discriminatory. Id., p. 47 and cases cited. A license tax applied to activities guaranteed by the First Amendment would have the same destructive effect. It is true that the First Amendment, like the commerce clause, draws no distinction between license taxes, fixed sum taxes, and other kinds of taxes. But that is no reason why we should shut our eyes to the nature of the tax and its destructive influence. The power to impose a license tax on the exercise of these freedoms is indeed as potent as the power of censorship which this Court has repeatedly struck down. Lovell v. Griffin, 303 U.S. 444; Schneider v. State, supra; Cantwell v. Connecticut, 310 U.S. 296, 306; Largent v. Texas, 318 U.S. 418; Jamison v. Texas, supra. It was for that reason that the dissenting opinion in Jones v. Opelika, supra, stressed the nature of this type of tax. 316 U.S. pp. 607-609, 620, 623. In that case, as in the present ones, we have something very different from a registration system under which those going from house to house are required to give their names, addresses and other marks of identification to the authorities. In all of these cases the issuance of the permit or license is dependent on the payment of a license tax. And the license tax is fixed in amount and unrelated to the scope of the activities of petitioners or to their realized revenues. It is not a nominal fee imposed as a regulatory measure to defray the expenses of policing the activities in question.[8] It is in no way apportioned. It is a flat license tax levied and collected as a condition to the pursuit of activities whose enjoyment is guaranteed by the First Amendment. Accordingly, it restrains in advance those constitutional liberties of press and religion and inevitably tends to suppress their exercise. That is almost uniformly recognized as the inherent vice and evil of this flat license tax. As stated by the Supreme Court of Illinois in a case involving this same sect and an ordinance similar to the present one, a person cannot be compelled "to purchase, through a license fee or a license tax, the privilege freely granted by the constitution."[9] Blue Island v. Kozul, 379 Ill. 511, 519, 41 N.E. 2d 515. So, it may not be said that proof is lacking that these license taxes either separately or cumulatively have restricted or are likely to restrict petitioners' religious activities. On their face they are a restriction of the free exercise of those freedoms which are protected by the First Amendment.

The taxes imposed by this ordinance can hardly help but be as severe and telling in their impact on the freedom of the press and religion as the "taxes on knowledge" at which the First Amendment was partly aimed. Grosjean v. American Press Co., supra, pp. 244-249. They may indeed operate even more subtly. Itinerant evangelists moving throughout a state or from state to state would feel immediately the cumulative effect of such ordinances as they become fashionable. The way of the religious dissenter has long been hard. But if the formula of this type of ordinance is approved, a new device for the suppression of religious minorities will have been found. This method of disseminating religious beliefs can be crushed and closed out by the sheer weight of the toll or tribute which is exacted town by town, village by village. The spread of religious ideas through personal visitations by the literature ministry of numerous religious groups would be stopped.

The fact that the ordinance is "nondiscriminatory" is immaterial. The protection afforded by the First Amendment is not so restricted. A license tax certainly does not acquire constitutional validity because it classifies the privileges protected by the First Amendment along with the wares and merchandise of hucksters and peddlers and treats them all alike. Such equality in treatment does not save the ordinance. Freedom of press, freedom of speech, freedom of religion are in a preferred position.

It is claimed, however, that the ultimate question in determining the constitutionality of this license tax is whether the state has given something for which it can ask a return. That principle has wide applicability. State Tax Commission v. Aldrich, 316 U.S. 174, and cases cited. But it is quite irrelevant here. This tax is not a charge for the enjoyment of a privilege or benefit bestowed by the state. The privilege in question exists apart from state authority. It is guaranteed the people by the Federal Constitution.

Considerable emphasis is placed on the kind of literature which petitioners were distributing--its provocative, abusive, and ill-mannered character and the assault which it makes on our established churches and the cherished faiths of many of us. See Douglas v. Jeannette, concurring opinion, post, p. 166. But those considerations are no justification for the license tax which the ordinance imposes. Plainly a community may not suppress, or the state tax, the dissemination of views because they are unpopular, annoying or distasteful. If that device were ever sanctioned, there would have been forged a ready instrument for the suppression of the faith which any minority cherished but which does not happen to be in favor. That would be a complete repudiation of the philosophy of the Bill of Rights.

Jehovah's Witnesses are not "above the law." But the present ordinance is not directed to the problems with which the police power of the state is free to deal. It does not cover, and petitioners are not charged with, breaches of the peace. They are pursuing their solicitations peacefully and quietly. Petitioners, moreover, are not charged with or prosecuted for the use of language which is obscene, abusive, or which incites retaliation. Cf. Chaplinsky v. New Hampshire, supra. Nor do we have here, as we did in Cox v. New Hampshire, supra, and Chaplinsky v. New Hampshire, supra, state regulation of the streets to protect and insure the safety, comfort, or convenience of the public. Furthermore, the present ordinance is not narrowly drawn to safeguard the people of the community in their homes against the evils of solicitations. See Cantwell v. Connecticut, supra, 306. As we have said, it is not merely a registration ordinance calling for an identification of the solicitors so as to give the authorities some basis for investigating strangers coming into the community. And the fee is not a nominal one, imposed as a regulatory measure and calculated to defray the expense of protecting those on the streets and at home against the abuses of solicitors. See Cox v. New Hampshire, supra, pp. 576-577. Nor can the present ordinance survive if we assume that it has been construed to apply only to solicitation from house to house.[10] The ordinance is not narrowly drawn to prevent or control abuses or evils arising from that activity. Rather, it sets aside the residential areas as a prohibited zone, entry of which is denied petitioners unless the tax is paid. That restraint and one which is city-wide in scope (Jones v. Opelika) are different only in degree. Each is an abridgment of freedom of press and a restraint on the free exercise of religion. They stand or fall together.

The judgment in Jones v. Opelika has this day been vacated. Freed from that controlling precedent, we can restore to their high, constitutional position the liberties of itinerant evangelists who disseminate their religious beliefs and the tenets of their faith through distribution of literature. The judgments are reversed and the causes are remanded to the Pennsylvania Superior Court for proceedings not inconsistent with this opinion.

Reversed.

NOTES

1. Two religious books--Salvation and Creation--were sold. Others were offered in addition to the Bible. The Watch Tower Bible & Tract Society is alleged to be a non-profit charitable corporation.

2. Petitioners paid three cents each for the pamphlets and, if they devoted only their spare time to the work, twenty cents each for the books. Those devoting full time to the work acquired the books for five cents each. There was evidence that some of the petitioners paid the difference between the sales price and the cost of the books to their local congregations which distributed the literature.

3. Purchased along with the record from the Watch Tower Bible & Tract Society.

4. The nature and extent of their activities throughout the world during the years 1939 and 1940 are to be found in the 1941 Yearbook of Jehovah's Witnesses, pp. 62-243.

5. Palmer, The Printing Press and the Gospel (1912).

6. White, The Colporteur Evangelist (1930); Home Evangelization (1850); Edwards, The Romance of the Book (1932) c. V; 12 Biblical Repository (1844) Art. VIII; 16 The Sunday Magazine (1887) pp.43-47; 3 Meliora (1861) pp. 311-319; Felice, Protestants of France (1853) pp. 53, 513; 3 D'Aubigne, History of The Reformation (1849) pp. 103, 152, 436-437; Report of Colportage in Virginia, North Carolina & South Carolina, American Tract Society (1855). An early type of colporteur was depicted by John Greenleaf Whittier in his legendary poem, The Vaudois Teacher. And see, Wylie, History of the Waldenses.

7. The General Conference of Seventh-Day Adventists, who filed a brief amicus curiae on the reargument of Jones v. Opelika, has given us the following data concerning their literature ministry: This denomination has 83 publishing houses throughout the world, issuing publications in over 200 languages. Some 9, 256 separate publications were issued in 1941. By printed and spoken word, the Gospel is carried into 412

countries in 824 languages. 1942 Yearbook, p. 287. During December 1941, a total of 1,018 colporteurs operated in North America. They delivered during that month $97,997.19 worth of gospel literature, and for the whole year of 1941 a total of $790,610.36--an average per person of about $65 per month. Some of these were students and temporary workers. Colporteurs of this denomination receive half of their collections, from which they must pay their traveling and living expenses. Colporteurs are specially trained and their qualifications equal those of preachers. In the field, each worker is under the supervision of a field missionary secretary to whom a weekly report is made. After fifteen years of continuous service, each colporteur is entitled to the same pension as retired ministers. And see Howell, The Great Advent Movement (1935), pp. 72-75.

8. The constitutional difference between such a regulatory measure and a tax on the exercise of a federal right has long been recognized. While a state may not exact a license tax for the privilege of carrying on interstate commerce (McGoldrick v. Berwind-White Co., supra, pp. 56-58), it may, for example, exact a fee to defray the cost of purely local regulations in spite of the fact that those regulations incidentally affect commerce. "So long as they do not impede the free flow of commerce and are not made the subject of regulation by Congress they are not forbidden. Clyde Mallory Lines v. Alabama, 296 U.S. 261, 267, and cases cited. And see South Carolina Highway Dept. v. Barnwell Bros., 303 U.S. 177, 185-188.

9. That is the view of most state courts which have passed on the question. McConkey v. Fredericksburg, 179 Va. 556, 19 S.E.2d 682; State v. Greaves, 112 Vt. 222, 22 A.2d 497; People v. Banks, 168 Misc. 515, 6 N.Y.S.2d 41. Contra: Cook v. Harrison, 180 Ark. 546, 21 S.W.2d 966.

## Saia v. New York, 334 U.S. 558 (1948)

The Supreme Court declares unconstitutional an ordinance forbidding the use of sound amplification devices except with permission of the chief of police, Douglas stating in the opinion of the Court: "Any abuses which loud-speakers create can be controlled by narrowly drawn statutes. When a city allows an official to ban them in his uncontrolled discretion, it sanctions a device for suppression of free communication of ideas. In this case a permit is denied because some persons were said to have found the sound annoying. In the next one a permit may be denied because some people find the ideas annoying. Annoyance at ideas can be cloaked in annoyance at sound. The power of censorship inherent in this type of ordinance reveals its vice.

"Courts must balance the various community interests in passing on the constitutionality of local regulations of the character involved here. But in that process they should be mindful to keep the freedoms of the First Amendment in a preferred position."

* * *

Opinion of the Court by MR. JUSTICE DOUGLAS, announced by MR. JUSTICE BLACK.

This case presents the question of the validity under the Fourteenth Amendment of a penal ordinance of the City of Lockport, New York, which forbids the use of sound amplification devices except with permission of the Chief of Police. [1]

Appellant is a minister of the religious sect known as Jehovah's Witnesses. He obtained from the Chief of Police permission to use sound equipment, mounted atop his car, to amplify lectures on religious subjects. The lectures were given at a fixed place in a public park, on designated Sundays. When this permit expired, he applied for another one but was refused on the ground that complaints had been made. Appellant nevertheless used his equipment as planned on four occasions, but without a permit. He was tried in Police

Court for violations of the ordinance. It was undisputed that he used his equipment to amplify speeches in the park and that they were on religious subjects. Some witnesses testified that they were annoyed by the sound, though not by the content of the addresses; others were not disturbed by either. The court upheld the ordinance against the contention that it violated appellant's rights of freedom of speech, assembly, and worship under the Federal Constitution. Fines and jail sentences were imposed. His convictions were affirmed without opinion by the County Court for Niagara County and by the New York Court of Appeals, 297 N.Y. 659, 76 N.E. 2d 323. The case is here on appeal.

We hold that § 3 of this ordinance is unconstitutional on its face, for it establishes a previous restraint on the right of free speech in violation of the First Amendment which is protected by the Fourteenth Amendment against State action. To use a loud-speaker or amplifier one has to get a permit from the Chief of Police. There are no standards prescribed for the exercise of his discretion. The statute is not narrowly drawn to regulate the hours or places of use of loud-speakers, or the volume of sound (the decibels) to which they must be adjusted. The ordinance therefore has all the vices of the ones which we struck down in Cantwell v. Connecticut, 310 U.S. 296; Lovell v. Griffin, 303 U.S. 444; and Hague v. C.I.O., 307 U.S. 496.

In the Cantwell case a license had to be obtained in order to distribute religious literature. What was religious was left to the discretion of a public official. We held that judicial review to rectify abuses in the licensing system did not save the ordinance from condemnation on the grounds of previous restraint. Lovell v. Griffin, supra, held void on its face an ordinance requiring a license for the distribution of literature. That ordinance, like the present one, was dressed in the garb of the control of a "nuisance." But the Court made short shrift of the argument, saying that approval of the licensing system would institute censorship "in its baldest form." In Hague v. C.I.O., supra, we struck down a city ordinance which required a license from a local official for a public assembly on the streets or highways or in the public parks or public buildings. The official was empowered to refuse the permit if in his opinion the refusal would prevent "riots, disturbances or disorderly assemblage." We held that the ordinance was void on its face because it could be made "the instrument of arbitrary suppression of free expression of views on national affairs." 307 U.S. p. 516.

The present ordinance has the same defects. The right to be heard is placed in the uncontrolled discretion of the Chief of Police. He stands athwart the channels of communication as an obstruction which can be removed only after criminal trial and conviction and lengthy appeal. A more effective previous restraint is difficult to imagine. Unless we are to retreat from the firm positions we have taken in the past, we must give freedom of speech in this case the same preferred treatment that we gave freedom of religion in the Cantwell case, freedom of the press in the Griffin case, and freedom of speech and assembly in the Hague case.[2]

Loud-speakers are today indispensable instruments of effective public speech. The sound truck has become an accepted method of political campaigning. It is the way people are reached. Must a candidate for governor or the Congress depend on the whim or caprice of the Chief of Police in order to use his sound truck for campaigning? Must he prove to that official that his noise will not be annoying?

The present ordinance would be a dangerous weapon if it were allowed to get a hold on our public life. Noise can be regulated by regulating decibels. The hours and place of public discussion can be controlled. But to allow the police to bar the use of loud-speakers because their use can be abused is like barring radio receivers because they too make a noise. The police need not be given the power to deny a man the use of his radio in order to protect a neighbor against sleepless nights. The same is true here.

Any abuses which loud-speakers create can be controlled by narrowly drawn statutes. When a city allows an official to ban them in his uncontrolled discretion, it sanctions a device for suppression of free communication of ideas. In this case a permit is denied because some persons were said to have found the sound annoying. In the next one a permit may be denied because some people find the ideas annoying. Annoyance at ideas can be cloaked in annoyance at sound. The power of censorship inherent in this type of ordinance reveals its vice.

Courts must balance the various community interests in passing on the constitutionality of local regulations of the character involved here. But in that process they should be mindful to keep the freedoms of the First Amendment in a preferred position. See Marsh v. Alabama, 326 U.S. 501, 509.

Reversed.

## NOTES

1. The ordinance, insofar as pertinent, reads as follows: "Section 2. Radio devices, etc. It shall be unlawful for any person to maintain and operate in any building, or on any premises or on any automobile, motor truck or other motor vehicle, any radio device, mechanical device, or loud speaker or any device of any kind whereby the sound therefrom is cast directly upon the streets and public places and where such device is maintained for advertising purposes or for the purpose of attracting the attention of the passing public, or which is so placed and operated that the sounds coming therefrom can be heard to the annoyance or inconvenience of travelers upon any street or public places or of persons in neighboring premises.

 "Section 3. Exception. Public dissemination, through radio loudspeakers, of items of news and matters of public concern and athletic activities shall not be deemed a violation of this section provided that the same be done under permission obtained from the Chief of Police."

 Appellant's conduct was regarded throughout as falling within the types of activity enumerated in § 3. We take the ordinance as construed by the State courts.

2. Cox v. New Hampshire, 312 U.S. 569, 577-578, did not depart from the rule of these earlier cases but re-emphasized the vice of the type of ordinance we have here. Davis v. Massachusetts, 167 U.S. 43, was distinguished in the Hague case, 397 U.S. pp. 514-516, which likewise involved an ordinance regulating the use of public streets and parks. It was there said, "We have no occasion to determine whether, on the facts disclosed, the Davis case was rightly decided, but we cannot agree that it rules the instant case. Wherever the title of streets and parks may rest, they have immemorially been held in trust for the use of the public and, time out of mind, have been used for purposes of assembly, communicating thoughts between citizens, and discussing public questions. Such use of the streets and public places has, from ancient times, been a part of the privileges, immunities, rights and liberties of citizens. The privilege of a citizen of the United States to use the streets and parks for communication of views on national questions may be regulated in the

interest of all; it is not absolute, but relative, and must be exercised in subordination to the general comfort and convenience, and in consonance with peace and good order; but it must not, in the guise of regulation, be abridged or denied."

We adhere to that view. Though the statement was that of only three Justices, it plainly indicated the route the majority followed, who on the merits did not consider the Davis case to be controlling.

Poulos v. New Hampshire, 345 U.S. 395 (1953)

The Supreme Court decides that a Portsmouth, N.H., city ordinance which forbade the holding of a religious meeting in a public park without a license did not violate the principles of the First Amendment. Douglas dissents, declaring: "There is no free speech in the sense of the constitution when permission must be obtained from an official before a speech can be made. That is a previous restraint condemned by history and at war with the First Amendment. The nature of the particular official who has the power to grant or deny the authority does not matter. Those who wrote the First Amendment conceived of the right to free speech as wholly independent of the prior restraint of anyone. The judiciary was not granted a privilege of restraint withheld from other officials. For history proved that judges too were sometimes tyrants."

* * *

MR. JUSTICE DOUGLAS, with whom MR. JUSTICE BLACK concurs, dissenting.

The Court concedes, as indeed it must under our decisions (see Royall v. Virginia, 116 U.S. 572; Thomas v. Collins, 323 U.S. 516), that if denial of the right to speak had been contained in a statute, appellant would have been entitled to flout the law, to exercise his constitutional right to free speech, to make the address on July 2, 1950, and when arrested and tried for violating the statute, to defend on the ground that the law was unconstitutional. An unconstitutional statute is not necessarily a nullity; it may have intermediate consequences binding upon people. See Chicot County Dist. v. Bank, 308 U.S. 371. But when a legislature undertakes to proscribe the exercise of a citizen's constitutional right to free speech, it acts lawlessly; and the citizen can take matters in his own hands and proceed on the basis that such a law is no law at all. See De Jonge v. Oregon, 299 U.S. 353, 365.

The reason is the preferred position granted freedom

of speech, freedom of press, freedom of assembly, and freedom of religion by the First Amendment. See Thomas v. Collins, supra, p. 530; Murdock v. Pennsylvania, 319 U. S. 105, 115. The command of the First Amendment (made applicable to the States by the Fourteenth) is that there shall be no law which abridges those civil rights. The matter is beyond the power of the legislature to regulate, control, or condition. The case is therefore quite different from a legislative program in the field of business, labor, housing, and the like where regulation is permissible and the claim of unconstitutionality usually can be determined only by the manner or degree of application of the statute to an aggrieved person.

A legislature that undertakes to license or censor the right of free speech is imposing a prior restraint (see Near v. Minnesota, 283 U. S. 697), odious in our history. The Constitution commands that government keep its hands off the exercise of First Amendment rights. No matter what the legislature may say, a man has the right to make his speech, print his handbill, compose his newspaper, and deliver his sermon without asking anyone's permission. The contrary suggestion is abhorrent to our traditions.

If the citizen can flout the legislature when it undertakes to tamper with his First Amendment rights, I fail to see why he may not flout the official or agency who administers a licensing law designed to regulate the exercise of the right of free speech. Defiance of a statute is hardly less harmful to an orderly society than defiance of an administrative order. The vice of a statute, which exacts a license for the right to make a speech, is that it adds a burden to the right. The burden is the same when the officials administering the licensing system withhold the license and require the applicant to spend months or years in the courts in order to win a right which the Constitution says no government shall deny.

It was said by way of dictum in Royall v. Virginia, supra, p. 582, that "as a general rule," if an officer, entrusted with a licensing power, has only "ministerial" duties to perform, "the remedy by mandamus would be appropriate to compel the officer" to issue the license. I do not agree that the present statute, as construed by the New Hampshire court, imposes merely a ministerial duty on the city council. The construction, by which we are bound, gives wide range to the discretion of the city council:

> The discretion thus vested in the authority is limited in its exercise by the bounds of reason, in uniformity of method of treatment upon the facts of each application, free from improper or inappropriate considerations and from unfair discrimination. A systematic, consistent and just order of treatment, with reference to the convenience of public use of the highways [here the parks], is the statutory mandate. The licensing authority has no delegation of power in excess of that which the legislature granting the power has and the legislature attempted to delegate no power it did not possess. [State v. Cox, 91 N.H. 137, 143, 16 A. 2d 508, 513.]

The requirement that the licensing authority stay within "the bounds of reason" and that it be "free from improper or inappropriate considerations and from unfair discrimination" is a command that it act reasonably, not capriciously or arbitrarily. But even a reasonable regulation of the right to free speech is not compatible with the First Amendment.[1] Of course, a state could deny the use of a park to one religious group if a prior application had been granted to another group and the meetings would conflict. But there is no suggestion by New Hampshire that its system of regulation vests the licensing authority with only that limited power. The gloss which the New Hampshire court has placed on the statute grants a power reasonably to regulate free speech. That unfortunately is a doctrine that has been slowly creeping into our constitutional law.[2] It has no place there. It is a doctrine dangerous to liberty and destructive of the great rights guaranteed by the First Amendment.

So, one answer to the Court's holding that appellant should have gone into court to compel the issuance of a license is that the licensing power was discretionary not ministerial and that a discretionary power to license free speech is unconstitutional.

There is another answer which is found in Cantwell v. Connecticut, 310 U.S. 296. In that case it was argued that a licensing power in a state statute be construed so as to limit the power of the licensing authority to ministerial acts. We rejected that offer on two grounds. In the first place, the statute had not been so narrowly construed by the state court. In the second place, the availability of judicial relief would not in any event save the statute. What Mr. Justice Roberts, writing for a unanimous Court, said was this (310 U.S., at 306):

> ... the availability of a judicial remedy for abuses in the system of licensing still leaves that system one of previous restraint which, in the field of free speech and press, we have held inadmissible. A statute authorizing previous restraint upon the exercise of the guaranteed freedom by judicial decision after trial is as obnoxious to the Constitution as one providing for like restraint by administrative action.

What Mr. Justice Roberts said needs to be repeated over and again. There is no free speech in the sense of the Constitution when permission must be obtained from an official before a speech can be made. That is a previous restraint condemned by history and at war with the First Amendment. The nature of the particular official who has the power to grant or deny the authority does not matter. Those who wrote the First Amendment conceived of the right to free speech as wholly independent of the prior restraint of anyone. The judiciary was not granted a privilege of restraint withheld from other officials. For history proved that judges too were sometimes tyrants.

NOTES

1. This marks a distinction between the present case and Cox v. New Hampshire, 312 U.S. 569. There the sole charge against appellants was that they were "taking part in a parade or procession" on public streets without a license. We only held that New Hampshire's method of controlling travel on the streets of cities was permissible under the police power of the states. We distinguished that problem from like cases arising under the First Amendment, p. 573,

   "The sole charge against appellants was that they were 'taking part in a parade or procession' on public streets without a permit as the statute required. They were not prosecuted for distributing leaflets, or for conveying information by placards or otherwise, or for issuing invitations to a public meeting, or for holding a public meeting, or for maintaining or expressing religious beliefs. Their right to do any one of these things apart from engaging in a 'parade or procession' upon a public street is not here involved and the question of the validity of a statute addressed to any other sort of conduct than that complained of is not before us."

2. Beauharnais v. Illinois, 343 U.S. 250; Dennis v. United States, 341 U.S. 494; Feiner v. New York, 340 U.S. 315. Cf. Breard v. Alexandria, 341 U.S. 622; American Communications Assn. v. Douds, 339 U.S. 382; Osman v. Douds, 339 U.S. 846.

Times Film Corp. v. Chicago, 365 U. S. 43 (1961)

The Supreme Court upholds a Chicago ordinance that requires all motion pictures for public exhibition be submitted to a city official empowered to prohibit the showing of the film, the Court asserting that freedom from prior restraint is not an absolute privilege under the First Amendment.

Justice Douglas dissents, declaring that "the First Amendment was designed to enlarge, not to limit freedom in literature and in the arts as well as in politics, economics, law, and other fields.... Its aim was to unlock all ideas for argument, debate, and dissemination. No more potent force in defeat of that freedom could be designed than censorship. It is a weapon that no minority or majority group, acting through government, should be allowed to wield over any of us."

* * *

MR. JUSTICE DOUGLAS, with whom THE CHIEF JUSTICE and MR. JUSTICE BLACK concur, dissenting.

My view that censorship of movies is unconstitutional because it is a prior restraint and violative of the First Amendment has been expressed on prior occasions. Superior Films v. Department of Education, 346 U. S. 587, 588-589 (concurring opinion); Kingsley Pictures Corp. v. Regents, 360 U. S. 684, 697 (concurring opinion).

While the problem of movie censorship is relatively new, the censorship device is an ancient one. It was recently stated, "There is a law of action and reaction in the decline and resurgence of censorship and control. Whenever liberty is in the ascendant, a social group will begin to resist it; and when the reverse is true, a similar resistance in favor of liberty will occur." Haney, Comstockery in America (1960), pp. 11-12.

Whether or not that statement of history is accurate, censorship has had many champions throughout time.

Socrates: "And shall we just carelessly allow children to hear any casual tales which may be devised by casual persons, and to receive into their minds ideas for the most part the very opposite of those which we should wish them to have when they are grown up?"

Glaucon: "We can not."

Socrates: "Then the first thing will be to establish a censorship of the writers of fiction, and let the censors receive any tale of fiction which is good, and reject the bad; and we will desire mothers and nurses to tell their children the authorized ones only. Let them fashion the mind with such tales, even more fondly than they mould the body with their hands; but most of those which are now in use must be discarded." Plato, Republic (The Dialogues of Plato, Jowett trans., Ox. Univ. Press, 1953) vol. 2, p. 221.

Hobbes was the censor's proponent: "... it is annexed to the sovereignty, to be judge of what opinions and doctrines are averse, and what conducing to peace; and consequently, on what occasions, how far, and what men are to be trusted withal, in speaking to multitudes of people; and who shall examine the doctrines of all books before they be published. For the actions of men proceed from their opinions; and in the well-governing of opinions, consisteth the well-governing of men's actions, in order to their peace, and concord." Leviathan (Oakeshott ed. 1947), p. 116.

Regimes of censorship are common in the world today. Every dictator has one; every Communist regime finds it indispensable.[1] One shield against world opinion that colonial powers have used was the censor, as dramatized by France in North Africa. Even England has a vestige of censorship in the Lord Chamberlain (32 Halsbury's Laws of England (2d ed. 1939), p. 68) who presides over the stage--a system that in origin was concerned with the barbs of political satire.[2] But the concern with political satire shifted to a concern with atheism and with sexual morality--the last being the concern evident in Chicago's system now before us.

The problems of the wayward mind concern the clerics, the psychiatrists, and the philosophers. Few groups have hesitated to create the political pressures that translate into secular law their notions of morality. Pfeffer, Creeds in Competition (1958), pp. 103-109. No more powerful weapon for sectarian control can be imagined than governmental censorship. Yet in this country the state is not the secular arm of any religious school of thought, as in some nations; nor is the church an instrument of the state. Whether--as here--city officials or--as in Russia--a political party lays claim to the power of governmental censorship, whether the pressures are for a conformist moral code or for a conformist political ideology, no such regime is permitted by the First Amendment.

The forces that build up demands for censorship are heterogeneous.

> The comstocks are not merely people with intellectual theories who might be convinced by more persuasive theories; nor are they pragmatists who will be guided by the balance of power among pressure groups. Many of them are so emotionally involved in the condemnation of what they find objectionable that they find rational arguments irrelevant. They _must_ suppress what is offensive in order to stabilize their own tremulous values and consciences. Panic rules them, and they cannot be calmed by discussions of legal rights, literary integrity, or artistic merit. [_Haney_, _op. cit. supra_, pp. 176-177.]

Yet as long as the First Amendment survives, the censor, no matter how respectable his cause, cannot have the support of government. It is not for government to pick and choose according to the standards of any religious, political, or philosophical group. It is not permissible, as I read the Constitution, for government to release one movie and refuse to release another because of an official's concept of the prevailing need or the public good. The Court in _Near v. Minnesota_, 283 U.S. 697, 713, said that the "chief purpose" of the First Amendment's guarantee of freedom of press was "to prevent previous restraints upon the publication."

A noted Jesuit has recently stated one reason against governmental censorship:

> The freedom toward which the American people are fundamentally orientated is a freedom under God, a freedom that knows itself to be bound by the imperatives of the moral law. Antecedently it is presumed that a man will make morally and socially responsible use of his freedom of expression;

> hence there is to be no prior restraint on it. However, if his use of freedom is irresponsible, he is summoned after the fact to responsibility before the judgment of the law. There are indeed other reasons why prior restraint on communications is outlawed; but none are more fundamental than this. [Murray, We Hold These Truths (1960), pp. 164-165.]

Experience shows other evils of "prior restraint." The regime of the censor is deadening. One who writes cannot afford entanglements with the man whose pencil can keep his production from the market. The result is a pattern of conformity. Milton made the point long ago: "For though a licenser should happen to be judicious more than ordinarily, which will be a great jeopardy of the next succession, yet his very office, and his commission enjoins him to let pass nothing but what is vulgarly received already." Areopagitica, 3 Harvard Classics (1909), p. 212.

Another evil of censorship is the ease with which the censor can erode liberty of expression. One stroke of the pen is all that is needed. Under a censor's regime the weights are cast against freedom.[3] If, however, government must proceed against an illegal publication in a prosecution, then the advantages are on the other side. All the protections of the Bill of Rights come into play. The presumption of innocence, the right to jury trial, proof of guilt beyond a reasonable doubt--these become barriers in the path of officials who want to impose their standard of morality on the author or producer. The advantage a censor enjoys while working as a supreme bureaucracy disappears. The public trial to which a person is entitled who violates the law gives a hearing on the merits, airs the grievance, and brings the community judgment to bear upon it. If a court sits in review of a censor's ruling, its function is limited. There is leeway left the censor, who like any agency and its _expertise_, is given a presumption of being correct.[4] That advantage disappears when the government must wait until a publication is made and then prove its case in the accepted manner before a jury in a public trial. All of this is anathema to the censor who prefers to work in secret, perhaps because, as Milton said, he is "either ignorant, imperious, and remiss, or basely pecuniary." Areopagitica, _supra_, p. 210.

The First Amendment was designed to enlarge, not to

limit, freedom in literature and in the arts as well as in politics, economics, law, and other fields. Hannegan v. Esquire, Inc., 327 U.S. 146, 151-159; Kingsley Pictures Corp. v. Regents, supra. Its aim was to unlock all ideas for argument, debate, and dissemination. No more potent force in defeat of that freedom could be designed than censorship. It is a weapon that no minority or majority group, acting through government, should be allowed to wield over any of us.[5]

## NOTES

1. "Nowhere have the Communists become simply a vote-getting party. They are organized around ideas and they care about ideas. They are the great heresy hunters of the modern world." Ways, Beyond Survival (1959), p. 199.

2. Ivor Brown in a recent summary of the work of the Lord Chamberlain states: "The licensing of plays was imposed not to protect the morals of the British public but to safeguard the reputation of politicians. This happened in 1737 when the Prime Minister, Sir Robert Walpole, infuriated by the stage lampoons of Henry Fielding and others, determined to silence these much enjoyed exposures of his alleged corruption and incompetence. This had the curiously beneficial result of driving Fielding away from the stage. He then became an excellent magistrate and a major creator of the English novel. But in the puritanical atmosphere of the nineteenth century the discipline was applied to the moral content of plays and applied so rigorously that that the dramatists were barred from serious treatment of 'straight sex,' as well as the abnormalities. The prissiness of respectable Victorian society was such that legs were hardly to be mentioned, let alone seen, and Charles Dickens wrote cumbrously of 'unmentionables' when he meant trousers." N.Y. Times, Jan. 1, 1961 § 2, p. X3. And see Knowles, The Censor, The Drama, and The Film (1934). As to British censorship of movies see 15 & 16 Geo. 6 & 1 Eliz. 2, c. 68.

3. John Galsworthy wrote in opposition to the British censorship of plays: "In this country the tongue and pen are subject to the law; so may it ever be! But in

this country neither tongue nor pen are in any other instance subject to the despotic judgments of a single man. The protest is not aimed at the single man who holds this office. He may be the wisest man in England, the best fitted for his despotic office. It is not he; it is the office that offends. It offends the decent pride and self-respect of an entire profession. To those who are surprised that dramatic authors should take themselves so seriously we say, What workman worthy of his tools does not believe in the honour of his craft? In this appeal for common justice we dramatists, one little branch of the sacred tree of letters, appeal to our brother branches. We appeal to the whole knighthood of the pen--scientists, historians, novelists, journalists. The history of the health of nations is the history of the freedom--not the license--of the tongue and pen. We are claiming the freedom--not the licence of our pens. Let those hold back in helping us who would tamely suffer their own pens to be warped and split as ours are before we take them up." London Times, Nov. 1, 1907, p. 7. And see the testimony of George Bernard Shaw in Report, Joint Select Committee of the House of Lords and the House of Commons on the Stage Plays (Censorship) (1909), p. 46 et seq. Shaw, three of whose plays had been suppressed, caused a contemporary sensation by asking, and being refused, permission to file with the Committee an attack on censorship that he had prepared. Shaw's version of the story and the rejected statement can be found as his preface to The Shewing-Up of Blanco Posnet. He says in his statement: "Any journalist may publish an article, any demagogue may deliver a speech without giving notice to the government or obtaining its license. The risk of such freedom is great; but as it is the price of our political liberty, we think it worth paying. We may abrogate it in emergencies ... just as we stop the traffic in a street during a fire or shoot thieves on sight after an earthquake. But when the emergency is past, liberty is restored everywhere except in the theatre. [Censorship is] a permanent proclamation of martial law with a single official subsituated for a court martial." The Shewing-Up of Blanco Posnet (Brentano's, 1913), p. 36.

4. See Note, 71 Harv. L. Rev. 326, 331. Cf. Glanzman v. Christenberry, 175 F. Supp. 485, with Grove Press,

Inc., v. Christenberry, 175 F. Supp. 488, as to the weight given to post-office determinations of nonmailability.

5. "First, within the larger pluralist society each minority group has the right to censor for its own members, if it so chooses, the content of the various media of communication, and to protect them, by means of its own choosing, from materials considered harmful according to its own standards.

"Second, in a pluralist society no minority group has the right to demand that government should impose a general censorship, affecting all the citizenry, upon any medium of communication, with a view to punishing the communication of materials that are judged to be harmful according to the special standards held within one group.

"Third, any minority group has the right to work toward the elevation of standards of public morality in the pluralist society, through the use of the methods of persuasion and pacific argument.

"Fourth, in a pluralist society no minority group has the right to impose its own religious or moral views on other groups, through the use of the methods of force, coercion, or violence." Murray, We Hold These Truths (1960), p. 168.

# BREACH

# OF

# THE

# PEACE

Terminiello v. Chicago, 337 U.S. 1 (1949)

The Supreme Court finds for a speaker who had been convicted of "disorderly conduct," Douglas stating in the opinion of the Court: "Accordingly a function of free speech under our system of government is to invite dispute. It may indeed best serve its high purpose when it induces a condition of unrest, creates dissatisfaction with conditions as they are, or even stirs people to anger. Speech is often provocative and challenging. It may strike at prejudices and preconceptions and have profound unsettling effects as it presses for acceptance of an idea. That is why freedom of speech, though not absolute ... is nevertheless protected against censorship or punishment, unless shown likely to produce a clear and present danger of a serious substantive evil that rises far above public inconvenience, annoyance, or unrest."

* * *

MR. JUSTICE DOUGLAS delivered the opinion of the Court.

Petitioner after jury trial was found guilty of disorderly conduct in violation of a city ordinance of Chicago[1] and fined. The case grew out of an address he delivered in an auditorium in Chicago under the auspices of the Christian Veterans of America. The meeting commanded considerable public attention. The auditorium was filled to capacity with over eight hundred persons present. Others were turned away. Outside of the auditorium a crowd of about one thousand persons gathered to protest against the meeting. A cordon of policemen was assigned to the meeting to maintain order; but they were not able to prevent several disturbances. The crowd outside was angry and turbulent.

Petitioner in his speech condemned the conduct of the crowd outside and vigorously, if not viciously, criticized various political and racial groups whose activities he denounced as inimical to the nation's welfare.

The trial court charged that "breach of the peace" consists of any "misbehavior which violates the public peace and decorum"; and that the "misbehavior may constitute a breach of the peace if it stirs the public to anger, invites dispute, brings about a condition of unrest, or creates a disturbance, or if it molests the inhabitants in the enjoyment of peace and quiet by arousing alarm." Petitioner did not take exception to that instruction. But he maintained at all times that the ordinance as applied to his conduct violated his right of free speech under the Federal Constitution. The judgment of conviction was affirmed by the Illinois Appellate Court (332 Ill. App. 17, 74 N.E. 2d 45) and by the Illinois Supreme Court. 396 Ill. 41, 71 N.E. 2d 2; 400 Ill. 23, 79 N.E. 2d 39. The case is here on a petition for certiorari which we granted because of the importance of the question presented.

The argument here has been focused on the issue of whether the content of petitioner's speech was composed of derisive, fighting words, which carried it outside the scope of the constitutional guarantees. See Chaplinsky v. New Hampshire, 315 U.S. 568; Cantwell v. Connecticut, 310 U.S. 296, 310. We do not reach that question, for there is a preliminary question that is dispositive of the case.

As we have noted, the statutory words "breach of the peace" were defined in instructions to the jury to include speech which "stirs the public to anger, invites a dispute, brings about a condition of unrest, or creates a disturbance ...." That construction of the ordinance is a ruling on a question of state law that is as binding on us as though the precise words had been written into the ordinance. See Hebert v. Louisiana, 272 U.S. 312, 317; Winters v. New York, 333 U.S. 507, 514.

The vitality of civil and political institutions in our society depends on free discussion. As Chief Justice Hughes wrote in De Jonge v. Oregon, 299 U.S. 353, 365, it is only through free debate and free exchange of ideas that government remains responsive to the will of the people and peaceful change is effected. The right to speak freely and to promote diversity of ideas and programs is therefore one of the chief distinctions that sets us apart from totalitarian regimes.

Accordingly a function of free speech under our system of government is to invite dispute. It may indeed best serve its high purpose when it induces a condition of unrest, creates dissatisfaction with conditions as they are, or even stirs people to anger. Speech is often provocative and challenging. It may strike at prejudices and preconceptions and have profound unsettling effects as it presses for acceptance of an idea. That is why freedom of speech, though not absolute, Chaplinsky v. New Hampshire, supra, pp. 571-572, is nevertheless protected against censorship or punishment, unless shown likely to produce a clear and present danger of a serious substantive evil that rises far above public inconvenience, annoyance, or unrest. See Bridges v. California, 314 U.S. 252, 262; Craig v. Harney, 331 U.S. 367, 373. There is no room under our Constitution for a more restrictive view. For the alternative would lead to standardization of ideas either by legislatures, courts, or dominant political or community groups.

The ordinance as construed by the trial court seriously invaded this province. It permitted conviction of petitioner if his speech stirred people to anger, invited public dispute, or brought about a condition of unrest. A conviction resting on any of those grounds may not stand.

The fact that petitioner took no exception to the instruction is immaterial. No exception to the instructions was taken in Stromberg v. California, 283 U.S. 359. But a judgment of conviction based on a general verdict under a state statute was set aside in that case, because one part of the statute was unconstitutional. The statute had been challenged as unconstitutional and the instruction was framed in its language. The Court held that the attack on the statute as a whole was equally an attack on each of its individual parts. Since the verdict was a general one and did not specify the ground upon which it rested, it could not be sustained. For one part of the statute was unconstitutional and it could not be determined that the defendant was not convicted under that part.

The principle of that case controls this one. As we have said, the gloss which Illinois placed on the ordinance gives it a meaning and application which are conclusive on us. We need not consider whether as construed it is defective in its entirety. As construed and applied it at least contains parts that are unconstitutional. The verdict was a general one; and we do not know on this record but what it may rest on the invalid clauses.

The statute as construed in the charge to the jury was passed on by the Illinois courts and sustained by them over the objection that as so read it violated the Fourteenth Amendment. The fact that the parties did not dispute its construction makes the adjudication no less ripe for our review, as the Stromberg decision indicates. We can only take the statute as the state courts read it. From our point of view it is immaterial whether the state law question as to its meaning was controverted or accepted. The pinch of the statute is in its application. It is that question which the petitioner has brought here. To say therefore that the question on this phase of the case is whether the trial judge gave a wrong charge is wholly to misconceive the issue.

But it is said that throughout the appellate proceedings the Illinois courts assumed that the only conduct punishable and punished under the ordinance was conduct constituting "fighting words." That emphasizes, however, the importance of the rule of the Stromberg case. Petitioner was not convicted under a statute so narrowly construed. For all anyone knows he was convicted under the parts of the ordinance (as construed) which, for example, make it an offense merely to invite dispute or to bring about a condition of unrest. We cannot avoid that issue by saying that all Illinois did was to measure petitioner's conduct, not the ordinance, against the Constitution. Petitioner raised both points--that his speech was protected by the Constitution; that the inclusion of his speech within the ordinance was a violation of the Constitution. We would, therefore, strain at technicalities to conclude that the unconstitutionality of the ordinance as construed and applied to petitoner was not before the Illinois courts. The record makes clear that petitioner at all times challenged the constitutionality of the ordinance as construed and applied to him.

Reversed.

NOTE

1. "All persons who shall make, aid, countenance, or assist in making any improper noise, riot, disturbance, breach of the peace, or diversion tending to a breach of the peace, within the limits of the city ... shall be deemed guilty of disorderly conduct, and upon conviction thereof, shall be severally fined not less than one dollar nor more than two hundred dollars for each offense." Municipal Code of Chicago, 1939, § 193-1.

Feiner v. New York, 340 U.S. 315 (1951)

The majority of the Court decides to uphold the conviction of a street-corner orator. Douglas dissents, declaring: "Public assemblies and public speech occupy an important role in American life. One high function of the police is to protect these lawful gatherings so that the speakers may exercise their constitutional rights. When unpopular causes are sponsored from the public platform, there will be mutterings and unrest and heckling from the crowd. When a speaker mounts a platform it is not unusual to find him resorting to exaggeration, to vilification of ideas and men, to the making of false charges. But those extravagances ... do not justify penalizing the speaker by depriving him of the platform or by punishing him for his conduct."

* * *

MR. JUSTICE DOUGLAS, with whom MR. JUSTICE MINTON concurs, dissenting.

Feiner, a university student, made a speech on a street corner in Syracuse, New York, on March 8, 1949. The purpose of the speech was to publicize a meeting of the Young Progressives of America to be held that evening. A permit authorizing the meeting to be held in a public school auditorium had been revoked and the meeting shifted to a local hotel.

Feiner delivered his speech in a small shopping area in a predominantly colored residential section of Syracuse. He stood on a large box and spoke over loudspeakers mounted on a car. His audience was composed of about 75 people, colored and white. A few minutes after he started two police officers arrived.

The speech was mainly devoted to publicizing the evening's meeting and protesting the revocation of the permit. It also touched on various public issues. The following are the only excerpts revealed by the record:

'Mayor Costello (of Syracuse) is a champagne-sipping bum; he does not speak for the negro people."

"The 15th Ward is run by corrupt politicians, and there are horse rooms operating there."

"President Truman is a bum."

'Mayor O'Dwyer is a bum."

"The American Legion is a Nazi Gestapo."

"The negroes don't have equal rights; they should rise up in arms and fight for their rights."

There was some pushing and shoving in the crowd and some angry muttering. That is the testimony of the police. But there were no fights and no "disorder" even by the standards of the police. There was not even any heckling of the speaker.

But after Feiner had been speaking about 20 minutes a man said to the police officers, "If you don't get that son of a bitch off, I will go over and get him off there myself." It was then that the police ordered Feiner to stop speaking; when he refused, they arrested him.

Public assemblies and public speech occupy an important role in American life. One high function of the police is to protect these lawful gatherings so that the speakers may exercise their constitutional rights. When unpopular causes are sponsored from the public platform, there will commonly be mutterings and unrest and heckling from the crowd. When a speaker mounts a platform it is not unusual to find him resorting to exaggeration, to vilification of ideas and men, to the making of false charges. But those extravagances, as we emphasied in Cantwell v. Connecticut, 310 U. S. 296, do not justify penalizing the speaker by depriving him of the platform or by punishing him for his conduct.

A speaker may not, of course, incite a riot any more than he may incite a breach of the peace by the use of "fighting words." See Chaplinsky v. New Hampshire, 315 U. S. 568. But this record shows no such extremes. It shows an unsympathotic audience and the threat of one man to haul the speaker from the stage. It is against that kind of threat that speakers need police protection. If they do not receive it and instead the police throw their weight on the side of those who would break up the meetings, the police become the new censors of speech. Police censorship has all the vices of the censorship from city halls which we have repeatedy struck down. See Lovell v. City of Griffin,

303 U.S. 444; Hague v. C.I.O., 307 U.S. 496; Cantwell v. Connecticut, supra; Murdock v. Pennsylvania, 319 U.S. 105; Saia v. New York, 334 U.S. 558.

## Grayned v. City of Rockford, 408 U.S. 104 (1972)

While the Supreme Court finds unconstitutional a Rockford, Illinois, antipicketing ordinance that describes "impermissible picketing not in terms of time, place, and manner, but in terms of subject matter," it finds constitutional an antinoise ordinance under which Grayned, who had taken part in a civil rights demonstration in front of a high school, was convicted. Douglas concurs in part and dissents in part.

* * *

MR. JUSTICE DOUGLAS, dissenting in part.

While I join Part I of the Court's opinion, I would also reverse the appellant's conviction under the antinoise ordinance.

The municipal ordinance on which this case turns is c. 28, § 19.2 (a) which provides in relevant part:

> That no person, while on public or private grounds adjacent to any building in which a school or any class thereof is in session, shall willfully make or assist in the making of any noise or diversion which disturbs or tends to disturb the peace or good order of such school session or class thereof.

Appellant was one of 200 people picketing a school and carrying signs promoting a black cause--"Black cheerleaders to cheer too," "Black history with black teachers," "We want our rights," and the like. Appellant, however, did not himself carry a picket sign. There was no evidence that he yelled or made any noise whatsoever. Indeed, the evidence reveals that appellant simply marched quietly and on one occasion raised his arm in the "power to the people" salute.

The pickets were mostly students; but they included

former students, parents of students, and concerned citizens. They had made proposals to the school board on their demands and were turned down. Hence the picketing. The picketing was mostly by black students who were counseled and advised by a faculty member of the school. The school contained 1, 800 students. Those counseling the students advised they must be quiet, walk hand in hand, no whispering, no talking.

Twenty-five policemen were stationed nearby. There was noise but most of it was produced by the police who used loudspeakers to explain the local ordinance and to announce that arrests might be made. The picketing did not stop, and some 40 demonstrators, including appellant, were arrested.

The picketing lasted 20 to 30 minutes and some students went to the windows of the classrooms to observe it. It is not clear how many there were. The picketing was, however, orderly or, as one officer testified, "very orderly." There was no violence. And appellant made no noise whatever.

What Mr. Justice Roberts said in Hague v. CIO, 307 U.S. 496, 515-516, has never been questioned:

> Wherever the title of streets and parks may rest, they have immemorially been held in trust for the use of the public and, time out of mind, have been used for purposes of assembly, communicating thoughts between citizens, and discussing public questions. Such use of the streets and public places has, from ancient times, been a part of the privileges, immunities, rights, and liberties of citizens. The privilege of a citizen of the United States to use the streets and parks for communication of views on national questions may be regulated in the interest of all; it is not absolute, but relative, and must be exercised in subordination to the general comfort and convenience, and in consonance with peace and good order; but it must not, in the guise of regulation, be abridged or denied.

We held in Cox v. Louisiana, 379 U.S. 536, 544-545, that a State could not infringe the right of free speech and free assembly by convicting demonstrators under a "disturbing the peace" ordinance where all that the students in that case did was to protest segregation and discrimination against blacks by peaceably assembling and marching to the courthouse where they sang, prayed, and listened to a speech, but where there was no violence, no rioting, no boisterous conduct.

The school where the present picketing occurred was the center of a racial conflict. Most of the pickets were indeed students in the school. The dispute doubtless disturbed the school; and the blaring of the loudspeakers of the police was certainly a "noise or diversion" in the meaning of the ordinance. But there was no evidence that appellant was noisy or boisterous or rowdy. He walked quietly and in an orderly manner. As I read this record, the disruptive force loosed at this school was an issue dealing with race--an issue that is preeminently one for solution by First Amendment means.[1] That is all that was done here; and the entire picketing, including appellant's part in it, was done in the best First Amendment tradition.

## NOTE

1. The majority asserts that "appellant's sole claim ... is that he was convicted under facially unconstitutional ordinances" and that there is, therefore, no occasion to consider whether his activities were protected by the First Amendment. Ante, at 106 n. 1. Appellant argues, however, that the ordinance is overly broad in that it punishes constitutionally protected activity. A statute may withstand an overbreadth attack "only if, as authoritatively construed ... ,it is not susceptible of application to speech ... that is protected by the First and Fourteenth Amendments." Gooding v. Wilson, 405 U.S. 518, 520 (1972). If the ordinance applies to appellant's activities and if appellant's activities are unconstitutionally protected, then the ordinance is overly broad and, thus, unconstitutional. There is no merit, therefore, to the Court's suggestion that the question whether "appellant's particular behavior was protected by the First Amendment," ante, at 106 n. 1, is not presented.

# SYMBOLIC

# SPEECH

Adderley v. Florida, 385 U.S. 39 (1966)

The Supreme Court upholds the trespass convictions of civil rights demonstrators protesting racial segregation. Douglas dissents, asserting that: "The jailhouse, like an executive mansion, a legislative chamber, a courthouse, or the statehouse itself ... is one of the seats of government, whether it be the Tower of London, the Bastille, or a small county jail. And when it houses political prisoners or those who many think are unjustly held, it is an obvious center for protest. The right to petition for the redress of grievances has an ancient history and is not limited to writing a letter or sending a telegram to a congressman; it is not confined to appearing before the local city council, or writing letters to the President or Governor or Mayor.... Conventional methods of petitioning may be, and often have been, shut off to large groups of our citizens.... Their methods should not be condemned as tactics of obstruction and harassment as long as the assembly and petition are peaceable, as these were."

* * *

MR. JUSTICE DOUGLAS, with whom THE CHIEF JUSTICE, MR. JUSTICE BRENNAN, and MR. JUSTICE FORTAS concur, dissenting.

The First Amendment, applicable to the States by reason of the Fourteenth (Edwards v. South Carolina, 372 U.S. 229, 235), provides that "Congress shall make no law ... abridging ... the right of the people peaceably to assemble, and to petition the Government for a redress of grievances." These rights, along with religion, speech, and press, are preferred rights of the Constitution, made so by reason of that explicit guarantee and what Edmond Cahn in Confronting Injustice (1966) referred to as "The Firstness of the First Amendment."[1] With all respect, therefore, the Court errs in treating the case as if it were an ordinary trespass case or an ordinary picketing case.

The jailhouse, like an executive mansion, a legislative chamber, a courthouse, or the statehouse itself (Edwards v. South Carolina, supra) is one of the seats of government, whether it be the Tower of London, the Bastille, or a small county jail. And when it houses political prisoners or those who many think are unjustly held, it is an obvious center for protest. The right to petition for the redress of grievances has an ancient history[2] and is not limited to writing a letter or sending a telegram to a congressman' it is not confined to appearing before the local city council, or writing letters to the President or Governor or Mayor. See N. A. A. C. P. v. Button, 371 U. S. 415, 429-431. Conventional methods of petitioning may be, and often have been, shut off to large groups of our citizens. Legislators may turn deaf ears; formal complaints may be routed endlessly through a bureaucratic maze; courts may let the wheels of justice grind very slowly. Those who do not control television and radio, those who cannot afford to advertise in newspapers or circulate elaborate pamphlets may have only a more limited type of access to public officials. Their methods should not be condemned as tactics of obstruction and harassment as long as the assembly and petition are peaceable, as these were.

There is no question that petitioners had as their purpose a protest against the arrest of Florida A. & M. students for trying to integrate public theatres. The sheriff's testimony indicates that he well understood the purpose of the rally. The petitioners who testified unequivocally stated that the group was protesting the arrests, and state and local policies of segregation, including segregation of the jail. This testimony was not contradicted or even questioned. The fact that no one gave a formal speech, that no elaborate handbills were distributed, and that the group was not laden with signs would seem to be immaterial. Such methods are not the sine qua non of petitioning for the redress of grievances. The group did sing "freedom" songs. And history shows that a song can be a powerful tool of protest. See Cox v. Louisiana, 379 U. S. 536, 546-548. There was no violence; no threat of violence; no attempted jail break; no storming of a prison; no plan or plot to do anything but protest. The evidence is uncontradicted that the petitioners' conduct did not upset the jailhouse routine; things went on as they normally would. None of the group entered the jail. Indeed, they moved back from the entrance as they were instructed. There was no shoving, no pushing, no disorder or threat of riot. It is said that some of the group blocked part of the driveway leading to the jail entrance. The chief jailer, to be sure, testified that vehicles would not have been able to use the driveway. Never did the students locate themselves so as to cause interference with persons or vehicles going to or coming from the jail. Indeed, it is undisputed that the sheriff and deputy sheriff, in separate cars, were able to drive up the driveway to the parking places near the entrance and that no one obstructed their path. Further, it is undisputed that the entrance to the jail was not blocked. And whenever the students were requested to move they did so. If there was congestion, the solution was a further request to move to lawns or parking areas, not complete ejection and arrest. The claim is made that a tradesman waited inside the jail because some of the protestants were sitting around and leaning on his truck. The only evidence supporting such a conclusion is the testimony of a deputy sheriff that the tradesman "came to the door ... and then did not leave." His remaining is just as consistent with a desire to satisfy his curiosity as it is with a restraint. Finally, the fact that some of the protestants may have felt their cause so just that they were willing to be arrested for making their protest outside the jail seems wholly irrelevant. A petition is nonetheless a petition, though its futility may make martyrdom attractive.

We do violence to the First Amendment when we permit this "petition for redress of grievances" to be turned into a trespass action. It does not help to analogize this problem to the problem of picketing. Picketing is a form of protest usually directed against private interests. I do not see how rules governing picketing in general are relevant to this express constitutional right to assemble and to petition for redress of grievances. In the first place the jailhouse grounds were not marked with "NO TRESPASSING!" signs, nor does respondent claim that the public was generally excluded from the grounds. Only the sheriff's fiat transformed lawful conduct into an unlawful trespass. To say that a private owner could have done the same if the rally has taken place on private property is to speak of a different case, as an assembly and a petition for redress of grievances run to government, not to private proprietors.

The Court forgets that prior to this day our decisions have drastically limited the application of state statutes inhibiting the right to go peacefully on public property to exercise First Amendment rights. As Mr. Justice Roberts wrote in Hague v. C.I.O., 307 U.S. 496, 515-516:

> ... Wherever the title of streets and parks may rest, they have immemorially been held in trust for the use of the public and, time out of mind, have been used for purposes of assembly, communicating thoughts between citizens, and discussing public questions. Such use of the streets and public places has, from ancient times, been a part of the privileges, immunities, rights, and liberties of citizens. The privilege of a citizen of the United States to use the streets and parks for communication of views on national questions may be regulated in the interest of all; it is not absolute, but relative, and must be exercised in subordination to the general comfort and convenience, and in consonance with peace and good order; but it must not, in the guise of regulation, be abridged or denied.

Such was the case of Edwards v. South Carolina, where aggrieved people "peaceably assembled at the site of the State Government" to express their grievances to the citizens of the State as well as to the legislature. Supra, at 235. Edwards was in the tradition of Cox v. New Hampshire, 312 U.S. 569, where the public streets were said to be "immemorially associated" with "the right of assembly and the opportunities for the communication of thought and the discussion of public questions." Id., at 574. When we allow Florida to construe her "malicious trespass" statute to bar a person from going on property knowing it is not his own and to apply that prohibition to public property, we discard Cox and Edwards. Would the case be any different if, as is common, the demonstration took place outside a building which housed both the jail and the legislative body? I think not.

There may be some public places which are so clearly committed to other purposes that their use for the airing of grievances is anomalous. There may be some instances in which assemblies and petitions for redress of grievances are not consistent with other necessary purposes of public property. A noisy meeting may be out of keeping with the serenity of the statehouse or the quiet of the courthouse. No one, for example, would suggest that the Senate gallery is the proper place for a vociferous protest rally. And in other cases it may be necessary to adjust the right to petition for redress of grievances to the other interests inhering in the uses to which the public property is normally put.

See Cox v. New Hampshire, supra; Poulos v. New Hampshire, 345 U.S. 395. But this is quite different from saying that all public places are off limits to people with grievances. See Hague v. C.I.O., supra; Cox v. New Hampshire, supra; Jamison v. Texas, 318 U.S. 413, 415-416; Edwards v. South Carolina, supra. And it is farther yet from saying that the "custodian" of the public property in his discretion can decide when public places shall be used for the communication of ideas, especially the constitutional right to assemble and petition for redress of grievances. See Hague v. C.I.O., supra; Schneider v. State, 308 U.S. 147, 163-164; Cantwell v. Connecticut, 310 U.S. 296; Largent v. Texas, 318 U.S. 418; Niemotko v. Maryland, 340 U.S. 268; Shuttlesworth v. City of Birmingham, 382 U.S. 87. For to place such discretion in any public official, be he the "custodian" of the public property or the local police commissioner (cf. Kunz v. New York, 340 U.S. 290), is to place those who assert their First Amendment rights at his mercy. It gives him the awesome power to decide whose ideas may be expressed and who shall be denied a place to air their claims and petition their government. Such power is out of step with all our decisions prior to today where we have insisted that before a First Amendment right may be curtailed under the guise of a criminal law, any evil that may be collateral to the exercise of the right, must be isolated and defined in a "narrowly drawn" statute (Cantwell v. Connecticut, supra, at 307) lest the power to control excesses of conduct be used to suppress the constitutional right itself. See Stromberg v. California, 283 U.S. 359, 369; Herndon v. Lowry, 301 U.S. 242, 258-259; Edwards v. South Carolina, supra, at 238; N.A.A.C.P. v. Button, supra, at 433.

That tragic consequence happens today when a trespass law is used to bludgeon those who peacefully exercise a First Amendment right to protest to government against one of the most grievous of all modern oppressions which some of our States are inflicting on our citizens.

What we do today disregards the admonition in De Jonge v. Oregon, 299 U.S. 353, 364-365:

> These [First Amendment] rights may be abused by using speech or press or assembly in order to incite to violence and crime. The people through their legislatures may protect themselves against that abuse. But the legislative intervention can find constitutional justification only

> by dealing with the abuse. The rights themselves must not be curtailed. The greater the importance of safeguarding the community from incitements to the overthrow of our institutions by force and violence, the more imperative is the need to preserve inviolate the constitutional rights of free speech, free press and free assembly in order to maintain the opportunity for free political discussion, to the end that government may be responsive to the will of the people and that changes, if desired, may be obtained by peaceful means. Therein lies the security of the Republic, the very foundation of constitutional government.

Today a trespass law is used to penalize people for exercising a constitutional right. Tomorrow a disorderly conduct statute, a breach-of-the-peace statute, a vagrancy statute will be put to the same end.[3] It is said that the sheriff did not make the arrests because of the views which petitioners espoused. That excuse is usually given, as we know from the many cases involving arrests of minority groups for breaches of the peace, unlawful assemblies, and parading without a permit. The charge against William Penn, who preached a nonconformist doctrine in a street in London, was that he caused "a great concourse and tumult of people" in contempt of the King and "to the great disturbance of his peace." 6 How. St. Tr. 951, 955. That was in 1670. In modern times, also, such arrests are usually sought to be justified by some legitimate function of government.[4] Yet by allowing these orderly and civilized protests against injustice to be suppressed, we only increase the forces of frustration which the conditions of second-class citizenship are generating amongst us.

NOTES

1. "Where would we really find the principal danger to civil liberty in a republic? Not in the governors as governors, not in the governed as governed, but in the governed unequipped to function as governors. The chief enemies of republican freedom are mental sloth, conformity, bigotry, superstition, credulity, monopoly in the market of ideas, and utter, benighted ignorance. Relying as it does on the consent of the governed, representative government cannot succeed unless the community receives enough information to grasp public

issues and make sensible decisions. As lights which may have been enough for the past do not meet the needs of the present, so present lights will not suffice for the more extensive and complex problems of the future. Heretofore public enlightenment may have been only a manifest desideratum; today it constitutes an imperative necessity. The First Amendment, says Justice Black, 'reflects the faith that a good society is not static but advancing, and that the fullest possible interchange of ideas and beliefs is essential to attainment of this goal.' [From Feldman v. United States, 322 U.S. 487, 501 (dissenting opinion).]" Cahn, supra, at 102.

2. The historical antecedents of the right to petition for the redress of grievances run deep, and strike to the heart of the democratic philosophy. C. 61 of the Magna Carta provided:

> [T]hat if we or our justiciar, or our bailiffs, or any of our servants shall have done wrong in any way toward any one, or shall have transgressed any of the articles of peace or security; and the wrong shall have been shown to four barons of the aforesaid twenty-five barons, let those four barons come to us or to our justiciar, if we are out of the kingdom, laying before us the transgression, and let them ask that we cause that transgression to be corrected without delay. Sources of Our Liberties 21 (Perry ed. 1959).

The representatives of the people vigorously exercised the right in order to gain the initiative in legislation and a voice in their government. See Pollard, The Evolution of Parliament 329-331 (1964). By 1669 the House of Commons had resolved that "it is an inherent right of every commoner of England to prepare and present Petitions to the house of commons in case of grievance," and "That no court whatsoever hath power to judge or censure any Petition presented...." 4 Parl. Hist. Eng. 432-433 (1669). The Bill of Rights of 1689 provided "That it is the right of the subjects to petition the king and all commitments and prosecutions for such petitioning are illegal." Adams & Stephens, Select Documents of English Constitutional History 464. The right to petition for a redress of grievances was early asserted in the Colonies. The

Stamp Act Congress of 1765 declared "That it is the right of the British subjects in these colonies, to petition the king or either house of parliament." Sources of Our Liberties 271 (Perry ed. 1959). The Declaration and Resolves of the First Continental Congress, adopted October 14, 1774, declared that Americans "have a right peaceably to assemble, consider their grievances, and petition the king; and that all prosecutions, prohibitory proclamations, and commitments for the same, are illegal." Id., at 288. The Declaration of Independence assigned as one of the reasons for the break from England the fact that "Our repeated Petitions have been answered only by repeated injury." The constitutions of four of the original States specifically guaranteed the right. Mass. Const., Art. 19 (1780); Pa. Const., Art IX, § 20 (1790); N. H. Const., Art. 32 (1784); N.C. Const., Art. 18 (1776).

3. In 1932 over 28,000 veterans demanding a bonus marched on Washington, D.C., paraded the streets, and camped mostly in parks and other public lands in the District, Virginia, and Maryland only to be routed by the Army. See Waters, B.E.F. (1933).

4. See, e.g., De Jonge v. Oregon, 299 U.S. 353; Feiner v. New York, 340 U.S. 315; Niemotko v. Maryland, 340 U.S. 268; Edwards v. South Carolina, 372 U.S. 229; Cox v. Louisiana, 379 U.S. 536; Shuttlesworth v. City of Birmingham, 382 U.S. 87. The same is true of other measures which inhibit First Amendment rights. See, e.g., N.A.A.C.P. v. Alabama, 357 U.S. 449; Bates v. City of Little Rock, 361 U.S. 516; Shelton v. Tucker, 364 U.S. 479; N.A.A.C.P. v. Button, 371 U.S. 415. If the invalidity of regulations and official conduct curtailing First Amendment rights turned on an unequivocal showing that the measure was intended to inhibit the rights, protection would be sorely lacking. It is not the intent or purpose of the measure but its effect on First Amendment rights which is crucial.

Brandenburg v. Ohio, 395 U.S. 444 (1969)

A leader of a Ku Klux Klan group gets First Amendment protection from the United States Supreme Court. The Klan leader had been convicted of advocating violence in a speech delivered at a Klan rally. The Supreme Court of Ohio upheld the conviction. The United States Supreme Court reversed, saying that "the constitutional guarantees of free speech and free press do not permit a state to forbid or proscribe advocacy of the use of force or of law violation except where such advocacy is directed to inciting or producing imminent lawless action and is likely to incite or produce such action." Douglas concurs, reviewing previous First Amendment cases dealing with the clear-and-present-danger test and with symbolic speech, declaring "Action is often a method of expression and within the protection of the First Amendment."

* * *

MR. JUSTICE DOUGLAS, concurring.

While I join the opinion of the Court, I desire to enter a caveat.

The "clear and present danger" test was adumbrated by Mr. Justice Holmes in a case arising during World War I--a war "declared" by the Congress, not by the Chief Executive. The case was Schenck v. United States, 249 U.S. 47, 52, where the defendant was charged with attempts to cause insubordination in the military and obstruction of enlistment. The pamphlets that were distributed urged resistance to the draft, denounced conscription, and impugned the motives of those backing the war effort. The First Amendment was tendered as a defense. Mr. Justice Holmes in rejecting that defense said:

> The question in every case is whether the words used are used in such circumstances and are of such a nature as to create a clear and

> present danger that they will bring about the substantive evils that Congress has a right to prevent. It is a question of proximity and degree.

Frohwerk v. United States, 249 U.S. 204, also authored by Mr. Justice Holmes, involved prosecution and punishment for publication of articles very critical of the war effort in World War I. Schenck was referred to as a conviction for obstructing security "by words of persuasion." Id., at 206. And the conviction in Frohwerk was sustained because "the circulation of the paper was in quarters where a little breath would be enough to kindle a flame." Id., at 209.

Debs v. United States, 249 U.S. 211, was the third of the trilogy of the 1918 Term. Debs was convicted of speaking in opposition to the war where his "opposition was so expressed that its natural and intended effect would be to obstruct recruiting." Id., at 215.

> If that was intended and if, in all the circumstances, that would be its probable effect, it would not be protected by reason of its being part of a general program and expressions of a general and conscientious belief. [Ibid.]

In the 1919 Term, the Court applied the Schenck doctrine to affirm the convictions of other dissidents in World War I. Abrams v. United States, 250 U.S. 616, was one instance. Mr. Justice Holmes, with whom Mr. Justice Brandeis concurred, dissented. While adhering to Schenck, he did not think that on the facts a case for overriding the First Amendment had been made out:

> It is only the present danger of immediate evil or an intent to bring it about that warrants Congress in setting a limit to the expression of opinion where private rights are not concerned. Congress certainly cannot forbid all effort to change the mind of the country. [Id., at 628]

Another instance was Schaefer v. United States, 251 U.S. 466, in which Mr. Justice Brandeis, joined by Mr. Justice Holmes, dissented. A third was Pierce v. United States, 252 U.S. 239, in which again Mr. Justice Brandeis, joined by Mr. Justice Holmes, dissented.

Those, then, were the World War I cases that put the

gloss of "clear and present danger" on the First Amendment. Whether the war power--the greatest leveler of them all--is adequate to sustain that doctrine is debatable. The dissents in Abrams, Schaefer, and Pierce show how easily "clear and present danger" is manipulated to crush what Brandeis called "[t]he fundamental right of free men to strive for better conditions through new legislation and new institutions" by argument and discourse (Pierce v. United States, supra, at 273) even in time of war. Though I doubt if the "clear and present danger" test is congenial to the First Amendment in time of a declared war, I am certain it is not reconcilable with the First Amendment in days of peace.

The Court quite properly overrules Whitney v. California, 274 U.S. 357, which involved advocacy of ideas which the majority of the Court deemed unsound and dangerous.

Mr. Justice Holmes, though never formally abandoning the "clear and present danger" test, moved closer to the First Amendment ideal when he said in dissent in Gitlow v. New York, 268 U.S. 652, 673:

> Every idea is an incitement. It offers itself for belief and if believed it is acted on unless some other belief outweighs it or some failure of energy stifles the movement at its birth. The only difference between the expression of an opinion and an incitement in the narrower sense is the speaker's enthusiasm for the result. Eloquence may set fire to reason. But whatever may be thought of the redundant discourse before us it had no chance of starting a present conflagration. If in the long run the beliefs expressed in proletarian dictatorship are destined to be accepted by the dominant forces of the community, the only meaning of free speech is that they should be given their chance and have their way.

We have never been faithful to the philosophy of that dissent.

The Court in Herndon v. Lowry, 301 U.S. 242, overturned a conviction for exercising First Amendment rights to incite insurrection because of lack of evidence of incitement. Id., at 259-261. And see Hartzel v. United States, 322 U.S. 680. In Bridges v. California, 314 U.S. 252, 261-263, we approved the "clear and present danger" test in an elaborate dictum that tightened it and confined it to a narrow category. But in Dennis v. United States, 341 U.S. 494, we opened wide the door, distorting the "clear and present danger" test beyond recognition.[1]

In that case the prosecution dubbed an agreement to teach the Marxist creed a "conspiracy." The case was submitted to a jury on a charge that the jury could not convict unless it found that the defendants "intended to overthrow the Government 'as speedily as circumstances would permit.'" Id., at 509-511. The Court sustained convictions under that charge, construing it to mean a determination of " 'whether the gravity of the "evil," discounted by its improbability, justifies such invasion of free speech as is necessary to avoid the danger.' "[2] Id., at 510, quoting from United States v. Dennis, 183 F. 2d 201, 212.

Out of the "clear and present danger" test came other offspring. Advocacy and teaching of forcible overthrow of government as an abstract principle is immune from prosecution. Yates v. United States, 354 U.S. 298. 318. But an "active" member, who has a guilty knowledge and intent of the aim to overthrow the Government by violence, Noto v. United States, 367 U.S. 290, may be prosecuted. Scales v. United States, 367 U.S. 203, 228. And the power to investigate, backed by the powerful sanction of contempt, includes the power to determine which of the two categories fits the particular witness. Barenblatt v. United States, 360 U.S. 109, 130. And so the investigator roams at will through all of the beliefs of the witness, ransacking his conscience and his innermost thoughts.

Judge Learned Hand, who wrote for the Court of Appeals in affirming the judgment in Dennis, coined the "not improbable" test, 183 F. 2d 201, 214, which this Court adopted and which Judge Hand preferred over the "clear and present danger" test. Indeed, in his book, The Bill of Rights 59 (1958), in referring to Holmes' creation of the "clear and present danger" test, he said, "I cannot help thinking that for once Homer nodded."

My own view is quite different. I see no place in the regime of the First Amendment for any "clear and present danger" test, whether strict and tight as some would make it, or free-wheeling as the Court in Dennis rephrased it.

When one reads the opinions closely and sees when and how the "clear and present danger" test has been applied, great misgivings are aroused. First, the threats were often loud but always puny and made serious only by judges so wedded to the status quo that critical analysis made them nervous. Second, the test was so twisted and perverted in Dennis as to make the trial of those teachers of Marxism an all-out political trial which was part and parcel of the cold war that has eroded substantial parts of the First Amendment.

Action is often a method of expression and within the protection of the First Amendment.

Suppose one tears up his own copy of the Constitution in eloquent protest to a decision of this Court. May he be indicted?

Suppose one rips his own Bible to shreds to celebrate his departure from one "faith" and his embrace of atheism. May he be indicted?

Last Term the Court held in United States v. O'Brien, 391 U.S. 367, 382, that a registrant under Selective Service who burned his draft card in protest of the war in Vietnam could be prosecuted. The First Amendment was tendered as a defense and rejected, the Court saying:

> The issuance of certificates indicating the registration and eligibility classification of individuals is a legitimate and substantial administrative aid in the functioning of this system. And legislation to insure the continuing availability of issued certificates serves a legitimate and substantial purpose in the system's administration. [391 U.S., at 377-378.]

But O'Brien was not prosecuted for not having his draft card available when asked for by a federal agent. He was indicted, tried, and convicted for burning the card. And this Court's affirmance of that conviction was not, with all respect, consistent with the First Amendment.

The act of praying often involves body posture and movement as well as utterances. It is nonetheless protected by the Free Exercise Clause. Picketing, as we have said on numerous occasions, is "free speech plus." See Bakery Drivers Local v. Wohl, 315 U.S. 769, 775 (Douglas, J., concurring); Giboney v. Empire Storage Co., 336 U.S. 490, 501; Hughes v. Superior Court, 339 U.S. 460, 465; Labor Board v.

Fruit Packers, 377 U.S. 58, 77 (Black, J., concurring), and id., at 93 (Harlan, J., dissenting); Cox v. Louisiana, 379 U.S. 559, 578 (opinion of Black, J.); Food Employees v. Logan Plaza, 391 U.S. 308, 326 (Douglas, J., concurring). That means that it can be regulated when it comes to the "plus" or "action" side of the protest. It can be regulated as to the number of pickets and the place and hours (see Cox v. Louisiana, supra), because traffic and other community problems would otherwise suffer.

But none of these considerations are implicated in the symbolic protest of the Vietnam war in the burning of a draft card.

One's beliefs have long been thought to be sanctuaries which government could not invade. Barenblatt is one example of the ease with which that sanctuary can be violated. The lines drawn by the Court between the criminal act of being an "active" Communist and the innocent act of being a nominal or inactive Communist mark the difference only between deep and abiding belief and casual or uncertain belief. But I think that all matters of belief are beyond the reach of subpoenas or the probings of investigators. That is why the invasions of privacy made by investigating committees were notoriously unconstitutional. That is the deep-seated fault in the infamous loyalty-security hearings which, since 1947 when President Truman launched them, have processed 20,000,000 men and women. Those hearings were primarily concerned with one's thoughts, ideas, beliefs, and convictions. They were the most blatant violations of the First Amendment we have ever known.

The line between what is permissible and not subject to control and what may be made impermissible and subject to regulation is the line between ideas and overt acts.

The example usually given by those who would punish speech is the case of one who falsely shouts fire in a crowded theatre.

This is, however, a classic case where speech is brigaded with action. See Speiser v. Randall, 357 U.S. 513, 536-537 (Douglas, J., concurring). They are indeed inseparable and a prosecution can be launched for the overt acts actually caused. Apart from rare instances of that kind, speech is, I think, immune from prosecution. Certainly there is no constitutional line between advocacy of abstract ideas as in Yates and advocacy of political action as in Scales. The quality of advocacy turns on the depth of the conviction; and government has no power to invade that sanctuary of belief and conscience.[3]

NOTES

1. See McKay, The Preference For Freedom, 34 N.Y.U.L. Rev. 1182, 1203-1212 (1959).

2. See Feiner v. New York, 340 U.S. 315, where a speaker was arrested for arousing an audience when the only "clear and present danger" was that the hecklers in the audience would break up the meeting.

3. See Mr. Justice Black, dissenting, in Communications Assn. v. Douds, 339 U.S. 382, 446, 449 et seq.

Eisenstadt v. Baird, 405 U.S. 438 (1972)

The Supreme Court finds for William Baird, who had been convicted in Massachusetts for "exhibiting contraceptive articles in the course of delivering a lecture on contraception to a group of students at Boston University and, second, for giving a young woman a package of Emko vaginal foam at the close of his address." Douglas concurs, stating: "First Amendment rights are not limited to verbal expression. The right to petition often involves the right to walk. The right of assembly may mean pushing or jostling. Picketing involves physical activity as well as a display of a sign. A sit-in can be a quiet, dignified protest that has First Amendment protection even though no speech is involved, as we held in Brown v. Louisiana, supra. Putting contraceptives on display is certainly an aid tc speech and discussion. Handing an article under discussion to a member of the audience is a technique known to all teachers and is commonly used. A handout may be on such a scale as to smack of a vendor's marketing scheme. But passing one article to an audience is merely a projection of the visual aid and should be a permissible adjunct of free speech. Baird was not making a prescription nor purporting to give medical advice. Handing out the article was not even a suggestion that the lady use it. At most it suggested that she become familiar with the product line."

* * *

MR. JUSTICE DOUGLAS, concurring.

While I join the opinion of the Court, there is for me a narrower ground for affirming the Court of Appeals. This to me is a simple First Amendment case, that amendment being applicable to the States by reason of the Fourteenth. Stromberg v. California, 283 U.S. 359.

Under no stretch of the law as presently stated could Massachusetts require a license for those who desire to lecture on planned parenthood, contraceptives, the rights of women, birth control, or any allied subject, or place a tax on that privilege. As to license taxes on First Amendment rights we said in Murdock v. Pennsylvania, 319 U. S. 105, 115:

> A license tax certainly does not acquire constitutional validity because it classifies the privileges protected by the First Amendment along with the wares and merchandise of hucksters and peddlers and treats them all alike. Such equality in treatment does not save the ordinance. Freedom of press, freedom of speech, freedom of religion are in a preferred position.

We held in Thomas v. Collins, 323 U. S. 516, that a person speaking at a labor union rally could not be required to register or obtain a license:

> As a matter of principle a requirement of registration in order to make a public speech would seem generally incompatible with an exercise of the rights of free speech and free assembly. Lawful public assemblies, involving no element of grave and immediate danger to an interest the State is entitled to protect, are not instruments of harm which require previous identification of the speakers. And the right either of workmen or of unions under these conditions to assemble and discuss their own affairs is as fully protected by the Constitution as the right of businessmen, farmers, educators, political party members or others to assemble and discuss their affairs and to enlist the support of others....
>
> ... If one who solicits support for the cause of labor may be required to register as a condition to the exercise of his right to make a public speech, so may he who seeks to rally support for any social, business, religious or political cause. We think a requirement that one must register before he undertakes to make a public speech to enlist support for a lawful movement is quite incompatible with the requirements of the First Amendment. [Id., at 539, 540.]

Baird addressed an audience of students and faculty at Boston University on the subject of birth control and overpopulation. His address was approximately one hour in length and consisted of a discussion of various contraceptive devices displayed by means of diagrams on two demonstration boards, as well as a display of contraceptive devices in their original packages. In addition, Baird spoke of the respective merits of various contraceptive devices; overpopulation in the world; crises throughout the world due to overpopulation; the large number of abortions performed on unwed mothers; and quack abortionists and the potential harm to women resulting from abortions performed by quack abortionists. Baird also urged members of the audience to petition the Massachusetts Legislature and to make known their feelings with regard to birth control laws in order to bring about a change in the laws. At the close of the address Baird invited members of the audience to come to the stage and help themselves to the contraceptive articles. We do not know how many accepted Baird's invitation. We only know that Baird personally handed one woman a package of Emko Vaginal Foam. He was then arrested and indicted (1) for exhibiting contraceptive devices and (2) for giving one such device away. The conviction for the first offense was reversed, the Supreme Judicial Court of Massachusetts holding that the display of the articles was essential to a graphic representation of the lecture. But the conviction for the giving away of one article was sustained. 355 Mass. 746, 247 N.E. 2d 574. The case reaches us by federal habeas corpus.

Had Baird not "given away" a sample of one of the devices whose use he advocated, there could be no question about the protection afforded him by the First Amendment. A State may not "contract the spectrum of available knowledge." Griswold v. Connecticut, 381 U.S. 479, 482. See also Thomas v. Collins, supra; Pierce v. Society of Sisters, 268 U.S. 510; Meyer v. Nebraska, 262 U.S. 390. However noxious Baird's ideas might have been to the authorities, the freedom to learn about them, fully to comprehend their scope and portent, and to weigh them against the tenets of the "conventional wisdom," may not be abridged. Terminiello v. Chicago, 337 U.S. 1. Our system of government requires that we have faith in the ability of the individual to decide wisely, if only he is fully apprised of the merits of a controversy.

> Freedom of discussion, if it would fulfill its historic function in this nation, must embrace all issues about which information is needed or appropriate to enable the members of society to cope with the exigencies of their period." [Thornhill v. Alabama, 310 U.S. 88, 102.]

The teachings of Baird and those of Galileo might be of a different order; but the suppression of either is equally repugnant.

As Milton said in the Areopagitica, "Give me the liberty to know, to utter, and to argue freely according to conscience, above all liberties."

It is said that only Baird's conduct is involved and United States v. O'Brien, 391 U.S. 367, is cited. That case involved a registrant under the Selective Service Act burning his Selective Service draft card. When prosecuted for that act, he defended his conduct as "symbolic speech." The Court held it was not.

Whatever may be thought of that decision on the merits,[1] O'Brien is not controlling here. The distinction between "speech" and "conduct" is a valid one, insofar as it helps to determine in a particular case whether the purpose of the activity was to aid in the communication of ideas, and whether the form of the communication so interferes with the rights of others that reasonable regulations may be imposed.[2] See Public Utilities Comm'n v. Pollak, 343 U.S. 451, 467 (Douglas, J., dissenting). Thus, excessive noise might well be "conduct"--a form of pollution--which can be made subject to precise, narrowly drawn regulations. See Adderley v. Florida, 385 U.S. 39, 54 (Douglas, J., dissenting). But "this Court has repeatedly stated, [First Amendment] rights are not confined to verbal expression. They embrace appropriate types of action...." Brown v. Louisiana, 383 U.S. 131, 141-142.

Baird gave an hour's lecture on birth control and as an aid to understanding the ideas which he was propagating he handed out one sample of one of the devices whose use he was endorsing. A person giving a lecture on coyote-getters would certainly improve his teaching technique if he passed one out to the audience; and he would be protected in doing so unless of course the device was loaded and ready to explode, killing or injuring people. The same holds true in my mind for mousetraps, spray guns, or any other article not dangerous per se on which speakers give educational lectures.

It is irrelevant to the application of these principles that Baird went beyond the giving of information about birth control and advocated the use of contraceptive articles. The

First Amendment protects the opportunity to persuade to action whether that action be unwise or immoral, or whether the speech incites to action. See, e.g., Brandenburg v. Ohio, 395 U.S. 444; Edwards v. South Carolina, 372 U.S. 229; Terminiello v. Chicago, supra.

In this case there was not even incitement to action.[3] There is no evidence or finding that Baird intended that the young lady take the foam home with her when he handed it to her or that she would not have examined the article and then returned it to Baird, had he not been placed under arrest immediately upon handing the article over.[4]

First Amendment rights are not limited to verbal expression.[5] The right to petition often involves the right to walk. The right of assembly may mean pushing or jostling. Picketing involves physical activity as well as a display of a sign. A sit-in can be a quiet, dignified protest that has First Amendment protection even though no speech is involved, as we held in Brown v. Louisiana, supra. Putting contraceptives on display is certainly an aid to speech and discussion. Handing an article under discussion to a member of the audience is a technique known to all teachers and is commonly used. A handout may be on such a scale as to smack of a vendor's marketing scheme. But passing one article to an audience is merely a projection of the visual aid and should be a permissible adjunct of free speech. Baird was not making a prescription nor purporting to give medical advice. Handing out the article was not even a suggestion that the lady use it. At most it suggested that she become familiar with the product line.

I do not see how we can have a Society of the Dialogue, which the First Amendment envisages, if time-honored teaching techniques are barred to those who give educational lectures.

NOTES

1. I have earlier expressed my reasons for believing that the O'Brien decision was not consistent with First Amendment rights. See Brandenburg v. Ohio, 395 U.S. 444, 455 (concurring opinion).

2. In Giboney v. Empire Storage Co., 336 U.S. 490, the

Court upheld a state court injunction against peaceful picketing carried on in violation of a state "anti-restraint-of-trade" law. Giboney, however, is easily distinguished from the present case. Under the circumstances there present, "There was clear danger, imminent and immediate, that unless restrained, appellants would succeed in making [state antitrust] policy a dead letter.... They were exercising their economic power together with that of their allies to compel Empire to abide by union rather than by state regulation of trade." Id., at 503 (footnote omitted; emphasis supplied). There is no such coercion in the instant case nor is there a similar frustration of state policy, see text at n. 4, infra. For an analysis of the state policies underlying the Massachusetts statute which Baird was convicted of having violated, see Dienes, The Progeny of Comstockery--Birth Control Laws Return to Court, 21 Am. U.L. Rev. 1, 3-44 (1971).

3. Even under the restrictive meaning which the Court has given the First Amendment, as applied to the States by the Fourteenth, advocacy of law violation is permissible "except where such advocacy is directed to inciting or producing imminent lawless action and is likely to incite or produce such action." Brandenburg v. Ohio, supra, n. 1, at 447.

Spence v. Washington, 418 U. S. 405 (1974)

A college student who had protested the U. S. invasion of Cambodia and the Kent State killings by taping a peace symbol onto each side of an American flag displayed upside down in his Seattle apartment window has his conviction for violating a Washington "improper use of the flag" statute reversed by the Supreme Court. Douglas states in his concurring opinion that the protester's action was symbolic speech.

* * *

MR. JUSTICE DOUGLAS, concurring.

I would reverse the judgment for substantially the same reasons given by the Iowa Supreme Court in State v. Kool, 212 N.W. 2d 518. In that case, the defendant hung a peace symbol made of cardboard and wrapped in tinfoil in the window of his home and hung a replica of the United States flag behind the peace symbol but in an upside-down position. The state statute made it a crime to "cast contempt upon, satirize, deride or burlesque [the] flag," Iowa Code § 32.1.

The court held that defendant's conduct constituted "symbolic speech." The court, in reversing the conviction, said:

> Someone in Newton might be so intemperate as to disrupt the peace because of this display. But if absolute assurance of tranquility is required, we may as well forget about free speech. Under such a requirement, the only 'free' speech would consist of platitudes. That kind of speech does not need constitutional protection. [212 N.W. 2d, at 521.]

That view is precisely my own. Hence I concur in reversing this judgment of conviction.

# OBSCENITY

Roth v. United States, 354 U.S. 476 (1957)

The majority decides that obscenity is not utterance within the area of protected speech and press. Douglas dissents, stating in his opinion: "Freedom of expression can be suppressed if, and to the extent that, it is so closely brigaded with illegal action as to be an inseparable part of it.... As a people, we cannot afford to relax that standard. For the test that suppresses a cheap tract today can suppress a literary gem tomorrow. All it need do is to incite a lascivious thought or arouse a lustful desire. The list of books that judges or juries can place in that category is endless.... I would give the broad sweep of the First Amendment full support. I have the same confidence in the ability of our people to reject noxious literature as I have in their capacity to sort out the true from the false in theology, economics, politics, or any other field."

* * *

MR. JUSTICE DOUGLAS, with whom MR. JUSTICE BLACK concurs, dissenting.

When we sustain these convictions, we make the legality of a publication turn on the purity of thought which a book or tract instills in the mind of the reader. I do not think we can approve that standard and be faithful to the command of the First Amendment, which by its terms is a restraint on Congress and which by the Fourteenth is a restraint on the States.

In the Roth case the trial judge charged the jury that the statutory words "obscene, lewd and lascivious" describe "that form of immorality which has relation to sexual impurity and has a tendency to excite lustful thoughts." He stated that the term "filthy" in the statute pertains "to that sort of treatment of sexual matters in such a vulgar and indecent way, so that it tends to arouse a feeling of disgust and revulsion." He went on to say that the material "must be calculated to corrupt and debauch the minds and morals" of "the average person in the community," not those of any particular class. "You judge the circulars, pictures and publications which have been put in evidence by present-day standards of the community. You may ask yourselves does it offend the common conscience of the community by present-day standards."

The trial judge who, sitting without a jury, heard the Alberts case and the appellate court that sustained the judgment of conviction, took California's definition of "obscenity" from People v. Wepplo, 78 Cal. App. 2d Supp. 959, 961, 178 P. 2d 853, 855. That case held that a book is obscene "if it has a substantial tendency to deprave or corrupt its readers by inciting lascivious thoughts or arousing lustful desire."

By these standards punishment is inflicted for thoughts provoked, not for overt acts nor antisocial conduct. This test cannot be squared with our decisions under the First Amendment. Even the ill-starred Dennis case conceded that speech to be punishable must have some relation to action which could be penalized by government. Dennis v. United States, 341 U.S. 494, 502-511. Cf. Chafee, The Blessings of Liberty (1956), p. 69. This issue cannot be avoided by saying that obscenity is not protected by the First Amendment. The question remains, what is the constitutional test of obscenity?

The tests by which these convictions were obtained require only the arousing of sexual thoughts. Yet the arousing of sexual thoughts and desires happens every day in normal life in dozens of ways. Nearly 30 years ago a questionnaire sent to college and normal school women graduates asked what things were most stimulating sexually. Of 409 replies, 9 said "music"; 18 said "pictures"; 29 said "dancing"; 40 said "drama"; 95 said "books"; and 218 said "man." Alpert, Judicial Censorship of Obscene Literature, 52 Harv. L. Rev. 40, 73.

The test of obscenity the Court endorses today gives the censor free range over a vast domain. To allow the State to step in and punish mere speech or publication that the judge or the jury thinks has an undesirable impact on thoughts but that is not shown to be a part of unlawful action is drastically to curtail the First Amendment. As recently stated by two of our outstanding authorities on obscenity, "The danger of influencing a change in the current moral standards of the community, or of shocking or offending readers, or of stimulating sex thoughts or desires apart from objective conduct, can never justify the losses to society that result from interference with literary freedom." Lockhart & McClure, Literature, The Law of Obscenity, and the Constitution, 38 Minn. L. Rev. 295, 387.

If we were certain that impurity of sexual thoughts impelled to action, we would be on less dangerous ground in punishing the distributors of this sex literature. But it is by no means clear that obscene literature, as so defined, is a significant factor in influencing substantial deviations from the community standards.

> There are a number of reasons for real and substantial doubts as to the soundness of that hypothesis. (1) Scientific studies of juvenile delinquency demonstrate that those who get into trouble, and are the greatest concern of the advocates of censorship, are far less inclined to read than those who do not become delinquent. The delinquents are generally the adventurous type, who have little use for reading and other non-active entertainment. Thus, even assuming that reading sometimes has an adverse effect upon moral conduct, the effect is not likely to be substantial, for those who are susceptible seldom read. (2) Sheldon and Eleanor Glueck, who are among the country's leading authorities on the treatment and causes of juvenile delinquency, have recently published the results of a ten year study of its causes. They exhaustively studied approximately 90 factors and influences that might lead to or explain juvenile delinquency, but the Gluecks gave no consideration to the type of reading material, if any read by the delinquents. This is, of course, consistent with their finding that delinquents read very little. When those who know so much about the problem of delinquency among youth--the very group about whom the advocates of censorship are most concerned--conclude that what delinquents read has so little effect upon their conduct that it is not worth investigating in an exhaustive study of causes, there is good reason for serious doubt concerning the basic hypothesis on which obscenity censorship is defended. (3) The many other influences in society that stimulate sexual desire are so much more frequent in their influence, and so much more potent in their effect, that the influence of reading is

> likely, at most, to be relatively insignificant in the composite of forces that lead an individual into conduct deviating from the community sex standards. The Kinsey studies show the minor degree to which literature serves as a potent sexual stimulant. And the studies demonstrating that sex knowledge seldom results from reading indicates [sic] the relative unimportance of literature in sex thoughts as compared with other factors in society. [Lockhart & McClure, op cit. supra, pp. 385-386.]

The absence of dependable information on the effect of obscene literature on human conduct should make us wary. It should put us on the side of protecting society's interest in literature, except and unless it can be said that the particular publication has an impact on action that the government can control.

As noted, the trial judge in the Roth case charged the jury in the alternative that the federal obscenity statute outlaws literature dealing with sex which offends "the common conscience of the community." That standard is, in my view, more inimical still to freedom of expression.

The standard of what offends "the common conscience of the community" conflicts, in my judgment, with the command of the First Amendment that "Congress shall make no law ... abridging the freedom of speech, or of the press." Certainly that standard would not be an acceptable one if religion, economics, politics or philosophy were involved. How does it become a constitutional standard when literature treating with sex is concerned?

Any test that turns on what is offensive to the community's standards is too loose, too capricious, too destructive of freedom of expression to be squared with the First Amendment. Under that test, juries can censor, suppress, and punish what they don't like, provided the matter relates to "sexual impurity" or has a tendency "to excite lustful thoughts." This is community censorship in one of its worst forms. It creates a regime where in the battle between the literati and the Philistines, the Philistines are certain to win. If experience in this field teaches anything it is that "censorship of obscenity has almost always been both irrational and indiscriminate." Lockhart & McClure, op. cit. supra, at 371. The test adopted here accentuates that trend.

I assume there is nothing in the Constitution which forbids Congress from using its power over the mails to proscribe conduct on the grounds of good morals. No one would suggest that the First Amendment permits nudity in public places, adultery, and other phases of sexual misconduct.

I can understand (and at times even sympathize) with programs of civic groups and church groups to protect and defend the existing moral standards of the community. I can understand the motives of the Anthony Comstocks who would impose Victorian standards on the community. When speech alone is involved, I do not think that government, consistently with the First Amendment, can become the sponsor of any of these movements. I do not think that government, consistently with the First Amendment, can throw its weight behind one school or another. Government should be concerned with antisocial conduct, not with utterances. Thus, if the First Amendment guarantee of freedom of speech and press is to mean anything in this field, it must allow protests even against the moral code that the standard of the day sets for the community. In other words, literature should not be suppressed merely because it offends the moral code of the censor.

The legality of a publication in this country should never be allowed to turn either on the purity of thought which it instills in the mind of the reader or on the degree to which it offends the community conscience. By either test the role of the censor is exalted, and society's values in literary freedom are sacrificed.

The Court today suggests a third standard. It defines obscene material as that "which deals with sex in a manner appealing to prurient interest." [1] Like the standards applied by the trial judges below, that standard does not require any nexus between the literature which is prohibited and action which the legislature can regulate or prohibit. Under the First Amendment, that standard is no more valid than those which the courts below adopted.

I do not think that the problem can be resolved by the Court's statement that "obscenity is not expression protected by the First Amendment." With the exception of Beauharnais v. Illinois, 343 U.S. 250, none of our cases has resolved problems of free speech and free press by placing any form of expression beyond the pale of the absolute prohibition of the First Amendment. Unlike the law of libel, wrongfully relied on in Beauharnais, there is no special historical evidence that literature dealing with sex was intended to be treated in a special manner by those who drafted the First Amendment. In fact, the first reported court decision in this country involving obscene literature was in 1821. Lockhart & McClure, op. cit. supra, at 324, n. 200. I reject too the implication that problems of freedom of speech and of the press are to be resolved by weighing against the values of free expression, the judgment of the Court that a particular form of that expression has "no redeeming social importance." The First Amendment, its prohibition in terms absolute, was designed to preclude courts as well as legislatures from weighing the values of speech against silence. The First Amendment puts free speech in the preferred position.

Freedom of expression can be suppressed if, and to the extent that, it is so closely brigaded with illegal action as to be an inseparable part of it. Giboney v. Empire Storage Co., 336 U.S. 490, 498; Labor Board v. Virginia Power Co., 314 U.S. 469, 477-478. As a people, we cannot afford to relax that standard. For the test that suppresses a cheap tract today can suppress a literary gem tomorrow. All it need do is to incite a lascivious thought or arouse a lustful desire. The list of books that judges or juries can place in that category is endless.

I would give the broad sweep of the First Amendment full support. I have the same confidence in the ability of our people to reject noxious literature as I have in their capacity to sort out the true from the false in theology, economics, politics, or any other field.

NOTE

1. The definition of obscenity which the Court adopts seems in substance to be that adopted by those who drafted the A.L.I., Model Penal Code. § 207.10 (2) (Tentative Draft No. 6, 1957).

"Obscenity is defined in terms of material which appeals predominantly to prurient interest in sexual matters and which goes beyond customary freedom of expression in these matters. We reject the prevailing tests of tendency to arouse lustful thoughts or desires because it is unrealistically broad for a society that plainly tolerates a great deal of erotic interest in literature, advertising, and art, and because regulation of thought or desire, unconnected with overt misbehavior, raises the most acute constitutional as well as practical difficulties." Id., at 10.

Memoirs v. Massachusetts, 383 U.S. 413 (1966)

The Supreme Court decides that Memoirs of a Woman of Pleasure (Fanny Hill) is not obscene. Justice Douglas writes a concurring opinion in which he states: "The censor is always quick to justify his function in terms that are protective of society. But the First Amendment, written in terms that are absolute, deprives the states of any power to pass on the value, the propriety, or the morality of a particular expression.... Perhaps the most frequently assigned justification for censorship is the belief that erotica produce antisocial sexual conduct. But the relationship has yet to be proven. Indeed, if one were to make judgments on the basis of speculation, one might guess that literature of the most pornographic sort would, in many cases, provide a substitute--not a stimulus--for antisocial sexual conduct.... As I read the First Amendment, Judges cannot gear the literary diet of an entire nation to whatever tepid stuff is incapable of triggering the most demented mind. The First Amendment demands more than a horrible example or two of the perpetrator of a crime of sexual violence, in whose pocket is found a pornographic book, before it allows the nation to be saddled with a regime of censorship."

* * *

MR. JUSTICE DOUGLAS, concurring in the judgment.

Memoirs of a Woman of Pleasure, or, as it is often titled, Fanny Hill, concededly is an erotic novel. It was first published in about 1749 and has endured to this date, despite periodic efforts to suppress it.[1] The book relates the adventures of a young girl who becomes a prostitute in London. At the end, she abandons that life and marries her first lover, observing:

> Thus, at length, I got snug into port, where, in the bosom of virtue, I gather'd the only uncorrupt sweets: where, looking back on the course of vice I had run, and comparing its infamous blandish-

> ments with the infinitely superior joys of innocence, I could not help pitying, even in point of taste, those who immers'd in gross sensuality, are insensible to the so delicate charms of VIRTUE, than which even PLEASURE has not a greater friend, nor than VICE a greater enemy. Thus temperance makes men lords over those pleasures that intemperance enslaves them to: The one, parent of health, vigour, fertility, cheerfulness, and every other desirable good of life; the other, of diseases, debility, barrenness, self-loathing, with only every evil incident to human nature.
>
> ... The paths of Vice are sometimes strew'd with roses, but then they are for ever infamous for many a thorn, for many a cankerworm: those of Virtue are strew'd with roses purely, and those eternally unfading ones.[2]

In 1963, an American publishing house undertook the publication of Memoirs. The record indicates that an unusually large number of orders were placed by universities and libraries; the Library of Congress requested the right to translate the book into Braille. But the Commonwealth of Massachusetts instituted the suit that ultimately found its way here, praying that the book be declared obscene so that the citizens of Massachusetts might be spared the necessity of determining for themselves whether or not to read it.

The courts of Massachusetts found the book "obscene" and upheld its suppression. This Court reverses, the prevailing opinion having seized upon language in the opinion of the Massachusetts Supreme Judicial Court in which it is candidly admitted that Fanny Hill has at least "some minimal literary value." I do not believe that the Court should decide this case on so disingenuous a basis as this. I base my vote to reverse on my view that the First Amendment does not permit the censorship of expression not brigaded with illegal action. But even applying the prevailing view of the Roth test, reversal is compelled by this record which makes clear that Fanny Hill is not "obscene." The prosecution made virtually no effort to prove that this book is "utterly without redeeming social importance." The defense, on the other hand, introduced considerable and impressive testimony to the effect that this was a work of literary, historical, and social importance.[3]

We are judges, not literary experts or historians or

philosophers. We are not competent to render an independent judgment as to the worth of this or any other book, except in our capacity as private citizens. I would pair my Brother Clark on Fanny Hill with the Universalist minister I quote in the Appendix. If there is to be censorship, the wisdom of experts on such matters as literary merit and historical significance must be evaluated. On this record, the Court has no choice but to reverse the judgment of the Massachusetts Supreme Judicial Court, irrespective of whether we would include Fanny Hill in our own libraries.

Four of the seven Justices of the Massachusetts Supreme Judicial Court conclude that Fanny Hill is obscene. 349 Mass. 69, 206 N. E. 2d 403. Four of the seven judges of the New York Court of Appeals conclude that it is not obscene. Larkin v. Putnam's Sons, 14 N.Y. 2d 399, 200 N. E. 2d 760. To outlaw the book on such a voting record would be to let majorities rule where minorities were thought to be supreme. The Constitution forbids abridgment of "freedom of speech, or of the press." Censorship is the most notorious form of abridgment. It substitutes majority rule where minority tastes or viewpoints were to be tolerated.

It is to me inexplicable how a book that concededly has social worth can nonetheless be banned because of the manner in which it is advertised and sold. However florid its cover, whatever the pitch of its advertisements, the contents remain the same.

Every time an obscenity case is to be argued here, my office is flooded with letters and postal cards urging me to protect the community or the Nation by striking down the publication. The messages are often identical even down to commas and semicolons. The inference is irresistible that they were all copied from a school or church blackboard. Dozens of postal cards often are mailed from the same precinct. The drives are incessant and the pressures are great. Happily we do not bow to them. I mention them only to emphasize the lack of popular understanding of our constitutional system. Publications and utterances were made immune from majoritarian control by the First Amendment, applicable to the States by reason of the Fourteenth. No exceptions were made, not even for obscenity. The Court's contrary conclusion in Roth, where obscenity was found to be "outside" the First Amendment, is without justification.

The extent to which the publication of "obscenity" was

a crime at common law is unclear. It is generally agreed that the first reported case involving obscene conduct is The King v. Sir Charles Sedley.[4] Publication of obscene literature, at first thought to be the exclusive concern of the ecclesiastical courts,[5] was not held to constitute an indictable offense until 1727.[6] A later case involved the publication of an "obscene and impious libel" (a bawdy parody of Pope's "Essay on Man") by a member of the House of Commons.[7] On the basis of these few cases, one cannot say that the common-law doctrines with regard to publication of obscenity were anything but uncertain. "There is no definition of the term. There is no basis of identification. There is no unity in describing what is obscene literature, or in prosecuting it. There is little more than the ability to smell it." Alpert, Judicial Censorship of Obscene Literature, 52 Harv. L. Rev. 40, 47 (1938).

But even if the common law had been more fully developed at the time of the adoption of the First Amendment, we would not be justified in assuming that the Amendment left the common law unscathed. In Bridges v. California, 314 U.S. 252, 264, we said:

> [T]o assume that English common law in this field became ours is to deny the generally accepted historical belief that 'one of the objects of the Revolution was to get rid of the English common law on liberty of speech and of the press.' [Schofield, Freedom of the Press in the United States, 9 Publications Amer. Sociol. Soc., 67, 76.]
>
> More specifically, it is to forget the environment in which the First Amendment was ratified. In presenting the proposals which were later embodied in the Bill of Rights, James Madison, the leader in the preparation of the First Amendment, said: 'Although I know whenever the great rights, the trial by jury, freedom of the press, or liberty of conscience, comes in question in that body [Parliament], the invasion of them is resisted by able advocates, yet their Magna Charta does not contain any one provision for the security of those rights, respecting which the people of America are most alarmed. The freedom of the press and rights of conscience, those choicest privileges of the people, are unguarded in the British Constitution.'

And see Grosjean v. American Press Co., 297 U.S. 233, 248-249.

It is true, as the Court observed in Roth, that obscenity laws appeared on the books of a handful of States at the time the First Amendment was adopted.[8] But the First Amendment was, until the adoption of the Fourteenth, a restraint only upon federal power. Moreover, there is an absence of any federal cases or laws relative to obscenity in the period immediately after the adoption of the First Amendment. Congress passed no legislation relating to obscenity until the middle of the nineteenth century.[9] Neither reason nor history warrants exclusion of any particular class of expression from the protection of the First Amendment on nothing more than a judgment that it is utterly without merit. We faced the difficult questions the First Amendment poses with regard to libel in New York Times v. Sullivan, 376 U. S. 254, 269, where we recognized that "libel can claim no talismanic immunity from constitutional limitations." We ought not to permit fictionalized assertions of constitutional history to obscure those questions here. Were the Court to undertake that inquiry, it would be unable, in my opinion, to escape the conclusion that no interest of society with regard to suppression of "obscene" literature could override the First Amendment to justify censorship.

The censor is always quick to justify his function in terms that are protective of society. But the First Amendment, written in terms that are absolute, deprives the States of any power to pass on the value, the propriety, or the morality of a particular expression. Cf. Kingsley Int'l Pictures Corp., v. Regents, 360 U.S. 684, 688-689; Joseph Burstyn, Inc. v. Wilson, 343 U.S. 495. Perhaps the most frequently assigned justification for censorship is the belief that erotica produce antisocial sexual conduct. But that relationship has yet to be proven.[10] Indeed, if one were to make judgments on the basis of speculation, one might guess that literature of the most pornographic sort would, in many cases, provide a substitute--not a stimulus--for antisocial sexual conduct. See Murphy, The Value of Pornography, 10 Wayne L. Rev. 655, 661 and n. 19 (1964). As I read the First Amendment, judges cannot gear the literary diet of an entire nation to whatever tepid stuff is incapable of triggering the most demented mind. The First Amendment demands more than a horrible example or two of the perpetrator of a crime of sexual violence, in whose pocket is found a pornographic book, before it allows the Nation to be saddled with a regime of censorship.[11]

Whatever may be the reach of the power to regulate

conduct, I stand by my view in Roth v. United States, supra, that the First Amendment leaves no power in government over expression of ideas.

## APPENDIX TO OPINION OF MR. JUSTICE DOUGLAS, CONCURRING

### Dr. Peale and Fanny Hill

An Address by
Rev. John R. Graham, First Universalist Church of Denver

December 1965

At the present point in the twentieth century, it seems to me that there are two books which symbolize the human quest for what is moral. Sin, Sex and Self-Control by Dr. Norman Vincent Peale, the well-known clergyman of New York City, portrays the struggle of contemporary middle-class society to arrive at a means of stabilizing behavior patterns. At the same time, there is a disturbing book being sold in the same stores with Dr. Peale's volume. It is a seventeenth century English novel by John Cleland and it is known as Fanny Hill: The Memoirs of a Woman of Pleasure.

Quickly, it must be admitted that it appears that the two books have very little in common. One was written in a day of scientific and technological sophistication, while the other is over two hundred years old. One is acclaimed in the pulpit, while the other is protested before the United States Supreme Court. Sin, Sex and Self-Control is authored by a Christian pastor, while Fanny Hill represents thoughts and experiences of a common prostitute. As far as the general public seems to be concerned, one is moral and the other is hopelessly immoral. While Dr. Peale is attempting to redeem the society, most people believe that Fanny Hill can only serve as another instance in an overall trend toward an immoral social order. Most parents would be pleased to find their children reading a book by Dr. Peale, but I am afraid that the same parents would be sorely distressed to discover a copy of Fanny Hill among the school books of their offspring.

Although one would not expect to find very many similarities between the thoughts of a pastor and those of a prostitute, the subject matter of the two books is, in many ways, strangely similar. While the contents are radically different, the concerns are the same. Both authors deal with human experience. They are concerned with people and what happens to them in the world in which they live each day. But most significantly of all, both books deal with the age-old question of "What is moral?" I readily admit that this concern with the moral is more obvious in Dr. Peale's book than it is in the one by John Cleland. The search for the moral in Fanny Hill is clothed in erotic passages which seem to equate morality with debauchery as far as the general public is concerned. At the same time, Dr. Peale's book is punctuated with such noble terms as "truth," "love," and "honesty."

These two books are not very important in themselves. They may or may not be great literature. Whether they will survive through the centuries to come is a question, although John Cleland has an historical edge on Norman Vincent Peale! However, in a symbolic way they do represent the struggle of the moral quest and for this reason they are important.

Dr. Peale begins his book with an analysis of contemporary society in terms of the moral disorder which is more than obvious today. He readily admits that the traditional Judeo-Christian standards of conduct and behavior no longer serve as strong and forceful guides. He writes:

> For more than forty years, ever since my ordination, I had been preaching that if a person would surrender to Jesus Christ and adopt strong affirmative attitudes toward life he would be able to live abundantly and triumphantly. I was still absolutely convinced that this was true. But I was also bleakly aware that the whole trend in the seventh decade of the twentieth century seemed to be away from the principles and practices of religion--not toward them. [Page 1.]

Dr. Peale then reflects on the various changes that have taken place in our day and suggests that although he is less than enthusiastic about the loss of allegiance to religion, he is, nevertheless, willing to recognize that one cannot live by illusion.

After much struggle, Dr. Peale then says that he was able to develop a new perspective on the current moral dilemma of our times. What first appeared to be disaster was really opportunity. Such an idea, coming from him, should not be very surprising, since he is more or less devoted to the concept of "positive thinking!" He concludes that our society should welcome the fact that the old external authorities have fallen. He does not believe that individuals should ever be coerced into certain patterns of behavior.

According to Dr. Peale, we live in a day of challenge. Our society has longed for a time when individuals would be disciplined by self-control, rather than being motivated by external compunction. Bravely and forthrightly, he announces that the time has now come when self-control can and must replace external authority. He is quick to add that the values contained in the Judeo-Christian tradition and "the American way of life" must never be abandoned for they emanate from the wellsprings of "Truth." What has previously been only an external force must now be internalized by individuals.

In many ways, Dr. Peale's analysis of the social situation and the solution he offers for assisting the individual to stand against the pressures of the times, come very close to the views of Sigmund Freud. He felt that society could and would corrupt the individual and, as a result, the only sure defense was a strong super-ego or conscience. This is precisely what Dr. Peale recommends.

Interestingly enough John Cleland, in Fanny Hill, is concerned with the same issues. Although the question of moral behavior is presented more subtly in his book, the problem with which he deals is identical. There are those who contend that the book is wholly without redeeming social importance. They feel that it appeals only to prurient interests.

I firmly believe that Fanny Hill is a moral, rather than an immoral, piece of literature. In fact, I will go as far as to suggest that it represents a more significant view of morality than is represented by Dr. Peale's book Sin, Sex and Self-Control. As is Dr. Peale, Cleland is concerned with the nature of the society and the relationship of the individual to it. Fanny Hill appears to me to be an allegory. In the story, the immoral becomes the moral and the unethical emerges as the ethical. Nothing is more distressing than to discover that what is commonly considered to be evil may, in reality, demonstrate characteristics of love and concern.

There is real irony in the fact that Fanny Hill, a

rather naive young girl who becomes a prostitute, finds warmth, understanding and the meaning of love and faithfulness amid surroundings and situations which the society, as a whole, condemns as debased and depraved. The world outside the brothel affirms its faith in the dignity of man, but people are often treated as worthless and unimportant creatures. However, within the world of prostitution, Fanny Hill finds friendship, understanding, respect and is treated as a person of value. When her absent lover returns, she is not a lost girl of the gutter. One perceives that she is a whole and healthy person who has discovered the ability to love and be loved in a brothel.

I think Cleland is suggesting that one must be cautious about what is condemned and what is held in honor. From Dr. Peale's viewpoint, the story of Fanny Hill is a tragedy because she did not demonstrate self-control. She refused to internalize the values inherent in the Judeo-Christian tradition and the catalog of sexual scenes in the book, fifty-two in all, are a symbol of the debased individual and the society in which he lives.

Dr. Peale and others, would be correct in saying that Fanny Hill did not demonstrate self-control. She did, however, come to appreciate the value of self-expression. At no time were her "clients" looked upon as a means to an end. She tried and did understand them and she was concerned about them as persons. When her lover, Charles, returned she was not filled with guilt and remorse. She accepted herself as she was and was able to offer him her love and devotion.

I have a feeling that many people fear the book Fanny Hill, not because of its sexual scenes, but because the author raises serious question with the issue of what is moral and what is immoral. He takes exception to the idea that repression and restraint create moral individuals. He develops the thought that self-expression is more human than self-control. And he dares to suggest that, in a situation which society calls immoral and debased, a genuine love and respect for life and for people, as human beings, can develop. Far from glorifying vice, John Cleland points an accusing finger at the individual who is so certain as to what it means to be a moral man.

There are those who will quickly say that this "message" will be missed by the average person who reads Fanny

Hill. But this is precisely the point. We become so accustomed to pre-judging what is ethical and what is immoral that we are unable to recognize that what we accept as good may be nothing less than evil because it harms people.

I know of no book which more beautifully describes meaningful relationships between a man and a woman than does Fanny Hill. In many marriages, men use a woman for sexual gratification and otherwise, as well as vice versa. But this is not the case in the story of Fanny Hill. The point is simply that there are many, many ways in which we hurt, injure and degrade people that are far worse than either being or visiting a prostitute. We do this all in the name of morality.

At the same time that Dr. Peale is concerned with sick people, John Cleland attempts to describe healthy ones. Fanny Hill is a more modern and certainly more valuable book than Sin, Sex and Self-Control because the author does not tell us how to behave, but attempts to help us understand ourselves and the nature of love and understanding in being related to other persons. Dr. Peale's writing emphasizes the most useful commodities available to man--self centeredness and self-control. John Cleland suggests that self-understanding and self-expression may not be as popular, but they are more humane.

The "Peale approach" to life breeds contentment, for it suggests that each one of us can be certain as to what is good and true. Standards for thinking and behavior are available and all we need to do is appropriate them for our use. In a day when life is marked by chaos and confusion, this viewpoint offers much in the way of comfort and satisfaction. There is only one trouble with it, however, and that is that it results in conformity, rigid behavior and a lack of understanding. It results in personality configurations that are marked with an intense interest in propositions about Truth and Right but, at the same time, build a wall against people. Such an attitude creates certainty, but there is little warmth. The idea develops that there are "my kind of people" and they are "right." It forces us to degrade, dismiss and ultimately attempt to destroy anyone who does not agree with us.

To be alive and sensitive to life means that we have to choose what we want. There is no possible way for a person to be a slave and free at the same time. Self-control and self-expression are at opposite ends of the continuum. As much as some persons would like to have both, it is necessary to make a choice, since restraint and openness are contradictory qualities. To internalize external values denies the possibility of self-expression. We must decide what we want, when it comes to conformity and creativity. If we want people to behave in a structured and predictable manner, then the ideal of creativity cannot have meaning....

Long ago Plato said, "What is honored in a country will be cultivated there." More and more, we reward people for thinking alike and as a result, we become frightened, beyond belief, of those who take exception to the current consensus. If our society collapses, it will not be because people read a book such as Fanny Hill. It will fall, because we will have refused to understand it. Decadence, in a nation or an individual, arises not because there is a lack of ability to distinguish between morality and immorality, but because the opportunity for self-expression has been so controlled or strangled that the society or the person becomes a robot.

The issue which a Dr. Peale will never understand, because he is a victim of it himself and which John Cleland describes with brilliant clarity and sensitive persuasion is that until we learn to respect ourselves enough that we leave each other alone, we cannot discover the meaning of morality.

Dr. Peale and Fanny Hill offer the two basic choices open to man. Man is free to choose an autocentric existence which is marked by freedom from ambiguity and responsibility. Autocentricity presupposes a "closed world" where life is predetermined and animal-like. In contrast to this view, there is the allocentric outlook which is marked by an "open encounter of the total person with the world." Growth, spontaneity and expression are the goals of such an existence.

Dr. Peale epitomizes the autocentric approach. He offers "warm blankets" and comfortable "cocoons" for those who want to lose their humanity. On the other hand, Fanny Hill represents the allocentric viewpoint which posits the possibility for man to raise his sights, stretch his imagination, cultivate his sensitiveness as well as deepen and broaden his perspectives. In discussing the autocentric idea, Floyd

W. Matson writes,

> Human beings conditioned to apathy and affluence may well prefer this regressive path of least resistance, with its promise of escape from freedom and an end to striving. But we know at least that it is open to them to choose otherwise: in a word, to choose themselves. [The Broken Image, page 193.]

In a day when people are overly sensitive in drawing lines between the good and the bad, the right and the wrong, as well as the true and the false, it seems to me that there is great irony in the availability of a book such as Fanny Hill. Prostitution may be the oldest profession in the world, but we are ever faced with a question which is becoming more and more disturbing: "What does a prostitute look like?"

NOTES

1. Memoirs was the subject of what is generally regarded as the first recorded suppression of a literary work in this country on grounds of obscenity. See Commonwealth v. Holmes, 17 Mass. 336 (1821). The edition there condemned differed from the present volume in that it contained apparently erotic illustrations.

2. Memoirs, at 213-214 (Putnam ed. 1963).

3. The defense drew its witnesses from the various colleges located within the Commonwealth of Massachusetts. These included: Fred Holly Stocking, Professor of English and Chairman of the English Department, Williams College; John M. Bullitt, Professor of English and Master of Quincy House, Harvard College; Robert H. Sproat, Associate Professor of English Literature, Boston University; Norman N. Holland, Associate Professor of English, Massachusetts Institute of Technology; and Ira Konigsberg, Assistant Professor of English and American Literature, Brandeis University.

   In addition, the defense introduced into evidence reviews of impartial literary critics. These are, in my opinion, of particular significance since their publication indicates that the book is of sufficient significance as to warrant serious critical comment. The reviews were by V. S. Pritchett, New York Review of Books, p. 1 (Oct. 31, 1963); Brigid Brophy, New Statesman, p. 710 (Nov. 15, 1963); and J. Donald Adams, New York Times Book Review, p. 2 (July 28, 1963). And the Appendix to this opinion contains another contemporary view.

4. There are two reports of the case. The first is captioned Le Roy v. Sr. Charles Sidney, 1 Sid. 168, pl. 29 (K. B. 1663); the second is titled Sir Charles Sydlyes Case, 1 Keble 620 (K. B. 1663). Sir Charles had made a public appearance on a London balcony while nude, intoxicated, and talkative. He delivered a lengthy speech to the assembled crowd, uttered profanity, and hurled bottles containing what was later described as an "offensive liquor" upon the crowd. The proximate source of the "offensive liquor" appears to have been Sir Charles. Alpert, Judicial Censorship of Obscene Literature, 52 Harv. L. Rev. 40-43 (1938).

5. The Queen v. Read, 11 Mod. 142 (Q. B. 1707).

6. Dominus Rex v. Curl, 2 Strange 789 (K. B. 1727). See Straus, The Unspeakable Curll (1927).

7. Rex v. Wilkes, 4 Burr. 2527 (K. B. 1770). The prosecution of Wilkes was a highly political action, for Wilkes was an outspoken critic of the government. See R. W. Postgate, That Devil Wilkes (1929). It has been suggested that the prosecution in this case was a convenient substitute for the less attractive charge of seditious libel. See Alpert, supra, at 45.

8. See 354 U. S., at 483 and n. 13. For the most part, however, the early legislation was aimed at blasphemy and profanity. See 354 U. S., at 482-483 and n. 12. The first reported decision involving the publication of obscene literature does not come until 1821. See Commonwealth v. Holmes, 17 Mass. 336. It was not until after the Civil War that state prosecutions of this sort became commonplace. See Lockhart & McClure, Literature, The Law of Obscenity, and the Constitution, 38 Minn. L. Rev. 295, 324-325 (1954).

9. Tariff Act of 1842, c. 270, § 28, 5 Stat. 566 (prohibiting importation of obscene "prints"). Other federal legislation followed; the development of federal law is

traced in Cairns, Paul & Wishner, Sex Censorship: The Assumptions of Anti-Obscenity Laws and the Empirical Evidence, 46 Minn. L. Rev. 1009, 1010 n. 2 (1962).

10. See Cairns, Paul & Wishner, supra, 1034-1041; Lockhart & McClure, supra, at 382-387. And see the summary of Dr. Jahoda's studies prepared by her for Judge Frank, reprinted in United States v. Roth, 237 F. 2d 796, 815-816 (concurring opinion). Those who are concerned about children and erotic literature would do well to consider the counsel of Judge Bok:

It will be asked whether one would care to have one's young daughter read these books. I suppose that by the time she is old enough to wish to read them she will have learned the biologic facts of life and the words that go with them. There is something seriously wrong at home if those facts have not been met and faced and sorted by then; it is not children so much as parents that should receive our concern about this. I should prefer that my own three daughters meet the facts of life and the literature of the world in my library than behind a neighbor's barn, for I can face the adversary there directly. If the young ladies are appalled by what they read, they can close the book at the bottom of page one; if they read further, they will learn what is in the world and in its people, and no parents who have been discerning with their children need fear the outcome. Nor can they hold it back, for life is a series of little battles and minor issues, and the burden of choice is on us all, every day, young and old. [Commonwealth v. Gordon, 66 Pa. D. & C. 101, 110.]

11. It would be a futile effort even for a censor to attempt to remove all that might possibly stimulate antisocial sexual conduct:

The majority [of individuals], needless to say, are somewhere between the over-scrupulous extremes of excitement and frigidity.... Within this variety, it is impossible to define 'hard-core' pornography, as if there were some singly lewd concept from which all profane ideas passed by imperceptible degrees into that sexuality called holy. But there is no 'hard-core.' Everything, every idea, is capable of being obscene if the personality perceiving it so apprehends it.

It is for this reason that books, pictures, charades, ritual, the spoken word, can and do lead directly to conduct harmful to the self indulging in it and to others. Heinrich Pommerenke, who was a rapist, abuser, and mass slayer of women in Germany, was prompted to his series of ghastly deeds by Cecil B. DeMille's The Ten Commandments. During the scene of the Jewish women dancing about the Golden Calf, all the doubts of his life came clear: Women were the source of the world's trouble and it was his mission to both punish them for this and to execute them. Leaving the theater, he slew his first victim in a park nearby. John George Haigh, the British vampire who sucked his victims' blood through soda straws and dissolved their drained bodies in acid baths, first had his murder-inciting dreams and vampire-longings from watching the 'voluptuous' procedure of--an Anglican High Church Service!" Murphy, supra, at 668.

Ginzburg v. United States, 383 U.S. 463 (1966)

The Supreme Court upholds the conviction of Ralph Ginzburg on the principle that the manner in which the "obscene" materials were advertised and disseminated could be used to determine whether the materials were constitutionally protected. Douglas dissents, declaring at the outset of his dissenting opinion: "Today's condemnation of the use of sex symbols to sell literature engrafts another exception on First Amendment rights that is as unwarranted as the judge-made exception concerning obscenity.... A book should stand on its own, irrespective of the reasons why it was written or the wiles used in selling it."

* * *

MR. JUSTICE DOUGLAS, dissenting.

Today's condemnation of the use of sex symbols to sell literature engrafts another exception on First Amendment rights that is as unwarranted as the judge-made exception concerning obscenity. This new exception condemns an advertising technique as old as history. The advertisements of our best magazines are chock-full of thighs, ankles, calves, bosoms, eyes and hair, to draw the potential buyer's attention to lotions, tires, food, liquor, clothing, autos, and even insurance policies. The sexy advertisement neither adds to nor detracts from the quality of the merchandise being offered for sale. And I do not see how it adds to or detracts one whit from the legality of the book being distributed. A book should stand on its own, irrespective of the reasons why it was written or the wiles used in selling it. I cannot imagine any promotional effort that would make chapters 7 and 8 of the Song of Solomon any the less or any more worthy of First Amendment protection than does their unostentatious inclusion in the average edition of the Bible.

I

The Court has, in a variety of contexts, insisted that

preservation of rights safeguarded by the First Amendment requires vigilance. We have recognized that a "criminal prosecution under a statute regulating expression usually involves imponderables and contingencies that themselves may inhibit the full exercise of First Amendment freedoms." Dombrowski v. Pfister, 380 U.S. 479, 486. Where uncertainty is the distinguishing characteristic of a legal principle--in this case the Court's "pandering" theory--"the free dissemination of ideas may be the loser." Smith v. California, 361 U.S. 147, 151. The Court today, however, takes the other course, despite the admonition in Speiser v. Randall, 357 U.S. 513, 525, that "[t]he separation of legitimate from illegitimate speech calls for ... sensitive tools." Before today, due regard for the frailties of free expression led us to reject insensitive procedures[1] and clumsy, vague, or overbroad substantive rules even in the realm of obscenity.[2] For as the Court emphasized in Roth v. United States, 354 U.S. 476, 488, "[t]he door barring federal and state intrusion into this area cannot be left ajar; it must be kept tightly closed and opened only the slightest crack necessary to prevent encroachment upon more important interests."

Certainly without the aura of sex in the promotion of these publications their contents cannot be said to be "utterly without redeeming social importance." Roth v. United States, supra, at 484.[3] One of the publications condemned today is the Housewife's Handbook on Selective Promiscuity, which a number of doctors and psychiatrists thought had clinical value. One clinical psychologist said: "I should like to recommend it, for example, to the people in my church to read, especially those who are having marital difficulities, in order to increase their tolerance and understanding for one another. Much of the book, I should think, would be very suitable reading for teen age people, especially teen age young women who could empathize strongly with the growing up period that Mrs. Rey [Anthony] relates, and could read on and be disabused of some of the unrealistic notions about marriage and sexual experiences. I should think this would make very good reading for the average man to help him gain a better appreciation of female sexuality."

The Rev. George Von Hilsheimer III, a Baptist minister,[4] testified that he has used the book "insistently in my pastoral counseling and in my formal psychological counseling":

> The book is a history, a very unhappy history, of a series of sexual and psychological misadventures

> and the encounter of a quite typical and average American woman with quite typical and average American men. The fact that the book itself is the history of a woman who has had sexual adventures outside the normally accepted bounds of marriage which, of course for most Americans today, is a sort of serial polygamy, it does not teach or advocate this, but gives the women to whom I give the book at least a sense that their own experiences are not unusual, that their sexual failures are not unusual, and that they themselves should not be guilty because they are, what they say, sexual failures.

I would think the Baptist minister's evaluation would be enough to satisfy the Court's test, unless the censor's word is to be final or unless the experts are to be weighed in the censor's scales, in which event one Anthony Comstock would too often prove more weighty than a dozen more detached scholars, or unless we, the ultimate Board of Censors, are to lay down standards for review that give the censor the benefit of the "any evidence" rule or the "substantial evidence" rule as in the administrative law field. Cf. Universal Camera Corp. v. Labor Board, 340 U.S. 474. Or perhaps we mean to let the courts sift and choose among conflicting versions of the "redeeming social importance" of a particular book, making sure that they keep their findings clear of doubt lest we reverse, as we do today in Memoirs v. Massachusetts, ante, p. 413, because the lower court in an effort to be fair showed how two-sided the argument was. Since the test is whether the publication is "utterly without redeeming social importance," then I think we should honor the opinion of the Baptist minister who testified as an expert in the field of counseling.

Then there is the newsletter Liaison. One of the defendants' own witnesses, critic Dwight Macdonald, testified that while, in his opinion, it did not go beyond the customary limits of candor tolerated by the community, it was "an extremely tasteless, vulgar and repulsive issue." This may, perhaps, overstate the case, but Liaison is admittedly little more than a collection of "dirty" jokes and poems, with the possible exception of an interview with Dr. Albert Ellis. As to this material, I find wisdom in the words of the late Judge Jerome Frank:

> Those whose views most judges know best are other lawyers. Judges can and should take judicial

> notice that, at many gatherings of lawyers at Bar Association or of alumni of our leading law schools, tales are told fully as 'obscene' as many of those distributed by men ... convicted for violation of the obscenity statute.... 'One thinks of the lyrics sung ... by a certain respected and conservative member of the faculty of a great law-school which considers itself the most distinguished and which is the Alma Mater of many judges sitting on upper courts.'[5]

Liaison's appeal is neither literary nor spiritual. But neither is its appeal to a "shameful or morbid interest in nudity, sex, or excretion." The appeal is to the ribald sense of humor which is--for better or worse--a part of our culture. A mature society would not suppress this newsletter as obscene but would simply ignore it.

Then there is EROS. The Court affirms the judgment of the lower court, which found only four of the many articles and essays to be obscene. One of the four articles consisted of numerous ribald limericks, to which the views expressed as to Liaison would apply with equal force. Another was a photo essay entitled "Black and White in Color" which dealt with interracial love: a subject undoubtedly offensive to some members of our society. Critic Dwight Macdonald testified:

> I suppose if you object to the idea of a Negro and a white person having sex together, then, of course, you would be horrified by it. I don't. From the artistic point of view I thought it was very good. In fact, I thought it was done with great taste, and I don't know how to say it--I never heard of him before, but he is obviously an extremely competent and accomplished photographer.

Another defense witness, Professor Horst W. Janson, presently the Chairman of the Fine Arts Department at New York University, testified:

> I think they are outstandingly beautiful and artistic photographs. I can not imagine the theme being treated in a more lyrical and delicate manner than it has been done here....
>
> I might add here that of course photography in

> appropriate hands is an artistic instrument and this particular photographer has shown a very great awareness of compositional devices and patterns that have a long and well-established history in western art....
>
> The very contrast in the color of the two bodies of course has presented him with certain opportunities that he would not have had with two models of the same color, and he has taken rather extraordinary and very delicate advantages of these contrasts.

The third article found specifically by the trial judge to be obscene was a discussion by Drs. Eberhard W. and Phyllis C. Kronhausen of erotic writing by women, with illustrative quotations.[6] The worth of the article was discussed by Dwight Macdonald, who stated:

> I thought [this was] an extremely interesting and important study with some remarkable quotations from the woman who had put down her sense of love-making, of sexual intercourse ... in an extremely eloquent way. I have never seen this from the woman's point of view. I thought the point they made, the difference between the man's and the woman's approach to sexual intercourse was very well made and very important.

Still another article found obscene was a short introduction to and a lengthy excerpt from My Life and Loves by Frank Harris, about which there is little in the record. Suffice it to say that this seems to be a book of some literary stature. At least I find it difficult on this record to say that it is "utterly without redeeming social importance."[7]

Some of the tracts for which these publishers go to prison concern normal sex, some homosexuality, some the masochistic yearning that is probably present in everyone and dominant in some. Masochism is a desire to be punished or subdued. In the broad frame of reference the desire may be expressed in the longing to be whipped and lashed, bound and gagged, and cruelly treated.[8] Why is it unlawful to cater to the needs of this group? They are, to be sure, somewhat offbeat, nonconformist, and odd. But we are not in the realm of criminal conduct, only ideas and tastes. Some like Chopin, others like "rock and roll." Some are "normal," some are masochistic, some deviant in other respects, such as the homosexual. Another group also represented here translates mundane articles into sexual symbols. This group, like those embracing masochism, are anathema to the so-called stable majority. But why is freedom of the press and expression denied them? Are they to be barred from communicating in symbolisms important to them? When the Court today speaks of "social value," does it mean a "value" to the majority? Why is not a minority "value" cognizable? The masochistic group is one; the deviant group is another. Is it not important that members of those groups communicate with each other? Why is communication by the "written word" forbidden? If we were wise enough, we might know that communication may have greater therapeutical value than any sermon that those of the "normal" community can ever offer. But if the communication is of value to the masochistic community or to others of the deviant community, how can it be said to be "utterly without redeeming social importance"? "Redeeming" to whom? "Importance" to whom?

We took quite a different stance in One, Inc. v. Olesen, 355 U.S. 371, where we unanimously reversed the decision of the Court of Appeals in 241 F. 2d 772 without opinion. Our holding was accurately described by Lockhart and McClure, Obscenity Censorship: The Core Constitutional Issue--What Is Obscene? 7 Utah L. Rev. 289, 293 (1961):

> [This] was a magazine for homosexuals entitled One--The Homosexual Magazine, which was definitely not a scientific or critical magazine, but appears to have been written to appeal to the tastes and interests of homosexuals.[9]

Man was not made in a fixed mould. If a publication caters to the idiosyncrasies of a minority, why does it not have some "social importance"? Each of us is a very temporary transient with likes and dislikes that cover the spectrum. However plebian my tastes may be, who am I to say that others' tastes must be so limited and that other tastes have no "social importance"? How can we know enough to probe the mysteries of the subconscious of our people and say that this is good for them and that is not? Catering to the most eccentric taste may have "social importance" in giving that minority an opportunity to express itself rather than to repress its inner desires, as I suggest in my separate opinion in Memoirs v. Massachusetts, ante, at 431-432. How can we know that this expression may not prevent anti-social conduct?

I find it difficult to say that a publication has no "social importance" because it caters to the taste of the most unorthodox amongst us. We members of this Court should be among the last to say what should be orthodox in literature. An omniscience would be required which few in our whole society possess.

II

This leads me to the conclusion, previously noted, that the First Amendment allows all ideas to be expressed--whether orthodox, popular, offbeat, or repulsive. I do not think it permissible to draw lines between the "good" and the "bad" and be true to the constitutional mandate to let all ideas alone. If our Constitution permitted "reasonable" regulation of freedom of expression, as do the constitutions of some nations,[10] we would be in a field where the legislative and the judiciary would have much leeway. But under our charter all regulation or control of expression is barred. Government does not sit to reveal where the "truth" is. People are left to pick and choose between competing offerings. There is no compulsion to take and read what is repulsive any more than there is to spend one's time poring over government bulletins, political tracts, or theological treatises. The theory is that people are mature enough to pick and choose, to recognize trash when they see it, to be attracted to the literature that satisfies their deepest need and hopefully to move from plateau to plateau and finally reach the world of enduring ideas.

I think this is the ideal of the Free Society written into our Constitution. We have no business acting as censors or endowing any group with censorship powers. It is shocking to me for us to send to prison anyone for publishing anything, especially tracts so distant from any incitement to action as the ones before us.

[This opinion applies also to <u>Mishkin v. New York, post</u>, p. 502.]

NOTES

1. <u>Marcus v. Search Warrant</u>, 367 U.S. 717; <u>A Quantity of Books v. Kansas</u>, 378 U.S. 205; <u>Freedman v. Maryland</u>, 380 U.S. 51.

2. Butler v. Michigan, 352 U.S. 380; Smith v. California, 361 U.S. 147; Manual Enterprises, Inc. v. Day, 370 U.S. 478 (opinion of Harlan, J.).

3. The Court's premise is that Ginzburg represented that his publications would be sexually arousing. The Court, however, recognized in Roth: "[S]ex and obscenity are not synonymous. Obscene material is material which deals with sex in a manner appealing to prurient interest ... i.e., a shameful or morbid interest in nudity, sex, or excretion...." Id., 487 and n. 20 (emphasis added). The advertisements for these publications, which the majority quotes (ante, at 468-469, n. 9), promised candor in the treatment of matters pertaining to sex, and at the same time proclaimed that they were artistic or otherwise socially valuable. In effect, then, these advertisements represented that the publications are not obscene.

4. Rev. Von Hilsheimer obtained an A.B. at the University of Miami in 1951. He did graduate work in psychology and studied analysis and training therapy. Thereafter, he did graduate work as a theological student, and received a degree as a Doctor of Divinity from the University of Chicago in 1957. He had extensive experience as a group counselor, lecturer, and family counselor. He was a consultant to President Kennedy's Study Group on National Voluntary Services, and a member of the board of directors of Mobilization for Youth.

5. United States v. Roth, 237 F. 2d 796, 822 and n. 58 (concurring opinion).

6. The Kronhausens wrote Pornography and the Law (1959).

7. The extensive literary comment which the book's publication generated demonstrates that it is not "utterly without redeeming social importance." See, e.g., New York Review of Books, p. 6 (Jan. 9, 1964); New Yorker, pp. 79-80 (Jan. 4, 1964); Library Journal, pp. 4743-4744 (Dec. 15, 1963); New York Times Book Review, p. 10 (Nov. 10, 1963); Time, pp. 102-104 (Nov. 8, 1963); Newsweek, pp. 98-100 (Oct. 28, 1963); New Republic, pp. 23-27 (Dec. 28, 1963).

8. See Krafft-Ebing, Psychopathia Sexualis, p. 89 et seq.

(1893); Eisler, Man Into Wolf, p. 23 et seq. (1951); Stekel, Sadism and Masochism (1929) passim; Bergler, Principles of Self-Damage (1959) passim; Reik, Masochism in Modern Man (1941) passim.

9. The Court of Appeals summarized the contents as follows:

"The article 'Sappho Remembered' is the story of a lesbian's influence on a young girl only twenty years of age but 'actually nearer sixteen in many essential ways of maturity,' in her struggle to choose between a life with the lesbian, or a normal married life with her childhood sweetheart. The lesbian's affair with her roommate while in college, resulting in the lesbian's expulsion from college, is recounted to bring in the jealousy angle. The climax is reached when the young girl gives up her chance for a normal married life to live with the lesbian. This article is nothing more than cheap pornography calculated to promote lesbianism. It falls far short of dealing with homosexuality from the scientific, historical and critical point of view.

"The poem 'Lord Samuel and Lord Montagu' is about the alleged homosexual activities of Lord Montagu and other British Peers and contains a warning to all males to avoid the public toilets while Lord Samuel is 'sniffing round the drains' of Piccadilly (London). . . .

"The stories 'All This and Heaven Too,' and 'Not Til the End,' pages 32-36, are similar to the story 'Sappho Remembered,' except that they relate to the activities of the homosexuals rather than lesbians." 241 F. 2d 772, 777, 778.

There are other decisions of ours which also reversed judgments condemning publications catering to a wider range of literary tastes than we seem to tolerate today. See, e.g., Mounce v. United States, 355 U.S. 180, vacating and remanding 247 F. 2d 148 (nudist magazines); Sunshine Book Co. v. Summerfield, 355 U.S. 372, reversing 101 U.S. App. D.C. 358, 249 F. 2d 114 (nudist magazine); Tralins v. Gerstein, 378 U.S. 576, reversing 151 So. 2d 19 (book titled "Pleasure Was My Business" depicting the happenings in a house of prostitution); Grove Press v. Gerstein, 378 U.S. 577, reversing 156 So. 2d 537 (book titled "Tropic of Cancer" by Henry Miller).

10. See, e.g., Constitution of the Union of Burma, Art. 17 (i), reprinted in I Peaslee, Constitutions of Nations, p. 281 (2d ed. 1956); Constitution of India, Art. 19 (2), II Peaslee, op. cit. supra, p. 227; Constitution of Ireland, Art. 40 (6) (1) (i), II Peaslee, op. cit. supra, p. 458; Federal Constitution of the Swiss Confederation, Art. 55, III Peaslee, op. cit supra, p. 344; Constitution of Libya, Art. 22, I Peaslee, Constitutions of Nations, p. 483 (3d ed. 1965); Constitution of Nigeria, Art. 25 (2), id., p. 605; Constitution of Zambia, Art. 22 (2), id., pp. 1040-1041.

Byrne v. Karalexis, 396 U.S. 976 (1969)

After being convicted in Massachusetts for possessing with the intent to exhibit the film "I Am Curious (Yellow)," theater-owner Karalexis gets a temporary injunction enjoining the District Attorney from interfering with exhibitions of the film pending a decision on the constitutionality of the conviction. The District Attorney requests the Supreme Court to stay the temporary injunction and the Court grants the motion for stay of the injunction. Douglas dissents, declaring in his opinion: "When our rewards go to people for thinking alike, it is no surprise that we become frightened at those who take exception to the current consensus. Then the hue and cry goes up for censors; and that is the start of an ominous trend. What can be done to literature under the banner of 'obscenity' can be done to other parts of the spectrum of ideas when party or majoritarian demands mount and propagandists start declaiming the law.... We forget today that under our constitutional system neither Congress nor the States have any power to pass on the value, the propriety, the Americanism, the soundness of any ideas or expression. It is that insulation from party or majoritarian control provided by the First Amendment--not our gross national product or mass production or pesticides or space ships or nuclear arsenal--that distinguishes our society from the other planetary regimes."

* * *

MR. JUSTICE DOUGLAS, dissenting.

Respondents are the owners and operators of a motion picture theatre which has been showing the film, "I Am Curious (Yellow)." On June 3, 1969, they were indicted by the Suffolk County, Mass., Grand Jury for possessing with intent to exhibit an obscene film in violation of Mass. Gen. Laws, c. 272 § 28A. On June 17, 1969, respondents brought an action in the United States District Court for the District of Massachusetts to enjoin future prosecutions for the showing of "I Am Curious (Yellow)" and to declare that prosecution and the Massachusetts statute unconstitutional. On June

24, 1969, the three-judge District Court enjoined the prosecution on the ground that the indictments did not allege scienter. The indictments were then dismissed, and new indictments were thereafter returned. Respondents' request for a temporary injunction barring the second prosecution was denied by the District Court on July 15, 1969. The court stated that it would not consider a claim that the film was not obscene as an evidentiary matter, but invited the parties to submit briefs on the question whether the Massachusetts statute was unconstitutional on its face.

Respondents were convicted of the state obscenity offense on November 12, 1969. The applicant in this proceeding, the District Attorney of Suffolk County, has not agreed that respondents may exhibit the film pending the appeal of their convictions. On November 19, 1969, applicant moved the District Court to abstain from deciding the constitutionality of the Massachusetts statute, pending the resolution of that issue in the state courts. On November 28, 1969, the District Court, by a 2-1 vote, denied the motion and authorized a temporary injunction enjoining applicant from interfering with respondents as respects future showings of the film, "I Am Curious (Yellow)," pending a final disposition by the District Court on the merits.

Applicant now requests this Court to stay the temporary injunction that was issued by the District Court.

The injunction issued by the District Court does not interfere in any way with the criminal conviction already obtained in the Massachusetts courts. That case will proceed unaffected by anything the federal court does, save for final execution of the state judgment. Dombrowski v. Pfister, 380 U.S. 479, is different. There we did not force petitioners to risk vindication of their constitutional rights in a state prosecution under an "overly broad" state statute. Id., at 486. But in this case that risk was faced and resolution of the constitutional issues is being undertaken in the state courts. All that the federal court proposes is protection of respondents against repeated prosecutions, while both the state courts and the federal courts are resolving the constitutional issues. Enjoining one state prosecution, though perhaps permissible under Ex parte Young, 209 U.S. 123, would not be in keeping with more recent decisions. Douglas v. Jeannette, 319 U.S. 157. But I read the sparse record before us differently from Mr. Justice Stewart and believe that we deal here with threats of repeated prosecutions; and those threats seem to me to be no less ominous to the federal constitutional regime than the threatened harassment of union leaders in Hague v. CIO, 307 U. S. 496, who were asserting First Amendment rights in explaining the purposes of the new National Labor Relations Act. See the opinion of Mr. Justice Roberts, in which Mr. Justice Black concurred, id., at 504-506.

There may in time be a collision between the two systems for us to resolve. Meanwhile I would let the two orderly processes go ahead. For I can imagine no better and smoother accommodation of the needs of the two regimes than that designed by the District Court.

Underlying the state case and the federal case is an important First Amendment question. Some people think that "obscenity" is not protected by the Free Speech and Free Press Clauses of the First Amendment. They believe that both Congress and the States can set up regimes of censorship to weed out "obscenity" from literature, movies, and other publications so as to rid the press of what they, the judges, deem to be beyond the pale.

I have consistently dissented from that course but not because, as frequently charged, I relish "obscenity." I have dissented before and now because I think the First Amendment bars all kinds of censorship. Ginsberg v. New York, 390 U.S. 629, 650 (Douglas, J., dissenting); Ginzburg v. United States, 383 U.S. 463, 482 (Douglas, J., dissenting); Roth v. United States, 354 U.S. 476, 508 (Douglas, J., dissenting). To impose a regime of censors requires, in my view, a constitutional amendment. "Obscenity" is no exception. "Obscenity" certainly was not an established exception to free speech and free press when the Bill of Rights was adopted. See my concurring opinion in Memoirs v. Massachusetts, 383 U.S. 413, 428-433. It is a relatively new arrival on the American scene, propelled by dedicated zealots to cleanse all thought.

Prior to the Bill of Rights, state law, when it spoke of freedom of the press, meant only freedom from prior restraint. But an author or publisher could be held accountable for publishing what the statehouse thought was against "the public good." In other words, the First Amendment did not build on existing law; it broke with tradition, set a new standard, and exalted freedom of expression. There is no trace of a suggestion that "obscenity," however defined, was excepted.

That does not mean that "obscenity" is good or that it should be encouraged. It only means that we cannot be faithful to our constitutional mandate and allow any form or shadow of censorship over speech and press. [1]

When our rewards go to people for thinking alike, it is no surprise that we become frightened at those who take exception to the current consensus. Then the hue and cry goes up for censors; and that is the start of an ominous trend. What can be done to literature under the banner of "obscenity" can be done to other parts of the spectrum of ideas when party or majoritarian demands mount and propagandists start declaiming the law.

The "obscenity" issue raises large questions. To what extent may government watch over one's shoulder as he reads?

Judge Jerome Frank said in Roth v. Goldman, 172 F. 2d 788, 792:

> I think that no sane man thinks socially dangerous the arousing of normal sexual desires. Consequently, if reading obscene books has merely that consequence, Congress, it would seem, can constitutionally no more suppress such books than it can prevent the mailing of many other objects, such as perfumes, for example, which notoriously produce that result. But the constitutional power to suppress obscene publications might well exist if there were ample reason to believe that reading them conduces to socially harmful sexual conduct on the part of normal human beings.... Macaulay, replying to demands for suppression of obscene books, said: 'We find it difficult to believe that in a world so full of temptations as this, any gentleman, whose life would have been virtuous if he had not read Aristophanes and Juvenal, will be made vicious by reading them.' Substitute 'Waggish Tales from the Czech' for 'Aristophanes and Juvenal,' and those remarks become relevant here.

If "obscenity" can be carved out of the First Amendment, what other like exceptions can be created? Is "sacrilege" also beyond the pale? Are utterances or publications made with "malice" unprotected? How about "seditious" speech or articles? False, scandalous, and malicious writings or utterances against the Congress or the President "with intent to defame" or to bring them "into contempt or disrepute" or to "excite" against them "the hatred of the good people" or "to stir up sedition," or to "excite" people to "resist, oppose, or defeat" any law were once made a crime. (1 Stat. 596-597.) Now that the First Amendment applies to the States, Stromberg v. California, 283 U.S. 359; Near v. Minnesota, 283 U.S. 697, may the States embark on such totalitarian controls over thought or over the press? May Congress do so?

We forget today that under our constitutional system neither Congress nor the States have any power to pass on the value, the propriety, the Americanism, the soundness of any idea or expression. It is that insulation from party or majoritarian control provided by the First Amendment--not our gross national product or mass production or pesticides or space ships or nuclear arsenal--that distinguishes our society from the other planetary regimes.

## NOTE

1. John Hohenberg recently stated this First Amendment philosophy in a slightly different setting:

"As Aleksandr Solzhenitsyn wrote in bitter response to his removal from the rolls of the Russian Writers' Union late in 1969 following the West's sympathetic reception of two of his novels that he could not have published in his own country: 'It is time to remember that the first thing we belong to is humanity. And humanity is separated from the animal world by thought and speech, and they should naturally be free. If they are fettered, we go back to being animals. Publicity and openness, honest and complete--that is the prime condition for the health of every society, and ours too.'

"Wherever freedom is denied, these words will live on." 52 Saturday Review 72 (Dec. 13, 1969).

## Dyson v. Stein, 401 U.S. 200 (1971)

The Supreme Court finds against a Dallas, Texas, newspaper publisher who had been charged with violating a Texas law prohibiting the possession of obscene materials and who had sought "an injunction to prevent the Dallas police from arresting him and seizing his property on obscenity grounds without a prior judicial determination of obscenity." Douglas dissents, stating in his opinion: "The Constitution contains no standards or suggestions of standards respecting the vast array of subjects that various vocal groups would like to have suppressed--obscenity, sacrilege, un-Americanism, anti-clerical ideas, atheistic or anti-ecclesiastical ideas, communism, racism, and so on. Under the Constitution as written there are no standards of 'good' or 'bad' for the press. Since there is no constitutional definition of obscenity, the definition must be largely, if not exclusively, for legislative determination. Absent a controlling constitutional standard, I would think that a legislature could treat literature as it treats sewage effluent or infectious disease. This is not a happy prospect, for some would put even the Song of Solomon under the ban. It is, I fear, where we end once we lose our First Amendment moorings. Administrative censorship, however, is one thing. Criminal punishment is quite another. Publishing 'obscene' literature cannot, as I view it, be made a crime under our constitutional standards."

* * *

MR. JUSTICE DOUGLAS, dissenting.

I

The two raids in this case were search-and-destroy missions in the Vietnamese sense of the phrase. In each case the police came at night. The first search warrant authorized a search and seizure of "obscene articles and materials, to-wit: pictures, photographs, drawings and obscene literature" concealed at a given address. The seizures included: two tons of a newspaper (Dallas Notes), one photograph enlarger, two portable typewriters, two electric typewriters, one camera, "numerous obscene photographs," and $5.43 in money.[1] The second warrant was issued 16 days later, in response to a claim that marihuana was concealed on the premises. It authorized the officers "to search for and seize the said narcotic drug and dangerous drug in accordance with the law in such cases provided." Not finding any marihuana on the premises, the sergeant asked instructions from his lieutenant. He was told to seize pornographic literature and any equipment used to make it. He "didn't know what to seize and what not to seize so [he] just took everything." "Everything" included a Polaroid camera, a Kodak Brownie, a Flocon camera, a Kodak lamp, a floating fixture lamp, a three-drawer desk containing printers' supplies, a drafting square, a drafting table, two drawing boards, a mailing tube, two telephones, a stapler, five cardboard boxes containing documents, one electric typewriter, and one typewriter desk. A poster of Mao Tse-tung, credit cards, costume jewelry, cans of spices, a brown sweater, and a statue of a man and woman in an embrace were also seized. Thus the newspaper Dallas Notes, a bi-monthly, was effectively put out of business.[2]

It would be difficult to find in our books a more lawless search-and-destroy raid, unless it be the one in Kremen v. United States, 353 U.S. 346. If this search-and-destroy technique can be employed against this Dallas newspaper, then it can be done to the New York Times, the Washington Post, the Seattle Post Intelligencer, the Yakima Herald-Republic, the Sacramento Bee, and all the rest of our newspapers. For, as I shall point out, the Texas statute governing "obscenity"[3] is plainly unconstitutional.

Government certainly has no power to close down newspapers. Even censorship--whether for obscenity, for irresponsible reporting or editorials, or otherwise--is taboo. As Chief Justice Hughes said in Near v. Minnesota, 283 U.S. 697, decided in 1931:

> [T]he administration of government has become more complex, the opportunities for malfeasance and corruption have multiplied, crime has grown to most serious proportions, and the danger of its protection by unfaithful officials and of the impairment of the fundamental security of life and property by criminal alliances and official neglect, emphasizes the primary need of a vigilant and

> courageous press, especially in great cities. The fact that the liberty of the press may be abused by miscreant purveyors of scandal does not make any the less necessary the immunity of the press from previous restraint in dealing with official misconduct. Subsequent punishment for such abuses as may exist is the appropriate remedy, consistent with constitutional privilege. [Id., at 719-720.]

I agree with that view.

It is said, however, that these issues are not before us as the case has been remanded to a single judge to pass on them. But we deal with plain error, as the state statute is unconstitutional on its face and we should put an end to lawless raids under it.[4]

II

The constitutional mandate that government[5] "shall make no law ... abridging the freedom of speech, or of the press" precludes in my view any form of censorship. Vicious, irresponsible, and depraved as the press often is, the constitutional remedy is not censorship.[6] The antidote is education, pinning our faith to the Jeffersonian creed that by education we may in time become a mature people.[7]

I have set forth my views over and over again as to why the First Amendment should be strictly construed; and they need not to be repeated here. It is difficult--indeed impossible--to read the constitutional mandate that government "shall make no law" abridging freedom of the press to mean that government "may make some laws" abridging that freedom. Certainly a strict constructionist cannot so read it.

> The Court says it has been trying to balance the interests of society in protecting itself from the supposed evils of obscene material with the real interest in freedom of expression. There is ample evidence that the clear and definite language of the first amendment was intended to preclude the very problem of balancing assumed by the Court. The first amendment holds that the interest of society in freedom of expression[8] is more important than the harm that might flow from obscene material.

> The very interest in protection from injury from obscene material would be better served by allowing each individual to make a free appraisal of pornographic material. A hallmark of an immature and insecure society is the censorship of ideas. Censorship, which insulates all from what some suppose to be evil, merely magnifies that insecurity. If society does such a poor job of educating itself so that four letter words and explicit pictures are dangerous, the remedy is to improve the educational process, not to outlaw certain publications. While the first amendment does not mandate better education it does prohibit the censorship of ideas. This use of a balancing test evidences a minsconception of the constitutional nature of society. There is nothing to balance. Society's security flows directly and solely from the freedom and security of each individual. [31 Albany L. Rev. 143, 151 (1967).]

If I am correct in concluding that a State can make "no law" censoring the press because of obscenity, then a publisher threatened by such a law can go into a federal court to enjoin state officials from enforcing the law, as I made clear in my dissent in Younger v. Harris, ante, at 59. The special circumstances where such federal intervention is permissible are not restricted to bad faith on the part of state officials or the threat of multiple prosecutions. As Mr. Justice Butler, writing for the Court, said in Terrace v. Thompson, 263 U.S. 197, 214:

> Equity jurisdiction will be exercised to enjoin the threatened enforcement of a state law which contravenes the Federal Constitution wherever it is essential in order effectually to protect property rights and the rights of persons against injuries otherwise irremediable; and in such a case a person, who as an officer of the State is clothed with the duty of enforcing its laws and who threatens and is about to commence proceedings, either civil or criminal, to enforce such a law against parties affected, may be enjoined from such action by a federal court of equity.

And see Watson v. Buck, 313 U.S. 387, 402.

No possible construction of this state law can save it.

This is not a situation where mere overbreadth of a state statute may have chilling or crippling effects on First Amendment rights. This is a case where Texas has entered a field which the Constitution bars all the States and the Federal Government from entering.

The Texas obscenity statute, as I view it, meets precisely the hypothetical statute we discussed in Watson v. Buck, 313 U.S. 387, 402:

> It is of course conceivable that a statute might be flagrantly and patently violative of express constitutional prohibitions in every clause, sentence and paragraph, and in whatever manner and against whomever an effort might be made to apply it.

No clearer case justifying federal intervention to prevent a state criminal trial can be imagined.

No pending prosecutions are sought to be enjoined, only future ones.[9] Such an injunction is not impermissible under 28 U.S.C. § 2283. See Dombrowski v. Pfister, 380 U.S. 479, 484 n. 2, and my dissent in Younger v. Harris, ante, at 65. Appellee also asked for declaratory relief. If Zwickler v. Koota, 389 U.S. 241, means anything, it means that such relief can also be granted.

III

If a publication deemed "obscene" is not under the umbrella of the First Amendment, then I do not see how it enjoys many constitutional safeguards. That which is out from under the First Amendment would normally be subject to the police power of the States. Yet the Constitution contains no standards or suggestions of standards respecting the vast array of subjects that various vocal groups would like to have suppressed--obscenity, sacrilege, un-Americanism, anti-clerical ideas, atheistic or anti-ecclesiastical ideas, Communism, racism, and so on. Under the Constitution as written there are no standards of "good" or "bad" for the press. Since there is no constitutional definition of obscenity, the definition must be largely, if not exclusively, for legislative determination. Absent a controlling constitutional standard, I would think that a legislature could treat literature as it treats sewage effluent or infectious disease. That is not a happy prospect, for some would put even the Song of Solomon under the ban. It is, I fear, where we end once we lose our First Amendment moorings. Administrative censorship, however, is one thing. Criminal punishment is quite another. Publishing "obscene" literature cannot, as I view it, be made a crime under our constitutional standards.

"Whatever 'obscenity' is, it is immeasurable as a crime and delineable only as a sin. As a sin, it is present only in the minds of some and not in the minds of others. It is entirely too subjective for legal sanction. There are as many different definitions of obscenity as there are men; and they are as unique to the individual as are his dreams." Note, The Substantive Law of Obscenity: An Adventure in Quicksand, 13 N.Y.L.F. 81, 131 (1967).

What appeals to "prurient interests" describes sin to some but not to others and seems to me to be far too vague to pass muster as a criminal, as distinguished from an administrative, statute.[10]

I see no help on the vagueness problem even if the test "utterly without redeeming social importance" were added to the criminal standard, as it was in Jacobellis v. Ohio, 378 U.S. 184, 191.[11] That is a measurement which again is wholly subjective. It cannot be related to anything but the judge's or jurors' sophistication or stage of cultural development. Nor do I think the problem is helped by introducing the concept of "contemporary community standards" whether that refers to the public at large or a local county or town standard. Id., at 193.

The two tests--this Court's and that of Texas--seem to me to be substantially identical. I do not see how either can be held to be constitutional. The standard of guilt is wholly subjective. The jurors can convict or acquit according to their own personal tastes, their cultural standard, their literacy, and their tolerance for opposed ideas. And the same would be true of judges. It means that a book that is hailed as wholesome in one county may be the cause of punishment in another county of the same State.

The evidence in obscenity prosecutions is usually expert testimony. Analysts, English literature scholars, and others often have helpful and informed views, one way or the other. It seems impossible, if we continue to sanction the use of these vague standards in criminal prosecutions, that verdicts will be rendered which are based on the record and not on the emotional factors reflecting the prejudices of the judge or jurors.

Uncertainty, rather than certainty, is the standard. The book, play, poem, or movie is approved or condemned on the basis of the personal beliefs of the judge or jurors, not on the ban of a statute containing clear and objective standards.

The concept of "utterly without redeeming social importance" will divide even the experts. It is risky and perilous business to send men to prison on such provocative issues, which confuse people and create irreconcilable differences even among the judges who sentence them or approve their convictions.

In these criminal cases dealing with obscenity, we leave people confused and in the dark as to whether they are or are not criminals. Criminal laws must give fair warning; and a person receives no real warning when he crosses the line between the lawful and the unlawful, under the Texas statute [12] or under the standard approved by the Court.

Where constitutional rights may be infringed, Winters v. New York, 333 U.S. 507, should be our guide. There an "obscene" magazine was defined to include those which "massed" stories of bloodshed and lust to incite crimes. Id., at 513. We held that standard to be too vague to satisfy constitutional standards.[13]

> The standards of certainty in statutes punishing for offenses is higher than in those depending primarily upon civil sanction for enforcement. The crime 'must be defined with appropriate definiteness.' ... There must be ascertainable standards of guilt. Men of common intelligence cannot be required to guess at the meaning of the enactment. The vagueness may be from uncertainty in regard to persons within the scope of the act, ... or in regard to the applicable tests to ascertain guilt. [Id., at 515-516.]

And see Wright v. Georgia, 373 U.S. 284, 292; Smith v. California, 361 U.S. 147, 151; United States v. Harriss, 347 U.S. 612; Beauharnais v. Illinois, 343 U.S. 250, 264; Williams v. United States, 341 U.S. 97; Cantwell v. Connecticut, 310 U.S. 296.

My view, however, is that any regime of censorship over literature whether expressed in a criminal statute[14] or an administrative[15] procedure is unconstitutional by reason of the command of the First Amendment.

NOTES

1. This indiscriminate seizure is hardly surprising since none of the officers knew what to seize, as the questioning of the lieutenant in charge of the raid shows:
"Q. What instructions did you give the officers in effecting this search and seizure as to what they were to do?
"A. They were to search for any obscene material they could find. All of our officers know what obscene material is.
"Q. What is obscene material?
"A. Well, I wish you hadn't ask [sic] that. I take that back. They don't know, neither do I.
"Q. What instructions had you given them in terms of what they were to do?
"A. To search for obscene material and seize it.
"Q. What definition, if any, did you give them as to obscene material?
"A. I didn't."

2. Appellee Stein has since reached an agreement with the Dallas Police Department by which it returned most of the property to him in return for his execution of an Indemnity and Release Agreement. The binding effect of such an agreement, which required Stein to choose between the return of his property so that he could continue publishing and assertion of his civil rights under such provisions as 42 U.S.C. § 1983, is not at issue here.

The Dallas Police Department still holds "film negatives, eight or ten photographs, one movie advertisement poster, one litho copy of paper, and a representative number of back issues of paper entitled 'Dallas Notes' or 'Notes from the Underground.'"

3. Article 527 defined "obscene" as follows in § 3:
"[W]hether to the average person, applying contemporary community standards, the dominant theme of the material taken as a whole appeals to prurient interests. Provided, further, for the purpose of this

article, the term 'contemporary community standards' shall in no case involve a territory or geographic area less than the State of Texas."

After the three-judge court decision, Art. 527 was amended to defind "obscene" as "material (a) the dominant theme of which, taken as a whole, appeals to a prurient interest; (b) which is patently offensive because it affronts contemporary community standards relating to the description or representation of sexual matters; and (c) which is utterly without redeeming social value."

And "prurient interest" was defined as "a shameful or morbid interest in nudity, sex, or excretion, which goes substantially beyond customary limits of candor in description or representation of such matters. If it appears from the character of the material or the circumstances of its dissemination that the subject matter is designed for a specially susceptible audience, the appeal of the subject matter shall be judged with reference to such audience." Tex. Penal Code, Art. 527, § 1 (Supp. 1970-1971).

4. The appellee did not appeal from the decision of the District Court to remand the issue of harassment to a one-judge court, apparently since the ruling that the statute was unconstitutional made such further relief unnecessary, as all the harassment resulted from the enforcement of the statute. In this Court appellee has argued that his "constitutional rights [are] threatened by the existence of the Texas obscenity statute and the overbearing means chosen to enforce it." He has raised the issue of harassment here and the documentary evidence in support of his claim is overwhelming.

5. The First Amendment, originally applicable only to the Federal Government, was by virtue of the Fourteenth Amendment made applicable to the States in 1931 in Stromberg v. California, 283 U.S. 350.

6. Thomas Jefferson wrote, "I deplore ... the putrid state into which our newspapers have passed, and the malignity, the vulgarity, and mendacious spirit of those who write them.... It is however an evil for which there is no remedy, our liberty depends on the freedom of the press, and that cannot be limited without being lost." Jefferson, Democracy, selected and arranged by S. Padover 150-151 (1939).

7. Mr. Justice Brandeis, concurring in Whitney V. California, 274 U.S. 357, 375-376, said:

"Those who won our independence ... believed that freedom to think as you will and to speak as you think are means indispensable to the discovery and spread of political truth; that without free speech and assembly discussion would be futile; that with them, discussion affords ordinarily adequate protection against the dissemination of noxious doctrine; that the greatest menace to freedom is an inert people; that public discussion is a political duty; and that this should be a fundamental principle of the American government.... Believing in the power of reason as applied through public discussion, they eschewed silence coerced by law--the argument of force in its worst form. Recognizing the occasional tyrannies of governing majorities, they amended the Constitution so that free speech and assembly should be guaranteed."

8. We deal with a large and considerable problem. There are those who believe that an "ethic of sexuality joined with an ethic of the wholeness of life" (F. Darling, Wilderness and Plenty 75 (1970) has a close relation not only to population control but to a reverence for both the land and animal life.

9. The amended complaint asked for an injunction only against future arrests and prosecutions under the Texas statute, Art. 527, and a declaration that the statute was unconstitutional. See n. 3, supra.

10. This business of leveling the power of the Federal or State Government against a person in a criminal prosecution is an "awesome" power as Mr. Justice Black has stated:

"Experience, and wisdom flowing out of that experience, long ago led to the belief that agents of government should not be vested with power and discretion to define and punish as criminal past conduct which had not been clearly defined as a crime in advance." Ginzburg v. United States, 383 U.S. 463, 477 (dissenting opinion).

11. See n. 3, supra.

12. Even the police have no guidance as to the kind of books to be seized. See n. 1, supra.

13. Even where First Amendment or other constitutional rights are not involved, no one may be required "to speculate as to the meaning of penal statutes." Lanzetta v. New Jersey, 306 U.S. 451, 453. Chief Justice Marshall said in United States v. Wiltberger, 5 Wheat. 76, 105, that in determining the certainty needed in a penal law for its validity the "probability" that the legislature may have desired to include a species of activity within an Act is not enough. And see United States v. Lacher, 134 U.S. 624, 628; Pierce v. United States, 314 U.S. 306.

14. See Mr. Justice Black's opinion in Kingsley International Pictures Corp. v. Regents, 360 U.S. 684, 690 (concurring).

See my opinions in Roth v. United States, 354 U.S. 476, 508 (dissenting); Smith v. California, 361 U.S. 147, 167 (concurring); Ginzburg v. United States, 383 U.S. 463, 482 (dissenting).

15. See Mr. Justice Black's separate opinion in A Quantity of Books v. Kansas, 378 U.S. 205, 213.

Miller v. California, 413 U.S. 15 (1973)

On June 21, 1973 the Supreme Court upholds five obscenity convictions in five different cases. Douglas dissents in all five, asserting in his Miller opinion: "The idea that the First Amendment permits government to ban publications that are 'offensive' to some people puts an ominous gloss on freedom of the press. That test would make it possible to ban any paper or any journal or magazine in some benighted place. The First Amendment was designed 'to invite dispute,' to induce 'a condition of unrest,' to 'create dissatisfaction with conditions as they are,' and even to stir 'people to anger.' ... the idea that the First Amendment permits punishment for ideas that are 'offensive' to the particular judge or jury sitting in judgment is astounding. No greater leveler of speech or literature has ever been designed. To give the power to the censor, as we do today, is to make a sharp and radical break with the traditions of a free society. The First Amendment was not fashioned as a vehicle for dispensing tranquilizers to the people. Its prime function was to keep debate open to 'offensive' as well as to 'staid' people."

* * *

MR. JUSTICE DOUGLAS, dissenting.

I

Today we leave open the way for California[1] to send a man to prison for distributing brochures that advertise books and a movie under freshly written standards defining obscenity which until today's decision were never the part of any law.

The Court has worked hard to define obscenity and concededly has failed. In Roth v. United States, 354 U.S. 476, it ruled that "[o]bscene material is material which deals with sex in a manner appealing to prurient interest." Id., at 487. Obscenity, it was said, was rejected by the

First Amendment because it is "utterly without redeeming social importance." *Id.*, at 484. The presence of a "prurient interest" was to be determined by "contemporary community standards." *Id.*, at 489. That test, it has been said, could not be determined by one standard here and another standard there, *Jacobellis v. Ohio*, 378 U.S. 184, 194, but "on the basis of a national standard." *Id.*, at 195. My Brother Stewart in *Jacobellis* commented that the difficulty of the Court in giving content to obscenity was that it was "faced with the task of trying to define what may be indefinable." *Id.*, at 197.

In *Memoirs v. Massachusetts*, 383 U.S. 413, 418, the *Roth* test was elaborated to read as follows: "[T]hree elements must coalesce: it must be established that (a) the dominant theme of the material taken as a whole appeals to a prurient interest in sex; (b) the material is patently offensive because it affronts contemporary community standards relating to the description or representation of sexual matters; and (c) the material is utterly without redeeming social value."

In *Ginzburg v. United States*, 383 U.S. 463, a publisher was sent to prison, not for the kind of books and periodicals he sold, but for the manner in which the publications were advertised. The "leer of the sensualist" was said to permeate the advertisements. *Id.*, at 468. The Court said, "Where the purveyor's sole emphasis is on the sexually provocative aspects of his publications, that fact may be decisive in the determination of obscenity." *Id.*, at 470. As Mr. Justice Black said in dissent, "... Ginzburg ... is now finally and authoritatively condemned to serve five years in prison for distributing printed matter about sex which neither Ginzburg nor anyone else could possibly have known to be criminal." *Id.*, at 476. That observation by Mr. Justice Black is underlined by the fact that the *Ginzburg* decision was five to four.

A further refinement was added by *Ginsberg v. New York*, 390 U.S. 629, 641, where the Court held that "it was not irrational for the legislature to find that exposure to material condemned by the statute is harmful to minors."

But even those members of this Court who had created the new and changing standards of "obscenity" could not agree on their application. And so we adopted a *per curiam* treatment of so-called obscene publications that seemed to pass constitutional muster under the several constitutional tests which had been formulated. See Redrup v. New York, 386 U.S. 767. Some condemn it if its "dominant tendency might be to 'deprave or corrupt' a reader."[2] Others look not to the content of the book but to whether it is advertised "'to appeal to the erotic interests of customers.'"[3] Some condemn only "hardcore pornography"; but even then a true definition is lacking. It has indeed been said of that definition, "I could never succeed in [defining it] intelligibly," but "I know it when I see it."[4]

Today we would add a new three-pronged test: "(a) whether 'the average person, applying contemporary community standards' would find that the work, taken as a whole, appeals to the prurient interest, ... (b) whether the work depicts or describes, in a patently offensive way, sexual conduct specifically defined by the applicable state law, and (c) whether the work, taken as a whole, lacks serious literary, artistic, political, or scientific value."

Those are the standards we ourselves have written into the Constitution.[5] Yet how under these vague tests can we sustain convictions for the sale of an article prior to the time when some court has declared it to be obscene?

Today the Court retreats from the earlier formulations of the constitutional test and undertakes to make new definitions. This effort, like the earlier ones, is earnest and well intentioned. The difficulty is that we do not deal with constitutional terms, since "obscenity" is not mentioned in the Constitution or Bill of Rights. And the First Amendment makes no such exception from "the press" which it undertakes to protect nor, as I have said on other occasions, is an exception necessarily implied, for there was no recognized exception to the free press at the time the Bill of Rights was adopted which treated "obscene" publications differently from other types of papers, magazines, and books. So there are no constitutional guidelines for deciding what is and what is not "obscene." The Court is at large because we deal with tastes and standards of literature. What shocks me may be sustenance for my neighbor. What causes one person to boil up in rage over one pamphlet or movie may reflect only his neurosis, not shared by others. We deal here with a regime of censorship which, if adopted, should be done by constitutional amendment after full debate by the people.

Obscenity cases usually generate tremendous emotional outbursts. They have no business being in the courts. If a constitutional amendment authorized censorship, the censor would probably be an administrative agency. Then criminal prosecutions could follow as if and when publishers defied the censor and sold their literature. Under the present regime--whether the old standards or the new ones are used--the criminal law becomes a trap. A brand new test would put a publisher behind bars under a new law improvised by the courts after the publication. That was done in Ginzburg and has all the evils of an ex post facto law.

My contention is that until a civil proceeding has placed a tract beyond the pale, no criminal prosecution should be sustained. For no more vivid illustration of vague and uncertain laws could be designed than those we have fashioned. As Mr. Justice Harlan has said:

> The upshot of all this divergence in viewpoint is that anyone who undertakes to examine the Court's decisions since Roth which have held particular material obscene or not obscene would find himself in utter bewilderment." [Interstate Circuit, Inc. v. Dallas, 390 U.S. 676, 707.]

In Bouie v. City of Columbia, 378 U.S. 347, we upset a conviction for remaining on property after being asked to leave, while the only unlawful act charged by the statute was entering. We held that the defendants had received no "fair warning, at the time of their conduct" while on the property "that the act for which they now stand convicted was rendered criminal" by the state statute. Id., at 355. The same requirement of "fair warning" is due here, as much as in Bouie. The latter involved racial discrimination; the present case involves rights earnestly urged as being protected by the First Amendment. In any case--certainly when constitutional rights are concerned--we should not allow men to go to prison or be fined when they had no "fair warning" that what they did was criminal conduct.

II

If a specific book, play, paper, or motion picture has in a civil proceeding been condemned as obscene and review of that finding has been completed, and thereafter a person publishes, shows, or displays that particular book or film, then a vague law has been made specific. There would remain the underlying question whether the First Amendment allows an implied exception in the case of obscenity. I do not think it does[6] and my views on the issue have been stated over and over again.[7] But at least a criminal prosecution brought at that juncture would not violate the time-honored void-for-vagueness test.[8]

No such protective procedure has been designed by California in this case. Obscenity--which even we cannot define with precision--is a hodge-podge. To send men to jail for violating standards they cannot understand, construe, and apply is a monstrous thing to do in a Nation dedicated to fair trials and due process.

III

While the right to know is the corollary of the right to speak or publish, no one can be forced by government to listen to disclosure that he finds offensive. That was the basis of my dissent in Public Utilities Comm'n v. Pollak, 343 U.S. 451, 467, where I protested against making streetcar passengers a "captive audience. There is no "captive audience" problem in these obscenity cases. No one is being compelled to look or to listen. Those who enter newsstands or bookstalls may be offended by what they see. But they are not compelled by the State to frequent those places; and it is only state or government action against which the First Amendment, applicable to the States by virtue of the Fourteenth, raises a ban.

The idea that the First Amendment permits government to ban publications that are "offensive" to some people puts an ominous gloss on freedom of the press. That test would make it possible to ban any paper or any journal or magazine in some benighted place. The First Amendment was designed "to invite dispute," to induce "a condition of unrest," to "create dissatisfaction with conditions as they are," and even to stir "people to anger." Terminiello v. Chicago, 337 U.S. 1, 4. The idea that the First Amendment permits punishment for ideas that are "offensive" to the particular judge or jury sitting in judgment is astounding. No greater leveler of speech or literature has ever been designed. To give the power to the censor, as we do today, is to make a sharp and radical break with the traditions of a free society. The First Amendment was not fashioned as a vehicle for dispensing tranquilizers to the people. Its prime function was to keep debate open to "offensive" as well as to "staid" people. The tendency throughout history has been to subdue the individual and to exalt the power of government. The use of the standard "offensive" gives authority to government that cuts the very vitals out of the First Amendment.[9] As is intimated by the Court's opinion, the materials before us may be garbage. But so is much of what is said in political campaigns, in the daily press, on TV, or over the radio. By reason of the First Amendment--and solely because of it--speakers and publishers have not been threatened or subdued because their thoughts and ideas may be "offensive" to some.

The standard "offensive" is unconstitutional in yet another way. In Coates v. City of Cincinnati, 402 U.S. 611, we had before us a municipal ordinance that made it a crime for three or more persons to assemble on a street and conduct themselves "in a manner annoying to persons passing by." We struck it down, saying: "If three or more people meet together on a sidewalk or street corner, they must conduct themselves so as not to annoy any police officer or other person who should happen to pass by. In our opinion this ordinance is unconstitutionally vague because it subjects the exercise of the right of assembly to an unascertainable standard, and unconstitutionally broad because it authorizes the punishment of constitutionally protected conduct.

"Conduct that annoys some people does not annoy others. Thus, the ordinance is vague, not in the sense that it requires a person to conform his conduct to an imprecise but comprehensive normative standard, but rather in the sense that no standard of conduct is specified at all." Id., at 614.

How we can deny Ohio the convenience of punishing people who "annoy" others and allow California power to punish people who publish materials "offensive" to some people is difficult to square with constitutional requirements.

If there are to be restraints on what is obscene, then a constitutional amendment should be the way of achieving the end. There are societies where religion and mathematics are the only free segments. It would be a dark day for America if that were our destiny. But the people can make it such if they choose to write obscenity into the Constitution and define it.

We deal with highly emotional, not rational, questions. To many the Song of Solomon is obscene. I do not think we, the judges, were ever given the constitutional power to make definitions of obscenity. If it is to be defined, let the people debate and decide by a constitutional amendment what they want to ban as obscene and what standards they want the legislatures and the courts to apply. Perhaps the people will decide that the path towards a mature, integrated society requires that all ideas competing for acceptance must have no censor. Perhaps they will decide otherwise. Whatever the choice, the courts will have some guidelines. Now we have none except our own predilections.

NOTES

1. California defines "obscene matter" as "matter, taken as a whole, the predominant appeal of which to the average person, applying contemporary standards, is to prurient interest, i.e., a shameful or morbid interest in nudity, sex, or excretion; and is matter which taken as a whole goes substantially beyond customary limits of candor in description or representation of such matters; and is matter which taken as a whole is utterly without redeeming social importance." Calif. Penal Code § 311 (a).

2. Roth v. United States, 354 U.S. 476, 502 (opinion of Harlan, J.).

3. Ginzburg v. United States, 383 U.S. 463, 467.

4. Jacobellis v. Ohio, 378 U.S. 184, 197 (Stewart, J., concurring).

5. At the conclusion of a two-year study, the U.S. Commission on Obscenity and Pornography determined that the standards we have written interfere with constitutionally protected materials:

   "Society's attempts to legislate for adults in the area of obscenity have not been successful. Present laws prohibiting the consensual sale or distribution of explicit sexual materials to adults are extremely unsatisfactory in their practical application. The Constitution permits material to be deemed 'obscene' for adults only if, as a whole, it appeals to the 'prurient' interest of the average person, is 'patently offensive' in light of 'community standards,' and lacks 'redeeming social value.' These vague and highly subjective aesthetic, psychological and moral tests do not provide meaningful guidance for law enforcement officials, juries or courts. As a result, law is inconsistently and sometimes erroneously applied and the distinctions made by courts between prohibited and permissible materials often appear indefensible. Errors in the application of the law and uncertainty about its scope also cause interference with the communication of constitutionally protected materials." Report of the Commission on Obscenity and Pornography 53 (1970).

6. It is said that "obscene" publications can be banned on authority of restraints on communications incident to decrees restraining unlawful business monopolies or unlawful restraints of trade, Sugar Institute v. United States, 297 U.S. 553, 597, or communications respecting the sale of spurious or fraudulent securities. Hall v. Geiger-Jones Co., 242 U.S. 539, 549; Caldwell v. Sioux Falls Stock Yards Co., 242 U.S. 559, 567; Merrick v. Halsey & Co., 242 U.S. 568, 584. The First Amendment answer is that whenever speech and conduct are brigaded--as they are when one shouts "Fire" in a crowded theater--speech can be outlawed. Mr. Justice Black, writing for a unanimous Court in Giboney v. Empire Storage Co., 336 U.S. 490, stated that labor unions could be restrained from picketing a firm in support of a secondary boycott which a State had validly outlawed. Mr. Justice Black said: "It rarely has been suggested that the constitutional freedom for speech and press extends its immunity to speech or writing used as an integral part of conduct in violation of a valid criminal statute. We reject the contention now." Id., at 498.

7. See United States v. 12 200-ft. Reels of Film, post, p. 123; United States v. Orito, post, p. 139; Kois v. Wisconsin, 408 U.S. 229; Byrne v. Karalexis, 396 U.S. 976, 977; Ginsberg v. New York, 390 U.S. 629, 650; Jacobs v. New York, 388 U.S. 431, 436; Ginzburg v. United States, 383 U.S. 463, 482; Memoirs v. Massachusetts, 383 U.S. 413, 424; Bantam Books, Inc. v. Sullivan, 372 U.S. 58, 72; Times Film Corp., v. Chicago, 365 U.S. 43, 78; Smith v. California, 361 U.S. 147, 167; Kingsley Pictures Corp. v. Regents, 360 U.S. 684, 697; Roth v. United States, 354 U.S. 476, 508; Kingsley Books, Inc. v. Brown, 354 U.S. 436, 446; Superior Films, Inc. v. Department of Education, 346 U.S. 587, 588; Gelling v. Texas, 343 U.S. 960.

8. The Commission on Obscenity and Pornography has advocated such a procedure:

"The Commission recommends the enactment, in all jurisdictions which enact or retain provisions prohibiting the dissemination of sexual materials to adults or young persons, of legislation authorizing prosecutors to obtain declaratory judgments as to whether particular materials fall within existing legal prohibitions....

"A declaratory judgment procedure ... would permit prosecutors to proceed civilly, rather than through the criminal process, against suspected violations of obscenity prohibition. If such civil procedures are utilized, penalities would be imposed for violation of the law only with respect to conduct occurring after a civil declaration is obtained. The Commission believes this course of action to be appropriate whenever there is any existing doubt regarding the legal status of materials; where other alternatives are available, the criminal process should not ordinarily be invoked against persons who might have reasonably believed, in good faith, that the books or films they distributed were entitled to constitutional protection, for the threat of criminal sanctions might otherwise deter the free distribution of constitutionally protected material." Report of the Commission on Obscenity and Pornography 63 (1970).

9. Obscenity law has had a capricious history:

"The white slave traffic was first exposed by W.T. Stead in a magazine article, 'The Maiden Tribute.' The English law did absolutely nothing to the profiteers in vice, but put Stead in prison for a year for writing about an indecent subject. When the law supplies no definite standard of criminality, a judge in deciding what is indecent or profane may consciously disregard the sound test of present injury, and proceeding upon an entirely different theory may condemn the defendant because his words express ideas which are thought liable to cause bad future consequences. Thus musical comedies enjoy almost unbridled license, while a problem play is often forbidden because opposed to our views of marriage. In the same way, the law of blasphemy has been used against Shelley's *Queen Mab* and the decorous promulgation of pantheistic ideas, on the ground that to attack religion is to loosen the bonds of society and endanger the state. This is simply a roundabout modern method to make heterodoxy in sex matters and even in religion a crime." Z. Chafee, Free Speech in the United States 151 (1942).

## Paris Adult Theatre I v. Slaton, 413 U.S. 49 (1973)

A majority (5-4) of the Supreme Court upholds an obscenity conviction, declaring that "obscene films do not acquire constitutional immunity from state regulation simply because they are exhibited for consenting adults only" and that "although there is no conclusive proof of a connection between antisocial behavior and obscene materials, the legislature of Georgia could quite reasonably determine that such a connection does or might exist." Douglas dissents, stating in his opinion: "... since we do not have here the unique series of problems raised by government-imposed or government-approved captive audiences..., I see no constitutional basis for fashioning a rule that makes a publisher, producer, bookseller, librarian, or movie house operator criminally responsible, when he fails to take affirmative steps to protect the consumer against literature, books or movies offensive to those who temporarily occupy the seats of the mighty."

* * *

MR. JUSTICE DOUGLAS, dissenting.

MY BROTHER BRENNAN is to be commended for seeking a new path through the thicket which the Court entered when it undertook to sustain the constitutionality of obscenity laws and to place limits on their application. I have expressed on numerous occasions my disagreement with the basic decision that held that "obscenity" was not protected by the First Amendment. I disagreed also with the definitions that evolved. Art and literature reflect tastes; and tastes, like musical appreciation, are hardly reducible to precise definitions. That is one reason I have always felt that "obscenity" was not an exception to the First Amendment. For matters of taste, like matters of belief, turn on the idiosyncrasies of individuals. They are too personal to define and too emotional and vague to apply, as witness the prison term for Ralph Ginzburg, Ginzburg v. United States, 383 U.S. 463, not for what he printed but for the sexy manner in which he advertised his creations.

The other reason I could not bring myself to conclude that "obscenity" was not covered by the First Amendment was that prior to the adoption of our Constitution and Bill of Rights the Colonies had no law excluding "obscenity" from the regime of freedom of expression and press that then existed. I could find no such laws; and more important, our leading colonial expert, Julius Goebel, could find none, J. Goebel, Development of Legal Institutions (1946); J. Goebel, Felony and Misdemeanor (1937). So I became convinced that the creation of the "obscenity" exception to the First Amendment was a legislative and judicial tour de force; that if we were to have such a regime of censorship and punishment, it should be done by constitutional amendment.

People are, of course, offended by many offerings made by merchants in this area. They are also offended by political pronouncements, sociological themes, and by stories of official misconduct. The list of activities and publications and pronouncements that offend someone is endless. Some of it goes on in private; some of it is inescapably public, as when a government official generates crime, becomes a blatant offender of the moral sensibilities of the people, engages in burglary, or breaches the privacy of the telephone, the conference room, or the home. Life in this crowded modern technological world creates many offensive statements and many offensive deeds. There is no protection against offensive ideas, only against offensive conduct.

"Obscenity" at most is the expression of offensive ideas. There are regimes in the world where ideas "offensive" to the majority (or at least to those who control the majority) are suppressed. There life proceeds at a monotonous pace. Most of us would find that world offensive. One of the most offensive experiences in my life was a visit to a nation where bookstalls were filled only with books on mathematics and books on religion.

I am sure I would find offensive most of the books and movies charged with being obscene. But in a life that has not been short, I have yet to be trapped into seeing or reading something that would offend me. I never read or see the materials coming to the Court under charges of "obscenity," because I have thought the First Amendment made it unconstitutional for me to act as a censor. I see ads in bookstores and neon lights over theaters that resemble bait for those who seek vicarious exhilaration. As a parent or a priest or as a teacher I would have no compunction in edging my children or wards away from the books and movies that did no more than excite man's base instincts. But I never supposed that government was permitted to sit in judgment on one's tastes or beliefs--save as they involved action within the reach of the police power of government.

I applaud the effort of my Brother BRENNAN to forsake the low road which the Court has followed in this field. The new regime he would inaugurate is much closer than the old to the policy of abstention which the First Amendment proclaims. But since we do not have here the unique series of problems raised by government-imposed or government-approved captive audiences, cf. Public Utilities Comm'n v. Pollak, 343 U.S. 451, I see no constitutional basis for fashioning a rule that makes a publisher, producer, bookseller, librarian, or movie house operator criminally responsible, when he fails to take affirmative steps to protect the consumer against literature, books, or movies offensive[1] to those who temporarily occupy the seats of the mighty.

When man was first in the jungle he took care of himself. When he entered a societal group, controls were necessarily imposed. But our society--unlike most in the world--presupposes that freedom and liberty are in a frame of reference that makes the individual, not government, the keeper of his tastes, beliefs, and ideas. That is the philosophy of the First Amendment; and it is the article of faith that sets us apart from most nations in the world.

NOTE

1. What we do today is rather ominous as respects librarians. The net now designed by the Court is so finely meshed that, taken literally, it could result in raids on libraries. Libraries, I had always assumed, were sacrosanct, representing every part of the spectrum. If what is offensive to the most influential person or group in a community can be purged from a library, the library system would be destroyed.

A few States exempt librarians from laws curbing distribution of "obscene" literature. California's law, however, provides: "Every person who, with knowledge that a person is a minor, or who fails to exercise reasonable care in ascertaining the true age of a minor, knowingly distributes to or sends or causes to be sent to, or exhibits to, or offers to distribute or exhibit any harmful matter to a minor, is guilty of a misdemeanor." Calif. Penal Code § 313.1.

A "minor" is one under 18 years of age; the word "distribute" means "to transfer possession"; "matter" includes "any book, magazine, newspaper, or other printed or written material." Id., §§ 313 (b), (d), (g).

"Harmful matter" is defined in § 313 (a) to mean "matter, taken as a whole, the predominant appeal of which to the average person, applying contemporary standards, is to prurient interest, i.e., a shameful or morbid interest in nudity, sex, or excretion; and is matter which taken as a whole goes substantially beyond customary limits of candor in description or representation of such matters; and is matter which taken as a whole is utterly without redeeming social importance for minors."

United States v. 12 200-Ft. Reels of Film, 413 U.S. 123 (1973)

In a 5-4 decision, the Supreme Court declares constitutional the federal statute prohibiting importation of "obscene" materials and upholds the conviction of a person who had brought into the United States, from Mexico, "obscene" materials that he claimed were for private and personal use only. Douglas dissents, stating in his opinion: "... it is ironic to me that in this Nation many pages must be written and many hours spent to explain why a person who can read whatever he desires, Stanley v. Georgia, 394 U.S. 557, may not without violating a law carry that literature in his briefcase or bring it home from abroad. Unless there is that ancillary right, one's Stanley rights could be realized, as has been suggested, only if one wrote or designed a tract in his attic and printed or processed it in his basement, so as to be able to read it in his study."

* * *

MR. JUSTICE DOUGLAS, dissenting.

I know of no constitutional way by which a book, tract, paper, postcard, or film may be made contraband because of its contents. The Constitution never purported to give the Federal Government censorship or oversight over literature or artistic productions, save as they might be governed by the Patent and Copyright Clause of Art. I, § 8, cl. 8, of the Constitution.[1] To be sure, the Colonies had enacted statutes which limited the freedom of speech, see Roth v. United States, 354 U.S. 476, 482-484, nn. 10-13, and in the early 19th century the States punished obscene libel as a common-law crime. Knowles v. State, 3 Day 103 (Conn. 1808) (signs depicting "monster"); Commonwealth v. Holmes, 17 Mass. 336 (1821) (John Cleland's Memoirs of a Woman of Pleasure); State v. Appling, 25 Mo. 315, 316 (1857) (utterance of words "too vulgar to be inserted in this opinion"); Commonwealth v. Sharpless, 2 S. & R. 91, 92 (1815) ("lewd, wicked, scandalous, infamous, ... and indecent posture with a woman").

To construe this history, as this Court does today in Miller v. California, ante, p. 15, as qualifying the plain import of the First Amendment is both a non sequitur and a disregard of the Tenth Amendment.

"[W]hatever may [have been] the form which the several States ... adopted in making declarations in favor of particular rights," James Madison, the author of the First Amendment, tells us, "the great object in view [was] to limit and qualify the powers of [the Federal] Government, by excepting out of the grant of power those cases in which the Government ought not to act, or to act only in a particular mode." 1 Annals of Cong. 437. Surely no one should argue that the retention by the States of vestiges of established religions after the enactment of the Establishment and Free Exercise Clauses saps these clauses of their meaning.[2] Yet it was precisely upon such reasoning that this Court, in Roth, exempted the bawdry from the protection of the First Amendment.

When it was enacted, the Bill of Rights applied only to the Federal Government, Barron v. Mayor of Baltimore, 7 Pet. 243, and the Tenth Amendment reserved the residuum of power to the States and the people. That the States, at some later date, may have exercised this reserved power in the form of laws restricting expression in no wise detracts from the express prohibition of the First Amendment. Only when the Fourteenth Amendment was passed did it become even possible to argue that through it the First Amendment became applicable to the States. But that goal was not attained until the ruling of this Court in 1931 that the reach of the Fourteenth Amendment included the First Amendment. See Stromberg v. California, 283 U.S. 359, 368.

At the very beginning, however, the First Amendment applied only to the Federal Government and there is not the slightest evidence that the Framers intended to put the newly created federal regime into the role of ombudsman over literature. Tying censorship to the movement of literature or films in interstate commerce or into foreign commerce would have been an easy way for a government of delegated powers to impair the liberty of expression. It was to bar such suppression that we have the First Amendment. I dare say Jefferson and Madison would be appalled at what the Court espouses today.

The First Amendment was the product of a robust,

not a prudish, age. The four decades prior to its enactment "saw the publication, virtually without molestation from any authority, of two classics of pornographic literature." D. Loth, The Erotic in Literature 108 (1961). In addition to William King's The Toast, there was John Cleland's Memoirs of a Woman of Pleasure which has been described as the "most important work of genuine pornography that has been published in English...." L. Markun, Mrs. Grundy 191 (1930). In England, Harris' List of Covent Garden Ladies, a catalog used by prostitutes to advertise their trade, enjoyed open circulation. N. St. John-Stevas, Obscenity and the Law 25 (1956). Bibliographies of pornographic literature list countless erotic works which were published in this time. See, e.g., A. Craig, Suppressed Books (1963); P. Fraxi, Catena Librorum Tacendorum (1885); W. Gallichan, The Poison of Prudery (1929); D. Loth, supra; L. Markun, supra. This was the age when Benjamin Franklin wrote his "Advice to a Young Man on Choosing a Mistress" and "A Letter to the Royal Academy at Brussels." "When the United States became a nation, none of the fathers of the country were any more concerned than Franklin with the question of pornography. John Quincy Adams had a strongly puritanical bent for a man of his literary interests, and even he wrote of Tom Jones that it was 'one of the best novels in the language.'" Loth, supra, at 120. It was in this milieu that Madison admonished against any "distinction between the freedom and licentiousness of the press." S. Padover, The Complete Madison 295 (1953). The Anthony Comstocks, the Thomas Bowdlers and Victorian hypocrisy--the predecessors of our present obscenity laws--had yet to come upon the stage.[3]

Julius Goebel, our leading expert on colonial law, does not so much as allude to punishment of obscenity.[4] J. Goebel, Development of Legal Institutions (1946); J. Goebel, Felony and Misdemeanor (1937); J. Goebel & T. Naughton, Law Enforcement in Colonial New York (1944).

Nor is there any basis in the legal history antedating the First Amendment for the creation of an obscenity exception. Memoirs v. Massachusetts, 383 U.S. 413, 424 (Douglas, J., concurring). The first reported case involving obscene conduct was not until 1663. There, the defendant was fined for "shewing himself naked in a balkony, and throwing down bottles (pist in) vi & armis among the people in Convent Garden, conta pacem, and to the scandal of the Government." Sir Charles Sydlyes Case, 83 Eng. Rep. 1146-1147 (K.B. 1663). Rather than being a fountainhead for a body of law proscribing obscene literature, later courts viewed this case simply as an instance of assault, criminal breach of the peace, or indecent exposure. E.g., Bradlaugh v. Queen, L.R. 3 Q. B. 569, 634 (1878); Rex v. Curl, 93 Eng. Rep. 849, 851 (K.B. 1727) (Fortescue, J., dissenting).

The advent of the printing press spurred censorship in England, but the ribald and the obscene were not, at first, within the scope of that which was officially banned. The censorship of the Star Chamber and the licensing of books under the Tudors and Stuarts was aimed at the blasphemous or heretical, the seditious or treasonous. At that date, the government made no effort to prohibit the dissemination of obscenity. Rather, obscene literature was considered to raise a moral question properly cognizable only by ecclesiastical, and not the common-law, courts.[5] "A crime that shakes religion (a), as profaneness on the stage, &c. is indictable (b); but writing an obscene book, as that intitled, 'The Fifteen Plagues of a Maidenhead,' is not indictable, but punishable only in the Spiritual Court (c)." Queen v. Read, 88 Eng. Rep. 953 (K.B. 1707). To be sure, Read was ultimately overruled and the crime of obscene libel established. Rex v. Curl, supra. It is noteworthy, however, that the only reported cases of obscene libel involved politically unpopular defendants. Ibid.; Rex v. Wilkes, 98 Eng. Rep. 327 (K.B. 1770).

In any event, what we said in Bridges v. California, 314 U.S. 252, 264-265, would dispose of any argument that earlier restrictions on free expression should be read into the First Amendment:

> [T]o assume that English common law in this field became ours is to deny the generally accepted historical belief that 'one of the objects of the Revolution was to get rid of the English common law on liberty of speech and of the press.' ...
>
> More specifically, it is to forget the environment in which the First Amendment was ratified. In presenting the proposals which were later embodied in the Bill of Rights, James Madison, the leader in the preparation of the First Amendment, said: 'Although I know whenever the great rights, the trial by jury, freedom of the press, or liberty of conscience, come in question in that body [Parliament], the invasion of them is resisted by able

> advocates, yet their Magna Charta does not contain any one provision for the security of those rights, respecting which the people of America are most alarmed. The freedom of the press and rights of conscience, those choicest privileges of the people, are unguarded in the British Constitution. '

This Court has nonetheless engrafted an exception upon the clear meaning of words written in the 18th century. But see ibid.; Grosjean v. American Press Co., 297 U.S. 233, 249.

Our efforts to define obscenity have not been productive of meaningful standards. What is "obscene" is highly subjective, varying from judge to judge, from juryman to juryman.

> The fireside banter of Chaucer's Canterbury Pilgrims was disgusting obscenity to Victorian-type moralists whose co-ed granddaughters shock the Victorian-type moralists of today. Words that are obscene in England have not a hint of impropriety in the United States, and vice versa. The English language is full of innocent words and phrases with obscene ancestry." [I. Brant, The Bill of Rights 490 (1965).]

So speaks our leading First Amendment historian; and he went on to say that this Court's decisions "seemed to multiply standards instead of creating one." Id., at 491. The reason is not the inability or mediocrity of judges.

> What is the reason for this multiple sclerosis of the judicial faculty? It is due to the fact stated above, that obscenity is a matter of taste and social custom, not of fact. [Id., at 491-492.]

Taste and custom are part of it, but, as I have said on other occasions,[6] the neuroses of judges, lawmakers, and of the so-called "experts" who have taken the place of Anthony Comstock, also play a major role.

Finally, it is ironic to me that in this Nation many pages must be written and many hours spent to explain why a person who can read whatever he desires, Stanley v. Georgia, 394 U.S. 557, may not without violating a law carry that literature in his briefcase or bring it home from abroad. Unless there is that ancillary right, one's Stanley rights could be realized, as has been suggested, only if one wrote or designed a tract in his attic and printed or processed it in his basement, so as to be able to read it in his study. United States v. Thirty-seven Photographs, 402 U.S. 363, 382 (Black, J., dissenting).

Most of the items that come this way denounced as "obscene" are in my view trash. I would find few, if any, that had by my standards any redeeming social value. But what may be trash to me may be prized by others.[7] Moreover, by what right under the Constitution do five of us have to impose our set of values on the literature of the day? There is danger in that course, the danger of bending the popular mind to new norms of conformity. There is, of course, also danger in tolerance, for tolerance often leads to robust or even ribald productions. Yet that is part of the risk of the First Amendment.

Irving Brant summed the matter up:

> Blessed with a form of government that requires universal liberty of thought and expression, blessed with a social and economic system built on that same foundation, the American people have created the danger they fear by denying to themselves the liberties they cherish. [Brant, supra, at 493.]

## NOTES

1. Even the copyright power is limited by the freedoms secured by the First Amendment. Lee v. Runge, 404 U.S. 887, 892-893 (Douglas, J., dissenting); Nimmer, Does Copyright Abridge the First Amendment Guarantees of Free Speech and Press?, 17 U.C.L.A.L. Rev. 1180 (1970).

2. Thus, the suggestion that most of the States that had ratified the Constitution punished blasphemy or profanity, is irrelevant to our inquiry here.

3. Separating the worthwhile from the worthless has largely been a matter of individual taste because significant governmental sanctions against obscene literature are of relatively recent vintage, not having developed until

the Victorian Age of the mid-19th century. N. St. John-Stevas, Obscenity and the Law 1-85 (1956). See T. Emerson, The System of Freedom of Expression 468-469 (1970); J. Paul & M. Schwartz, Federal Censorship, c. 1 (1961); Report of the Commission on Obscenity and Pornography 349-354 (1970). In this country, the first federal prohibition on obscenity was not until the Tariff Act of 1842, c. 270, § 28, 5 Stat. 566. England, which gave us the infamous Star Chamber and a history of licensing of publishing, did not raise a statutory bar to the importation of obscenity until 1853, Customs Consolidation Act, 16 & 17 Vict., c. 107, and waited until 1857 to enact a statute which banned obscene literature outright. Lord Campbell's Act, 20 & 21 Vict., c. 83.

4. The only colonial statute mentioning the word "obscene" was Acts and Laws of the Province of Mass. Bay, c. CV, § 8 (1712) in Mass. Bay Colony Charter & Laws 399 (1814). It did so, however, in the context of "composing, writing, printing or publishing ... any filthy, obscene, or profane song, pamphlet, libel or mock sermon, in imitation or in mimicking of preaching, or any other part of divine worship" and must, therefore, be placed with the other colonial blasphemy laws. E.g., An Act for the Punishment of divers capital and other Felonies, Conn. Acts, Laws, Charter & Articles of Confederation 66, 67 (1784); Act of 1723, c. 16, § 1, Digest of the Laws of Md. 92 (Herty 1799).

5. Lord Coke's De Libellis Famosis, 77 Eng. Rep. 250 (1605), for example, was the definitive statement of the common law of libel but made no mention of the misdemeanor of obscene libel.

6. Ginsberg v. New York, 390 U.S. 629, 655-656, 661-671 (Douglas, J., dissenting).

7. Ginzburg v. United States, 383 U.S. 463, 491 (Douglas, J., dissenting).

United States v. Orito, 413 U.S. 139 (1973)

A majority (5-4) of the Supreme Court decides that interstate transportation of "obscene" films is prohibited, declaring: "... we cannot say that the Constitution forbids comprehensive federal regulation of interstate transportation of obscene material merely because such transport may be by private carriage, or because the material is intended for private use of the transporter." Douglas dissents, stating in his opinion that the court had held in Stanley v. Georgia, 394 U.S. 557 (1969) "that an individual reading or examining 'obscene' materials in the privacy of his home is protected against state prosecution by reason of the First Amendment made applicable to the states by reason of the Fourteenth." Douglas contends that "a person who reads an 'obscene' book on an airline or bus or train is protected. So is he who carries an 'obscene' book in his pocket during a journey for his intended personal enjoyment. So is he who carries the book in his baggage or has a trucking company move his household effects to a new residence."

* * *

MR. JUSTICE DOUGLAS, dissenting.

We held in Stanley v. Georgia, 394 U.S. 557, that an individual reading or examining "obscene" materials in the privacy of his home is protected against state prosecution by reason of the First Amendment made applicable to the States by reason of the Fourteenth. We said:

> These are the rights that appellant is asserting in the case before us. He is asserting the right to read or observe what he pleases--the right to satisfy his intellectual and emotional needs in the privacy of his own home. He is asserting the right to be free from state inquiry into the contents of his library. Georgia contends that appellant does not have these rights, that there are certain types of materials that the individual may not read or even possess. Georgia justifies this assertion by arguing

> that the films in the present case are obscene. But we think that mere categorization of these films as 'obscene' is insufficient justification for such a drastic invasion of personal liberties guaranteed by the First and Fourteenth Amendments. Whatever may be the justifications for other statutes regulating obscenity, we do not think they reach into the privacy of one's own home. If the First Amendment means anything, it means that a State has no business telling a man, sitting alone in his own house, what books he may read or what films he may watch. Our whole constitutional heritage rebels at the thought of giving government the power to control men's minds. [Id., at 565.]

By that reasoning a person who reads an "obscene" book on an airline or bus or train is protected. So is he who carries an "obscene" book in his pocket during a journey for his intended personal enjoyment. So is he who carries the book in his baggage or has a trucking company move his household effects to a new residence. Yet 18 U.S.C. § 1462[1] makes such interstate carriage unlawful. Appellee therefore moved to dismiss the indictment on the ground that § 1462 is so broad as to cover "obscene" material designed for personal use.

The District Court granted the motion, holding that § 1462 was overbroad and in violation of the First Amendment.

The conclusion is too obvious for argument, unless we are to overrule Stanley. I would abide by Stanley and affirm the judgment dismissing the indictment.

NOTE

1. "Whoever brings into the United States, or any place subject to the jurisdiction thereof, or knowingly uses any express company or other common carrier, for carriage in interstate or foreign commerce--
   "(a) any obscene, lewd, lascivious, or filthy book, pamphlet, picture, motion-picture film, paper, letter, writing, print, or other matter of indecent character."

Hamling v. United States, 418 U.S. 87 (1974)

The Supreme Court upholds the convictions of Hamling and others who had used the mails and conspired to use the mails to carry "obscene" brochures advertising their publication The Illustrated Presidential Report of the Commission on Obscenity and Pornography. Douglas dissents, saying that "if officials may constitutionally report on obscenity, I see nothing in the First Amendment that allows us to bar the use of a glossary factually to illustrate what the report discusses."

* * *

MR. JUSTICE DOUGLAS, dissenting.

In 1970 the President's Commission on Obscenity and Pornography issued its report. Dean William D. Lockhart was chairman. Eighteen others were members. It was a 646-page report. One member, Charles H. Keating, Jr., filed a dissenting report of some 60 pages with at least as many pages of exhibits. The report contains many references to many facets of sex: e.g., petting, coitus, oral sexuality, masturbation, and homosexual activities.

What petitioners did was to supply the report with a glossary--not in dictionary terms but visually. Every item in the glossary depicted explicit sexual material within the meaning of that term as used in the report. Perhaps we should have no reports on obscenity. But imbedded in the First Amendment is the philosophy that the people have the right to know.[1] Sex is more important to some than to others but it is of some importance to all. If officials may constitutionally report on obscenity, I see nothing in the First Amendment that allows us to bar the use of a glossary factually to illustrate what the report discusses.

NOTE

1. The Constitution of India (Mar. 1, 1963) provides in Art.

19 (1) that "[a]ll citizens shall have the right--(a) to freedom of speech and expression"; but Art. 19 (2) provides that nothing in that clause bars "reasonable restrictions on the exercise" of those rights "in the interests of ... decency or morality." Our First Amendment contains no such qualification and certainly when Jefferson and Madison drafted it, sex had as great a potential for vulgarity as for beauty. If they had wanted a federal censor to edit our publications, they certainly would have made it explicit.

# LOYALTY OATHS

# AND

# DISCLAIMER AFFIDAVITS

Garner v. Los Angeles Board, 341 U.S. 716 (1951)

The Supreme Court decides that a city of Los Angeles loyalty oath required of all municipal employees is constitutional. Douglas dissents, stating in his opinion: "Petitioners were disqualified from office not for what they are today, not because of any program they currently espouse ..., not because of standards related to fitness for the office ..., but for what they once advocated."

* * *

MR. JUSTICE DOUGLAS, with whom MR. JUSTICE BLACK joins, dissenting.

Petitioners are citizens of the United States and civil service employees of the City of Los Angeles. In 1948 the City of Los Angeles passed Ordinance No. 94,004 which requires each of its employees to subscribe to an oath of loyalty which included, inter alia, an affirmation that he does not advise, advocate, or teach, and has not within the five years prior to the effective date of the ordinance "advised, advocated or taught, the overthrow by force, violence or other unlawful means, of the Government of the United States of America or of the State of California," and that he is not and has not within that period been "a member of or affiliated with any group, society, association, organization or party which advises, advocates or teaches, or has, within said period, advised, advocated or taught, the overthrow by force, violence or other unlawful means of the Government of the United States of America, or of the State of California."

The ordinance also requires each employee to execute an affidavit stating "whether or not he is or ever was a member of the Communist Party of the United States of America or of the Communist Political Association, and if he is or was such a member, stating the dates when he became, and the periods during which he was, such a member."

The ordinance was passed to effectuate the provisions

of §432 of the Charter of Los Angeles (Cal. Stat. 1941, c. 67, p. 3409) which provides, inter alia, that no person who has within five years prior to the adoption of §432 advised, advocated or taught the overthrow by force or violence of the government of the United States or of California, or who during that time has been a member of or affiliated with any group or party which has advised, advocated, or taught that doctrine, shall hold or retain or be eligible for any employment in the service of the city. Thus the ordinance and § 432 of the Charter read together make plain that prior advocacy or membership is without more a disqualification for employment. Both the oath and the affidavit are methods for enforcement of that policy.

Fifteen of the petitioners refused to sign either the oath or the affidavit. Two took the oath but refused to sign the affidavit. All seventeen were discharged--the sole ground being their refusal to sign the affidavit or to sign and to take the oath, as the case may be. They had an administrative review, which afforded them no relief. This suit was thereupon instituted in the California court, claiming reinstatement and unpaid salaries. Relief was denied by the District Court of Appeal, 98 Cal. App. 2d 493, 220 P. 2d 958; and a hearing was denied by the Supreme Court, three justices dissenting. The case is here on certiorari.

The case is governed by Cummings v. Missouri, 4 Wall. 277, and Ex parte Garland, 4 Wall. 333, which struck down test oaths adopted at the close of the Civil War. The Cummings case involved provisions of the Missouri Constitution requiring public officials and certain classes of professional people, including clergymen, to take an oath that, inter alia, they had never been "in armed hostility" to the United States; that they had never "by act or word" manifested their "adherence to the cause" of enemies of the country or their "desire" for the triumph of its enemies; that they had never "knowingly and willingly harbored, aided, or countenanced" an enemy; that they had never been a "member of, or connected with, any order, society, or organization inimical to the government of the United States" or engaged "in guerilla warfare" against its inhabitants; that they had never left Missouri "for the purpose of avoiding enrolment for or draft into the military service of the United States" or become enrolled as a southern sympathizer.

The Garland case involved certain Acts of Congress requiring public officials and attorneys practicing before the federal courts to take an oath that they had "voluntarily given no aid, countenance, counsel, or encouragement to persons engaged in armed hostility" against the United States and that they had "neither sought nor accepted, nor attempted to exercise the functions of any office whatever, under any authority or pretended authority in hostility to the United States." The Court amended its rules of admission to require this oath.

Cummings, a Catholic priest, was indicted and convicted for teaching and preaching without having first taken the oath.

Garland, a member of the Bar of the Court, had served in the Confederate Government, for which he had received a pardon from the President conditioned on his taking the customary oath of loyalty. He applied for permission to practice before the Court without taking the new oath.

Article I, § 10 of the Constitution forbids any state to "pass any Bill of Attainder" or any "ex post facto Law." Article I, § 9 curtails the power of Congress by providing that "No Bill of Attainder or ex post facto Law shall be passed." The Court ruled that the test oaths in the Cummings and Garland cases were bills of attainder and ex post facto laws within the meaning of the Constitution. "A bill of attainder," wrote Mr. Justice Field for the Court, "is a legislative act which inflicts punishment without a judicial trial."[1] Cummings v. Missouri, supra, p. 323; and see United States v. Lovett, 328 U.S. 303, 317, 318. The Court held that deprivation of the right to follow one's profession is punishment. A bill of attainder, though generally directed against named individuals, may be directed against a whole class. Bills of attainder usually declared the guilt; here they assumed the guilt and adjudged the punishment conditionally, i.e., they deprived the parties of their right to preach and to practice law unless the presumption were removed by the expurgatory oath. That was held to be as much a bill of attainder as if the guilt had been irrevocably pronounced. The laws were also held to be ex post facto since they imposed a penalty for an act not so punishable at the time it was committed.

There are, of course, differences between the present case and the Cummings and Garland cases. Those condemned by the Los Angeles ordinance are municipal employees; those condemned in the others were professional people.

Here the past conduct for which punishment is exacted is single--advocacy within the past five years of the overthrow of the Government by force and violence. In the other cases the acts for which Cummings and Garland stood condemned covered a wider range and involved some conduct which might be vague and uncertain. But those differences, seized on here in hostility to the constitutional provisions, are wholly irrelevant. Deprivation of a man's means of livelihood by reason of past conduct, not subject to this penalty when committed, is punishment whether he is a professional man, a day laborer who works for private industry, or a government employee. The deprivation is nonetheless unconstitutional whether it be for one single past act or a series of past acts. The degree of particularity with which the past is defined is not the criterion. We are not dealing here with the problem of vagueness in criminal statutes. No amount of certainty would have cured the laws in the Cummings and Garland cases. They were stricken down because of the mode in which punishment was inflicted.

Petitioners were disqualified from office not for what they are today, not because of any program they currently espouse (cf. Gerende v. Board of Supervisors, 341 U. S. 56), not because of standards related to fitness for the office (cf. Dent v. West Virginia, 129 U. S. 114; Hawker v. New York, 170 U. S. 189), but for what they once advocated. They are deprived of their livelihood by legislative act, not by judicial processes. We put the case in the aspect most invidious to petitioners. Whether they actually advocated the violent overthrow of Government does not appear. But here, as in the Cummings case, the vice is in the presumption of guilt which can only be removed by the expurgatory oath. That punishment, albeit conditional, violates here as it did in the Cummings case the constitutional prohibition against bills of attainder. Whether the ordinance also amounts to an ex post facto law is a question we do not reach.

NOTE

1. Mr. Justice Field continued: "If the punishment be less than death, the act is termed a bill of pains and penalties. Within the meaning of the Constitution, bills of attainder include bills of pains and penalties. In these cases the legislative body, in addition to its legitimate functions, exercises the powers and office of judge; it assumes, in the language of the text-books,

judicial magistracy; it pronounces upon the guilt of the party, without any of the forms or safeguards of trial; it determines the sufficiency of the proofs produced, whether conformable to the rules of evidence or otherwise; and it fixes the degree of punishment in accordance with its own notions of the enormity of the offence." 4 Wall. p. 323.

In addition to the history of bills of attainder in England, the draftsmen of the Constitution had before them recent examples of such legislation by the Revolutionary governments of the states. Legislative action against persons of known or suspected Loyalist sympathies included outright attaint of treason or subversion (e.g., Georgia, Act of March 1, 1778; Pennsylvania Laws 1778, c. 49; New York Laws 1779, Third Session, c. 25); proscription and banishment (e.g., Massachusetts, Act of Sept. 1778, Charters and Gen. Laws, c. 48; New Hampshire Laws 1778, Fourth Session, c. 9); confiscation (e.g., Delaware Laws 1778, c. 29b; New Jersey, Act of Dec. 11, 1778, Laws, p. 40); as well as numerous test oaths involving, among other penalties, disqualification from holding office or practicing certain professions. See laws collected in Van Tyne, The Loyalists in the American Revolution, App. B, C; and generally, Thompson, Anti-Loyalist Legislation During the American Revolution, 3 Ill. L. Rev. 81, 147.

## Adler v. Board of Education, 342 U.S. 485 (1952)

The Supreme Court finds constitutional a New York statute requiring teachers to abide by a "loyalty oath." Douglas dissents, declaring in his opinion: "What happens under this law is typical of what happens in a police state. Teachers are under constant surveillance; their pasts are combed for signs of disloyalty; their utterances are watched for clues to dangerous thoughts. A pall is cast over the classrooms. There can be no real academic freedom in that environment. Where suspicion fills the air and holds scholars in line for fear of their jobs, there can be no exercise of the free intellect. Supineness and dogmatism take the place of inquiry .... A problem can no longer be pursued with impunity to its edges. Fear stalks the classroom. The teacher is no longer a stimulant to adventurous thinking; she becomes instead a pipeline for safe and sound information. A deadening dogma takes the place of free inquiry. Instruction tends to become sterile; pursuit of knowledge is discouraged; discussion often leaves off where it should begin."

* * *

MR. JUSTICE DOUGLAS, with whom MR. JUSTICE BLACK concurs, dissenting.

I have not been able to accept the recent doctrine that a citizen who enters the public service can be forced to sacrifice his civil rights.[1] I cannot for example find in our constitutional scheme the power of a state to place its employees in the category of second-class citizens by denying them freedom of thought and expression. The Constitution guarantees freedom of thought and expression to everyone in our society. All are entitled to it; and none needs it more than the teacher.

The public school is in most respects the cradle of our democracy. The increasing role of the public school is seized upon by proponents of the type of legislation represented by New York's Feinberg law as proof of the importance and need for keeping the school free of "subversive influences." But that is to misconceive the effect of this type of legislation. Indeed the impact of this kind of censorship on the public school system illustrates the high purpose of the First Amendment in freeing speech and thought from censorship.

The present law proceeds on a principle repugnant to our society--guilt by association. A teacher is disqualified because of her membership in an organization found to be "subversive." The finding as to the "subversive" character of the organization is made in a proceeding to which the teacher is not a party and in which it is not clear that she may even be heard. To be sure, she may have a hearing when charges of disloyalty are leveled against her. But in that hearing the finding as to the "subversive" character of the organization apparently may not be reopened in order to allow her to show the truth of the matter. The irrebuttable charge that the organization is "subversive" therefore hangs as an ominous cloud over her own hearing. The mere fact of membership in the organization raises a prima facie case of her own guilt. She may, it is said, show her innocence. But innocence in this case turns on knowledge; and when the witch hunt is on, one who must rely on ignorance leans on a feeble reed.

The very threat of such a procedure is certain to raise havoc with academic freedom. Youthful indiscretions, mistaken causes, misguided enthusiasms--all long forgotten--become the ghosts of a harrowing present. Any organization committed to a liberal cause, any group organized to revolt against an hysterical trend, any committee launched to sponsor an unpopular program becomes suspect. These are the organizations into which Communists often infiltrate. Their presence infects the whole, even though the project was not conceived in sin. A teacher caught in that mesh is almost certain to stand condemned. Fearing condemnation, she will tend to shrink from any association that stirs controversy. In that manner freedom of expression will be stifled.

But that is only part of it. Once a teacher's connection with a listed organization is shown, her views become subject to scrutiny to determine whether her membership in the organization is innocent or, if she was formerly a member, whether she has bona fide abandoned her membership.

The law inevitably turns the school system into a spying project. Regular loyalty reports on the teachers must be made out. The principals become detectives; the students, the parents, the community become informers. Ears are cocked for tell-tale signs of disloyalty. The prejudices of the community come into play in searching out the disloyal. This is not the ususal type of supervision which checks a teacher's competency; it is a system which searches for hidden meanings in a teacher's utterances.

What was the significance of the reference of the art teacher to socialism? Why was the history teacher so openly hostile to Franco Spain? Who heard overtones of revolution in the English teacher's discussion of the Grapes of Wrath? What was behind the praise of Soviet progress in metallurgy in the chemistry class? Was it not "subversive" for the teacher to cast doubt on the wisdom of the venture in Korea?

What happens under this law is typical of what happens in a police state. Teachers are under constant surveillance; their pasts are combed for signs of disloyalty; their utterances are watched for clues to dangerous thoughts. A pall is cast over the classrooms. There can be no real academic freedom in that environment. Where suspicion fills the air and holds scholars in line for fear of their jobs, there can be no exercise of the free intellect. Supineness and dogmatism take the place of inquiry. A "party line"--as dangerous as the "party line" of the Communists--lays hold. It is the "party line" of the orthodox view, of the conventional thought, of the accepted approach. A problem can no longer be pursued with impunity to its edges. Fear stalks the classroom. The teacher is no longer a stimulant to adventurous thinking; she becomes instead a pipe line for safe and sound information. A deadening dogma takes the place of free inquiry. Instruction tends to become sterile; pursuit of knowledge is discouraged; discussion often leaves off where it should begin.

This, I think, is what happens when a censor looks over a teacher's shoulder. This system of spying and surveillance with its accompanying reports and trials cannot go hand in hand with academic freedom. It produces standardized thought, not the pursuit of truth. Yet it was the pursuit of truth which the First Amendment was designed to protect. A system which directly or inevitably has that effect is alien to our system and should be struck down. Its survival is a real threat to our way of life. We need be bold and adventuresome in our thinking to survive. A school system producing students trained as robots threatens to rob a generation of the versatility that has been perhaps our greatest distinction. The Framers knew the danger of dogmatism; they also knew the strength that comes when the mind is free, when ideas may be pursued wherever they lead. We forget these teachings of the First Amendment when we sustain this law.

Of course the school systems of the country need not become cells for Communist activities; and the classrooms need not become forums for propagandizing the Marxist creed. But the guilt of the teacher should turn on overt acts. So long as she is a law-abiding citizen, so long as her performance within the public school system meets professional standards, her private life, her political philosophy, her social creed should not be the cause of reprisals against her.

## NOTE

1. United Public Workers v. Mitchell, 330 U.S. 75; Garner v. Board of Public Works of Los Angeles, 341 U.S. 716.

## Speiser v. Randall, 357 U.S. 513 (1958)

The Supreme Court declares unconstitutional a California loyalty oath required of veterans wishing to qualify for property-tax exemptions. Douglas writes a concurring opinion in which he declares: "I. The State by the device of the loyalty oath places the burden of proving loyalty on the citizen. That procedural device goes against the grain of our constitutional system, for every man is presumed innocent until guilt is established. This technique is an ancient one that was denounced in an early period in our history.... II. If the aim of the law is not to apprehend criminals but to penalize advocacy, it likewise must fall. Since the time that Alexander Hamilton wrote concerning these oaths, the Bill of Rights was adopted; and then much later came the Fourteenth Amendment. As a result of the latter a rather broad range of liberties was newly guaranteed to the citizen against state action. Included were those contained in the First Amendment--the right to speak freely, the right to believe what one chooses, the right of conscience.... What a man thinks is of no concern to government. 'The First Amendment gives freedom of mind the same security as freedom of conscience.' Advocacy and belief go hand in hand. For there can be no true freedom of mind if thoughts are secure only when they are pent up."

* * *

MR. JUSTICE DOUGLAS, with whom MR. JUSTICE BLACK agrees, concurring.

While I substantially agree with the opinion of the Court, I will state my reasons more fully and more explicitly.

I. The State by the device of the loyalty oath places the burden of proving loyalty on the citizen. That procedural device goes against the grain of our constitutional system, for every man is presumed innocent until guilt is established. This technique is an ancient one that was denounced in an early period of our history.

Alexander Hamilton, writing in 1784 under the name Phocion, said: "... let it be supposed that instead of the mode of indictment and trial by jury, the Legislature was to declare, that every citizen who did not swear he had never adhered to the King of Great Britain, should incur all the penalties which our treason laws prescribe. Would this not be ... a direct infringement of the Constitution? ... it is substituting a new and arbitrary mode of prosecution to that ancient and highly esteemed one, recognized by the laws and the Constitution of the State,--I mean the trial by jury." 4 The Works of Alexander Hamilton (Fed. ed. 1904) 269-270.

Hamilton compared that hypothetical law to an actual one passed by New York on March 27, 1778, whereby a person who had served the King of England in enumerated ways was declared "to be utterly disabled disqualified and incapacitated to vote either by ballot or viva voce at any election" in New York. N. Y. Laws 1777-1784, 35. An oath was required[1] in enforcement of that law.[2]

Hamilton called this "a subversion of one great principle of social security: to wit, that every man shall be preseumed innocent until he is proved guilty." 4 The Works of Alexander Hamilton (Fed. ed. 1904) 269. He went on to say "This was to invert the order of things; and, instead of obliging the State to prove the guilt in order to inflict the penalty, it was to oblige the citizen to establish his own innocence to avoid the penalty. It was to excite scruples in the honest and conscientious, and to hold out a bribe to perjury." Ibid.

If the aim is to apprehend those who have lifted a hand against the Government, the procedure is unconstitutional.

If one conspires to overthrow the Government, he commits a crime. To make him swear he is innocent to avoid the consequences of a law is to put on him the burden of proving this innocence. That method does not square with our standards of procedural due process, as the opinion of the Court points out.

The Court in Cummings v. Missouri, 4 Wall. 277, 328, denounced another expurgatory oath that had some of the vices of the present one.

"The clauses in question subvert the presumptions of

innocence, and alter the rules of evidence, which heretofore, under the universally recognized principles of the common law, have been supposed to be fundamental and unchangeable. They assume that the parties are guilty; they call upon the parties to establish their innocence; and they declare that such innocence can be shown only in one way--by an inquisition, in the form of an expurgatory oath, into the consciences of the parties."

II. If the aim of the law is not to apprehend criminals but to penalize advocacy, it likewise must fall. Since the time that Alexander Hamilton wrote concerning these oaths, the Bill of Rights was adopted; and then much later came the Fourteenth Amendment. As a result of the latter a rather broad range of liberties was newly guaranteed to the citizen against state action. Included were those contained in the First Amendment--the right to speak freely, the right to believe what one chooses, the right of conscience. Stromberg v. California, 283 U.S. 359; Murdock v. Pennsylvania, 319 U.S. 105; Staub v. City of Baxley, 355 U.S. 313. Today what one thinks or believes, what one utters and says have the full protection of the First Amendment. It is only his actions that government may examine and penalize. When we allow government to probe his beliefs and withhold from him some of the privileges of citizenship because of what he thinks, we do indeed "invert the order of things," to use Hamilton's phrase. All public officials--state and federal--must take an oath to support the Constitution by the express command of Article VI of the Constitution. And see Gerende v. Election Board, 341 U.S. 56. But otherwise the domains of conscience and belief have been set aside and protected from government intrusion. Board of Education v. Barnette, 319 U.S. 624. What a man thinks is of no concern to government. "The First Amendment gives freedom of mind the same security as freedom of conscience." Thomas v. Collins, 323 U.S. 516, 531. Advocacy and belief go hand in hand. For there can be no true freedom of mind if thoughts are secure only when they are pent up.

In Murdock v. Pennsylvania, supra, we stated, "Plainly a community may not suppress, or the state tax, the dissemination of views because they are unpopular, annoying or distasteful." 319 U.S., at 116. If the Government may not impose a tax upon the expression of ideas in order to discourage them, it may not achieve the same end by reducing the individual who expresses his views to second-class citizenship by withholding tax benefits granted others. When government denies a tax exemption because of the citizen's belief, it penalizes that belief. That is different only in form, not substance, from the "taxes on knowledge" which have had a notorious history in the English-speaking world. See Grosjean v. American Press Co., 297 U.S. 233, 246-247.

We deal here with a type of advocacy which, to say the least, lies close to the "constitutional danger zone." Yates v. United States, 354 U. S. 298, 319. Advocacy which is in no way brigaded with action should always be protected by the First Amendment. That protection should extend even to the ideas we despise. As Mr. Justice Holmes wrote in dissent in Gitlow v. New York, 268 U.S. 652, 673, "If in the long run the beliefs expressed in proletarian dictatorship are destined to be accepted by the dominant forces of the community, the only meaning of free speech is that they should be given their chance and have their way." It is time for government--state or federal--to become concerned with the citizen's advocacy when his ideas and beliefs move into the realm of action.

The California oath is not related to unlawful action. To get the tax exemption the taxpayer must swear he "does not advocate the overthrow of the Government of the United States or of the State of California by force or violence or other unlawful means nor advocate the support of a foreign government against the United States in event of hostilities."[3] The Court construes the opinion of the California Supreme Court as applying the same test of illegal advocacy as was sustained against constitutional challenge in Dennis v. United States, 341 U.S. 494. That case held that advocacy of the overthrow of government by force and violence was not enough, that incitement to action, as well as clear and present danger, were also essential ingredients. Id., at 512, 509-510. As Yates v. United States, supra, makes clear, there is still a clear constitutional line between advocacy of abstract doctrine and advocacy of action. The California Supreme Court said, to be sure, that the oath in question "is concerned" with that kind of advocacy.[4] But it nowhere says that oath is limited to that kind of advocacy. It seemed to think that advocacy was itself action for it said, "What one may merely believe is not prohibited. It is only advocates of the subversive doctrines who are affected. Advocacy constitutes action and the instigation of action, not mere belief or opinion."[5]

However the California opinion may be read, these judgments should fall. If the construction of the oath is the one I prefer, then the Supreme Court of California has obliterated the line between advocacy of abstract doctrine and advocacy of action. If the California oath has been limited by judicial construction to the type of advocacy condemned in Dennis, it still should fall. My disagreement with that decision has not abated. No conspiracy to overthrow the Government was involved. Speech and speech alone was the offense. I repeat that thought and speech go hand in hand. There is no real freedom of thought if ideas must be suppressed. There can be no freedom of the mind unless ideas can be uttered.

I know of no power that enables any government under our Constitution to become the monitor of thought, as this statute would have it become.

## NOTES

1. The oath was prescribed by the Council in charge of the Southern District of New York. The Council, authorized by the Act of October 23, 1779, was composed of the Governor, President of the Senate, Chancellor, Supreme Court judges, Senators, Assemblymen, Secretary of State, Attorney General, and County Court judges. The Council was to assume authority "whenever the enemy shall abandon or be dispossessed of the same, and until the legislature can be convened," N.Y. Laws 1777-1784, 192. The Council governed from November 25, 1783, to February 5, 1784. See Barck, New York City 1776-1783 (1931), 220-221. Among the powers of the Council was control of elections.

   The election oath prescribed by the Council read as follows:

   "I .................. do solemnly, without any mental Reservation or Equivocation whatsoever, swear and declare, and call God to witness (or if of the People called Quakers, affirm) that I renounce and abjure all Allegiance to the King of Great-Britain; and that I will bear true Faith and Allegiance to the State of New-York, as a Free and Independent State, and that I will in all Things, to the best of my Knowledge and Ability, do my Duty as a good and faithful Subject of the said State ought to do. So help me God." Independent Gazette, Dec. 13, 1783.

The Council further provided:

"That if any Person presenting himself to give his Vote, shall be suspected of, or charged with having committed any of the Offences above specified, it shall be Lawful for the Inspectors, or Superintendents (as the Case may be) to inquire into and determine the Fact whereof such Person shall be suspected, or wherewith he shall be charged, as the Cause of Disqualification, on the Oath of one or more Witnesses, or on the Oath of the Party so suspected or charged, at their Discretion; and if such Fact shall, in the Judgement of the Inspectors or Superintendents, be established, it shall be lawful for them, and they are hereby required, to reject the Vote of such Person at such Election." Independent Gazette, Dec. 13, 1783.

2. Other loyalty oaths appeared during this early period. Suspected persons were required to take a loyalty oath. N.Y. Laws 1777-1784, 87. The same was required of lawyers. Id., at 155, 420. And see Flick, Loyalism in New York During the American Revolution, 14 Studies in History, Economics and Public Law (Columbia Univ. 1901) 9 (passim).

3. Calif. Rev. & Tax Code, § 32; and see Calif. Const., Art. XX, § 19.

4. 48 Cal. 2d 419, 311 P. 2d 508, 520.

Elfbrandt v. Russell, 384 U.S. 11 (1966)

The Supreme Court finds an Arizona loyalty oath unconstitutional, Justice Douglas writing for the majority (5-4) stating: "Those who join an organization but do not share its unlawful purposes and who do not participate in its unlawful activities surely pose no threat, either as citizens or as public employees. Laws such as this which are not restricted in scope to those who join with the 'specific intent' to further illegal action impose, in effect, a conclusive presumption that the member shares the unlawful aims of the organization."

* * *

MR. JUSTICE DOUGLAS delivered the opinion of the Court.

This case, which involves questions concerning the constitutionality of an Arizona Act requiring an oath from state employees has been here before. We vacated the judgment of the Arizona Supreme Court which had sustained the oath (94 Ariz. 1, 381 P. 2d 554) and remanded the cause for reconsideration in light of Baggett v. Bullitt, 377 U.S. 360. See 378 U.S. 127. On reconsideration the Supreme Court of Arizona reinstated the original judgment. 97 Ariz. 140, 397 P. 2d 944. The case is here on certiorari. 382 U.S. 810.

The oath reads in conventional fashion as follows:[1]

> "I, (type or print name) do solemnly swear (or affirm) that I will support the Constitution of the United States and the Constitution and laws of the State of Arizona; that I will bear true faith and allegiance to the same, and defend them against all enemies, foreign and domestic, and that I will faithfully and impartially discharge the duties of the office of (name of office) according to the best of my ability, so help me God (or so I do affirm)."

The Legislature put a gloss on the oath[2] by subjecting to a prosecution for perjury and for discharge from public office anyone who took the oath and who "knowingly and wilfully becomes or remains a member of the communist party of the United States or its successors or any of its subordinate organizations" or "any other organization" having for "one of its purposes" the overthrow of the government of Arizona or any of its political subdivisions where the employee had knowledge of the unlawful purpose. Petitioner, a teacher and a Quaker, decided she could not in good conscience take the oath, not knowing what it meant and not having a chance to get a hearing at which its precise scope and meaning could be determined. This suit for declaratory relief followed. On our remand the Arizona Supreme Court said that the gloss on the oath is "not afflicted" with the many uncertainties found potentially punishable in Baggett v. Bullitt, supra.

> Nor does it reach endorsements or support for Communist candidates for office nor a lawyer who represents the Communist Party, or its members, nor journalists who defend the Communist Party, its rights, or its members. Such conduct is neither an act nor in aid of an act attempting to overthrow the government by force and violence.
>
> It is our conclusion that the portions of the Arizona act here considered do not forbid or require conduct in terms so vague that men of common intelligence must necessarily guess at the meaning and differ as to their application. [97 Ariz., at 147, 397 P. 2d, at 948.]

Mr. Justice Bernstein, in dissent, responded that the majority had failed to consider the so-called "membership clause" of the oath and accompanying statutory gloss:

> Let us consider a scientist, a teacher in one of our universities. He could not know whether membership is prohibited in an international scientific organization which includes members from neutralist nations and Communist bloc nations--the latter admittedly dedicated to the overthrow of our government and which control the organization--even though access to the scientific information of the organization is available only to its members....
>
> Though all might agree that the principal purpose of such an organization is scientific, the statute makes his membership a crime if any subordinate purpose is the overthrow of the state government. The vice of vagueness here is that the scientist cannot know whether membership in the organiza-

> tion will result in prosecution for a violation of § 38-231, subd. E or in honors from his university for the encyclopedic knowledge acquired in his field in part through his membership. [Id., at 147-148, 397 P. 2d, at 949.]

We recognized in Scales v. United States, 367 U.S. 203, 229, that "quasi-political parties or other groups ... may embrace both legal and illegal aims." We noted that a "blanket prohibition of association with a group having both legal and illegal aims" would pose "a real danger that legitimate political expression or association would be impaired." The statute with which we dealt in Scales, the so-called "membership clause" of the Smith Act (18 U.S.C. § 2385), was found not to suffer from this constitutional infirmity because, as the Court construed it, the statute reached only "active" membership (id., at 222) with the "specific intent" of assisting in achieving the unlawful ends of the organization (id., at 229-230). The importance of this limiting construction from a constitutional standpoint was emphasized in Noto v. United States, 367 U.S. 290, 299-300, decided the same day:

> [I]t should also be said that this element of the membership crime [the defendant's 'personal criminal purpose to bring about the overthrow of the Government by force and violence'], like its others, must be judged strictissimi juris, for otherwise there is a danger that one in sympathy with the legitimate aims of such an organization, but not specifically intending to accomplish them by resort to violence, might be punished for his adherence to lawful and constitutionally protected purposes, because of other and unprotected purposes which he does not necessarily share. [3]

Any lingering doubt that proscription of mere knowing membership, without any showing of "specific intent," would run afoul of the Constitution was set at rest by our decision in Aptheker v. Secretary of State, 378 U.S. 500. We dealt there with a statute which provided that no member of a Communist organization ordered by the Subversive Activities Control Board to register shall apply for or use a passport. We concluded that the statute would not permit a narrow reading of the sort we gave § 2385 in Scales. See 378 U.S., at 511, n. 9. The statute, as we read it, covered membership which was not accompanied by a specific intent to further the unlawful aims of the organization, and we held it unconstitutional.

The oath and accompanying statutory gloss challenged here suffer from an identical constitutional infirmity. One who subscribes to this Arizona oath and who is, or thereafter becomes, a knowing member of an organization which has as "one of its purposes" the violent overthrow of the government, is subject to immediate discharge and criminal penalties. Nothing in the oath, the statutory gloss, or the construction of the oath and statutes given by the Arizona Supreme Court, purports to exclude association by one who does not subscribe to the organization's unlawful ends. Here as in Baggett v. Bullitt, supra, the "hazard of being prosecuted for knowing but guiltless behavior" (id., at 373) is a reality. People often label as "communist" ideas which they oppose; and they often make up our juries. "[P]rosecutors too are human." Cramp v. Board of Public Instruction, 368 U.S. 278, 287. Would a teacher be safe and secure in going to a Pugwash Conference?[4] Would it be legal to join a seminar group predominantly Communist and therefore subject to control by those who are said to believe in the overthrow of the Government by force and violence? Juries might convict though the teacher did not subscribe to the wrongful aims of the organization. And there is apparently no machinery provided for getting clearance in advance.[5]

Those who join an organization but do not share its unlawful purposes and who do not participate in its unlawful activities surely pose no threat, either as citizens or as public employees. Laws such as this which are not restricted in scope to those who join with the "specific intent" to further illegal action impose, in effect, a conclusive presumption that the member shares the unlawful aims of the organization. See Aptheker v. Secretary of State, supra, at 511. The unconstitutionality of this Act follows a fortiori from Speiser v. Randall, 357 U.S. 513, where we held that a State may not even place on an applicant for a tax exemption the burden of proving that he has not engaged in criminal advocacy.

This Act threatens the cherished freedom of association protected by the First Amendment, made applicable to the States through the Fourteenth Amendment. Baggett v. Bullitt, supra; Cramp v. Board of Public Instruction, supra. Cf. N.A.A.C.P. v. Alabama, 357 U.S. 449, 460 et seq.; Gibson v. Florida Legislative Committee, 372 U.S. 539, 543-546. And, as a committee of the Arizona Legislature which urged adoption of this law itself recognized, public employees of character and integrity may well forgo their calling rather than risk prosecution for perjury or compromise their commitment to intellectual and political freedom:

> The communist trained in fraud and perjury has no qualms in taking an oath; the loyal citizen, conscious of history's oppressions, may well wonder whether the medieval rack and torture wheel are next for the one who declines to take an involved negative oath as evidence that he is a True Believer.[6]

A statute touching those protected rights must be "narrowly drawn to define and punish specific conduct as constituting a clear and present danger to a substantial interest of the State." Cantwell v. Connecticut, 310 U.S. 296, 311. Legitimate legislative goals "cannot be pursued by means that broadly stifle fundamental personal liberties when the end can be more narrowly achieved." Shelton v. Tucker, 364 U.S. 479, 488. And see Louisiana v. N.A.A.C.P., 366 U.S. 293, 296-297. As we said in N.A.A.C.P. v. Button, 371 U.S. 415, 432-433:

> The objectionable quality of ... overbreadth does not depend upon absence of fair notice to a criminally accused or upon unchanneled delegation of legislative powers, but upon the danger of tolerating, in the area of First Amendment freedoms, the existence of a penal statute susceptible of sweeping and improper application.... These freedoms are delicate and vulnerable, as well as supremely precious in our society. The threat of sanctions may deter their exercise almost as potently as the actual application of sanctions....

A law which applies to membership without the "specific intent" to further the illegal aims of the organization infringes unnecessarily on protected freedoms. It rests on the doctrine of "guilt by association" which has no place here. See Schneiderman v. United States, 320 U.S. 118, 136; Schware v. Board of Bar Examiners, 353 U.S. 232, 246. Such a law cannot stand.

Reversed.

NOTES

1. Ariz. Rev. Stat. § 38-231 (1965 Supp.).

2. Id., § E reads as follows:
"Any officer or employee as defined in this section

having taken the form of oath or affirmation prescribed by this section, and knowingly or wilfully at the time of subscribing the oath or affirmation, or at any time thereafter during his term of office or employment, does commit or aid in the commission of any act to overthrow by force or violence the government of this state or of any of its political subdivisions, or advocates the overthrow by force or violence of the government of this state or of any of its political subdivisions, or during such term of office or employment knowingly and wilfully becomes or remains a member of the communist party of the United States or its successors or any of its subordinate organizations or any other organization having for one of its purposes the overthrow by force or violence of the government of the state of Arizona or any of its political subdivisions, and said officer or employee as defined in this section prior to becoming or remaining a member of such organization or organizations, shall be guilty of a felony and upon conviction thereof shall be subject to all the penalties for perjury; in addition, upon conviction under this section, the officer or employee shall be deemed discharged from said office or employment and shall not be entitled to any additional compensation or any other emoluments or benefits which may have been incident or appurtenant to said office or employment."

3. Cf. Rowoldt v. Perfetto, 355 U.S. 115, 120; Gastelum-Quinones v. Kennedy, 374 U.S. 469.

4. The Pugwash Conferences, A Staff Analysis, Subcommittee to Investigate the Administration of the Internal Security Act, Senate Committee on the Judiciary, Commitee Print, 87th Cong., 1st Sess. (1961); Rabinowitch, Pugwash--History and Outlook, 13 Bull. Atomic Sci. 243 (1957); Topchiev, Comments on Pugwash: From the East, 14 Bull. Atomic Sci. 118 (1958); Thirring, Comments on Pugwash: From the West, id., at 121; Rabinowitch, The Stowe Conferences, 17 Bull. Atomic Sci. 382 (1961); Statement of International Pugwash Continuing Committee: Pugwash XIII, Bull. Atomic Sci. 43-45 (December 1964); Documents of Second Pugwash Conference of Nuclear Scientists (March 31-April 11, 1958).

5. Petitioner would, of course, have a hearing at a perjury

trial, after the event. And one member of the Arizona Supreme Court felt that petitioner, having tenure, would be entitled to a hearing before she was discharged from her teaching position. See Elfbrandt v. Russell, 94 Ariz. 1, 17-18, 381 P. 2d 554, 565 (Bernstein, C.J., concurring). But even that is not authoritatively decided by the court; indeed, another opinion states this to be a minority view, 94 Ariz., at 18, 381 P. 2d, at 566 (separate opinion of Jennings, J.).

6. Report of the Judiciary Committee in Support of the Committee Amendment to H.B. 115, Journal of the Senate, 1st Reg. Sess., 25th Legislature of the State of Arizona, p. 424 (1961).

Whitehill v. Elkins, 389 U.S. 54 (1967)

The Supreme Court decides that a Maryland teacher's loyalty oath is unconstitutional, Douglas delivering the opinion of the court, stating that sections of Maryland's Ober Act are "befogged": "the lines between permissible and impermissible conduct are quite indistinct. Precision and clarity are not present. Rather we find an overbreadth that makes possible oppressive or capricious application as regimes change. That very threat, as we said in another context ..., may deter the flowering of academic freedom as much as successive suits for perjury. Like the other oath cases mentioned, we have another classic example of the need for 'narrowly drawn' legislation ... in this sensitive and important First Amendment area."

* * *

MR. JUSTICE DOUGLAS delivered the opinion of the Court.

This suit for declaratory relief that a Maryland teacher's oath required of appellant was unconstitutional was heard by a three-judge court and dismissed. 258 F. Supp. 589. We noted probable jurisdiction. 386 U.S. 906.

Appellant, who was offered a teaching position with the University of Maryland, refused to take the following oath:

> I, ____________, do hereby (Print Name--including middle initial) certify that I am not engaged in one way or another in the attempt to overthrow the Government of the United States, or the State of Maryland, or any political subdivision of either of them, by force or violence.
>
> I further certify that I understand the aforegoing statement is made subject to the penalties of perjury prescribed in Article 27, Section 439 of the Annotated Code of Maryland (1957 edition).

The question is whether the oath is to be read in isolation or in connection with the Ober Act (Art. 85A, Md. Ann. Code, 1957) which by § § 1 and 13 defines a "subversive" as "... any person who commits, attempts to commit, or aids in the commission, or advocates, abets, advises or teaches by any means any person to commit, attempt to commit, or aid in the commission of any act intended to overthrow, destroy or *alter*, or to assist in the overthrow, destruction or *alteration* of, the constitutional form of the government of the United States, or of the State of Maryland, or any political subdivision of either of them, *by revolution, force, or violence*; or who is a *member of a subversive organization* or a foreign subversive organization, as more fully defined in this article." (Italics supplied.) Section 1 defines the latter terms: "subversive organization" meaning a group that would, *inter alia,* "alter" the form of government "by revolution, force or violence"; "foreign subversive organization" is such a group directed, dominated, or controlled by a foreign government which engages in such activities.

The oath was prepared by the Attorney General and approved by the Board of Regents that has exclusive management of the university. It is conceded that the Board had authority to provide an oath, as § 11 of the Act directs every agency of the State which appoints, employs, or supervises officials or employees to establish procedures designed to ascertain before a person is appointed or employed that he or she "is not a subversive person." And that term is, as noted, defined by § § 1 and 13. Our conclusion is that, since the authority to prescribe oaths is provided by § 11 of the Act and since it is in turn tied to § § 1 and 13, we must consider the oath with reference to § § 1 and 13, not in isolation. Nor can we assume that the Board of Regents meant to encompass less than the Ober Act, as construed, sought to cover.

If the Federal Constitution is our guide, a person who might wish to "alter" our form of government may not be cast into the outer darkness. For the Constitution prescribes the method of "alteration" by the amending process in Article V; and while the procedure for amending it is restricted, there is no restraint on the kind of amendment that may be offered. Moreover, the First Amendment, which protects a controversial as well as a conventional dialogue (*Terminiello v. Chicago,* 337 U.S. 1), is as applicable to the States as it is to the Federal Government; and it extends to petitions for redress of grievances (Edwards v. South Carolina, 372 U.S. 229, 235) as well as to advocacy and debate. So if § §1 and 13 of the Ober Act are the frame of reference in which the challenged oath is to be adjudged, we have important questions to resolve.

We are asked to treat § § 1 and 13 as if they barred only those who seek to overthrow or destroy the Government by force or violence. Reference is made to Gerende v. Election Board, 341 U.S. 56, where, in considering the definition of "subversive" person applicable to § 15 of the Act, governing candidates for office, we accepted the representation of the Attorney General that he would advise the proper authorities in Maryland to take and adopt the narrower version of the term "subversive." The Court of Appeals of Maryland had indicated in Shub v. Simpson, 196 Md. 177, 76A. 2d 332, that the purpose of the Act was to reach that group, and that the words "revolution, force, or violence" in § 1 did not include a peaceful revolution but one accomplished by force or violence. Id., at 190-191, 76 A. 2d, at 337-338. In that view the "alteration" defined would be an alteration by force and violence. That construction had not yet been fashioned into an oath or certificate when Gerende reached us. That case involved an attempt by a candidate for public office in Maryland to require the election officials to dispense with an oath that incorporated the statutory language. The Court of Appeals refused the relief asked. We referred to the narrow construction of § § 1 and 15 given in the Shub case saying:

> We read this decision to hold that to obtain a place on a Maryland ballot a candidate need only make oath that he is not a person who is engaged 'in one way or another in the attempt to overthrow the government by force or violence,' and that he is not knowingly a member of an organization engaged in such an attempt. [196] Md. at [192], 76 A. 2d at 338. At the bar of this Court the Attorney General of the State of Maryland declared that he would advise the proper authorities to accept an affidavit in these terms as satisfying in full the statutory requirement. Under these circumstances and with this understanding, the judgment of the Maryland Court of Appeals is affirmed. [341 U.S., at 56-57.]

As we said in Baggett v. Bullitt, 377 U.S. 360, 368, n. 7, we did not pass upon or approve the statutory definition of a "subversive" person in the Gerende case. Rather we accepted the narrowing construction tendered by the Attorney General during oral argument so as to avoid the constitutional issue that was argued.

It is, however, urged that § 18 of the Act which contains a severability clause makes it possible for the Maryland Attorney General and for us to separate the wheat from the chaff that may be in §§ 1 and 13. The District Court found merit in the point. 258 F. Supp., at 596. But our difficulty goes deeper. As we have said in like situations, the oath required must not be so vague and broad as to make men of common intelligence speculate at their peril on its meaning. Baggett v. Bullitt, supra; Elfbrandt v. Russell, 384 U.S. 11; Keyishian v. Board of Regents, 385 U.S. 589. And so we are faced with the kind of problem which we thought we had avoided in Gerende.

As we have seen, §§ 1 and 13 reach (1) those who would "alter" the form of government "by revolution, force, or violence" and (2) those who are members of a subversive organization or a foreign subversive organization.

The prescribed oath requires, under threat of perjury, a statement that the applicant is not engaged "in one way or another" in an attempt to overthrow the Government by force or violence. Though we assume arguendo that the Attorney General and the Board of Regents were authorized so to construe the Act as to prescribe a narrow oath (1) that excluded "alteration" of the Government by peaceful "revolution" and (2) that excluded all specific reference to membership in subversive groups, we still are beset with difficulties. Would a member of a group that was out to overthrow the Government by force or violence be engaged in that attempt "in one way or another" within the meaning of the oath, even though he was ignorant of the real aims of the group and wholly innocent of any illicit purpose? We do not know; nor could a prospective employee know, save as he risked a prosecution for perjury.

We are in the First Amendment field. The continuing surveillance[1] which this type of law places on teachers is hostile to academic freedom. As we said in Sweezy v. New Hampshire, 354 U.S. 234, 250:

> The essentiality of freedom in the community of American universities is almost self-evident.

> No one should underestimate the vital role in a democracy that is played by those who guide and train our youth. To impose any straitjacket upon the intellectual leaders in our colleges and universities would imperil the future of our Nation. No field of education is so thoroughly comprehended by man that new discoveries cannot yet be made. Particularly is that true in the social sciences, where few, if any, principles are accepted as absolutes. Scholarship cannot flourish in an atmosphere of suspicion and distrust. Teachers and students must always remain free to inquire, to study and to evaluate, to gain new maturity and understanding; otherwise our civilization will stagnate and die.

The restraints on conscientious teachers are obvious. As we noted in the Elfbrandt case, even attendance at an international conference might be a trap for the innocent if that conference were predominantly composed of those who would overthrow the Government by force or violence. 384 U.S., at 16-17. "Juries might convict though the teacher did not subscribe to the wrongful aims of the organization." Id., at 17.

In sum, we read the oath as an integral part of the Ober Act; and we undertake to read §§ 1 and 13 of that Act in light of the gloss that the Maryland courts have placed on it. We know that the Shub case says that "[a] person who advocates the overthrow of the Government of the United States ... through force or violence could scarcely in good faith, take the constitutional oath of office...." 196 Md., at 190, 76 A. 2d, at 337. (Italics supplied.) Yet that case does little more than afford the basis for argument that membership in a subversive organization means that the member must advocate a violent overthrow. This, however, is speculation, not certainty. Another Maryland case bearing on the question is Character Committee v. Mandras, 233 Md. 285, 196 A. 2d 630. There an applicant for admission to the Maryland bar answered "No" to the question "Are you now or have you ever been a subversive person as defined by the [Ober Act]?" He had apparently at one time been a member of the Communist Party. At a hearing he testified he had joined the party because he was interested in the candidacy of Henry Wallace and in the cause of civil liberties; but he denied he had been a subversive person or that he had advocated violent overthrow of the Government. The

Court of Appeals affirmed the Board of Law Examiners, finding that the applicant was not a subversive person. So it can be argued that passive membership as a matter of Maryland law does not make a person a subversive. Yet, as we read § § 1 and 13 of the Ober Act, the alteration clause and membership clause are still befogged.[2] The lines between permissible and impermissible conduct are quite indistinct. Precision and clarity are not present. Rather we find an overbreadth that makes possible oppressive or capricious application as regimes change. That very threat, as we said in another context (NAACP v. Button, 371 U. S. 415, 432-433), may deter the flowering of academic freedom as much as successive suits for perjury.

Like the other oath cases mentioned, we have another classic example of the need for "narrowly drawn" legislation (Cantwell v. Connecticut, 310 U. S. 296, 311) in this sensitive and important First Amendment area.

Reversed.

NOTES.

1. There is not only the provision for perjury prescribed in § 11, but also § 14 which provides in part that "Reasonable grounds on all the evidence to believe that any person is a subversive person, as defined in this article, shall be cause for discharge" of the employee. See Anti-Fascist Committee v. McGrath, 341 U. S. 123, 175, n. 1 (concurring opinion).

2. Art. 15, § 11, of the Maryland Constitution reads: "No person who is a member of an organization that advocates the overthrow of the Government of the United States or of the State of Maryland through force or violence shall be eligible to hold any office, be it elective or appointive, or any other position of profit or trust in the Government of or in the administration of the business of this State or of any county, municipality or other political subdivision of this State."

Shub tells us that the Ober Act was enacted pursuant to this state constitutional provision. 196 Md., at 192, 76 A. 2d, at 338. Our attention is not drawn to, nor have we found, any severability clause applicable to this constitutional provision. It is certainly dubious, then, whether the severability clause of the Ober Act can operate to "sever" the membership clause in the definition of subversive person so that it reads more narrowly than the constitutional provision upon which the Ober Act rests.

Cole v. Richardson, 405 U.S. 676 (1972)

A Massachusetts loyalty oath required of all public employees in that state is held to be constitutional by the Supreme Court, the oath reading: "I do solemnly swear (or affirm) that I will uphold and defend the Constitution of the United States of America and the Constitution of the Commonwealth of Massachusetts and that I will oppose the overthrow of the government of the United States of America or of this Commonwealth by force, violence, or by any illegal or unconstitutional method." Douglas dissents, declaring in his opinion: "Advocacy of basic fundamental changes in government which might popularly be described as 'overthrow,' is within the protection of the First Amendment even when it is restrictively construed.... The present oath makes such advocacy a possible offense under a restrictive reading of the First Amendment."

* * *

MR. JUSTICE DOUGLAS, dissenting.

The part of the oath that says "I will oppose the overthrow of the government of the United States of America or of this Commonwealth by force, violence or by any illegal or unconstitutional method" is plainly unconstitutional by our decisions. See Board of Education v. Barnette, 319 U.S. 624, 634.

Advocacy of basic fundamental changes in government, which might popularly be described as "overthrow," is within the protection of the First Amendment even when it is restrictively construed. In Brandenburg v. Ohio, 395 U.S. 444, a case involving criminal syndicalism, this Court ruled that a State may not "forbid or proscribe advocacy of the use of force or of law violation except where such advocacy is directed to inciting or producing imminent lawless action and is likely to incite or produce such action." Id., at 447. The same idea was put in somewhat different words in Noto v. United States, 367 U.S. 290, 297-298, that "abstract teaching" of overthrow is protected activity as contrasted to "preparing a group for violent action and steeling it to such action." And see Yates v. United States, 354 U.S. 298, 318.

The present oath makes such advocacy a possible offense under a restrictive reading of the First Amendment.

The views expressed by Mr. Justice Black and me give the First Amendment a more expansive reading. We have condemned loyalty oaths as "manifestation[s] of a national network of laws aimed at coercing and controlling the minds of men. Test oaths are notorious tools of tyranny. When used to shackle the mind they are, or at least they should be, unspeakably odious to a free people." Wieman v. Updegraff, 344 U.S. 183, 193 (Black, J., concurring). And see Speiser v. Randall, 357 U.S. 513, 532 (Douglas, J., concurring). We said in Brandenburg that the protection of the First Amendment as applied to the States through the Fourteenth does not depend on the "quality of advocacy," since that "turns on the depth of the conviction." 395 U.S., at 457 (Douglas, J., concurring). The line between the permissible control by a State and the impermissible control is "the line between ideas and overt acts." Id., at 456. "The First Amendment ... leaves the way wide open for people to favor, discuss, advocate, or incite causes and doctrines however obnoxious and antagonistic such views may be to the rest of us." Yates v. United States, supra, at 344 (Black, J., concurring and dissenting). This oath, however, requires that appellee "oppose" that which she has an indisputable right to advocate.[1] Yet the majority concludes that the promise of "opposition"--exacted as a condition of public employment[2]--is a mere redundancy which does not impair appellee's freedom of expression.[3]

It is suggested, however, that because only the second portion of the oath is unconstitutional we should sever the two clauses and uphold the first. Even on this assumption, the entire oath must fall. This Court should, of course, base its decisions upon local law where, in so doing, we may avoid deciding federal constitutional questions. Here, we have been cited to no evidence of a legislative intent to separate the two clauses of the oath. This case is thus governed by Pedlosky v. Massachusetts Institute of Technology, 352 Mass. 127, 224 N.E. 2d 414 (1967), where the Supreme Judicial Court of Massachusetts was confronted with a two-part test oath similar in effect to the one before us.[4] "The substance of the oath [was] not confined merely to a declaration of support of the Federal and State Constitutions. It equally concern[ed] an undertaking by the plaintiff that 'I will faithfully discharge the duties of the position of assistant professor of mathematics according to the best of my ability.'" Id., at 128-129, 224 N.E. 2d, at 416. Finding the oath to be "altogether too vague a standard to enforce judicially" and being without evidence "whether the Legislature would have enacted [it] without the [invalid] provision," the court was unable to hold that the provisions were severable, and thus unanimously struck down the entire oath. Id., at 129, 224 N.E. 2d, at 416.

I would follow the lead of the Supreme Judicial Court of Massachusetts--the court which has the final word on how the statutes of that State are to be construed--and hold that the entire oath must fall.

I conclude that whether the First Amendment is read restrictively or literally as Jefferson would have read it, the oath which the District Court struck down, 300 F. Supp. 1321, is plainly unconstitutional. I would affirm its judgment.

NOTES

1. The majority makes the suggestion that "we might be faced with a different question" if there were "a record of actual prosecutions or harassment through threatened prosecutions." Ante, at 685. Here, appellee has been discharged from employment and denied her source of livelihood because of her refusal to subscribe to an unconstitutional oath. If the oath suffers from constitutional infirmities, then it matters not whether the penalties imposed for refusing to subscribe to it were criminal or the denial of employment.

2. The Court is correct when it says "there is no constitutionally protected right to overthrow a government by force, violence, or illegal or unconstitutional means," ante, at 686, but that has no bearing on the present case. What is involved here is appellee's right to espouse and advocate ideas which may be unpopular to some. How we can honor that right to advocate while exacting the promise to "oppose," the Court leaves unanswered.

3. The majority first chides the District Court for taking "a literal approach" and "giv[ing] [the word 'oppose'] a dictionary meaning." The majority then reads "oppose" to be a mere "negative implication of th[e] notion" of "a commitment to abide by our constitutional system" not requiring "specific, positive action." Ante, at 683, 684. Having thus emasculated the word, the majority then labels it as "redundant" and a "repetiton," ibid., and concludes that the oath, in its entirety, is simply "to abide by the constitutional system in the future." Ante, at 686.

If the oath is void for vagueness or overbreadth, it is because the common meaning of its words is so imprecise or so farreaching as to place a "chilling effect" upon constitutionally protected expression. This vice--readily apparent in the present oath--is emphasized rather than avoided by the majority's opinion. The tortured route which the majority takes to give this oath a supposedly constitutional interpretation merely emphasizes the unconstitutional effect those words would have were they to be given their natural meaning.

4. The oath provided: "I do solemnly swear (or affirm) that I will support the Constitution of the United States and the Constitution of the Commonwealth of Massachusetts, and that I will faithfully discharge the duties of the position of (insert name of position) according to the best of my ability."

# GOVERNMENTAL SURVEILLANCE, INVESTIGATING COMMITTEES, AND "SUBVERSIVE SPEECH"

## Dennis v. United States, 341 U.S. 494 (1951)

The Supreme Court upholds the convictions of leaders of the U.S. Communist Party, who had been convicted of violating that part of the "Smith Act" "which makes it unlawful 'to organize or help to organize any society, group, or assembly of persons who teach, advocate, or encourage the overthrow or destruction of any government in the United States by force or violence.'" The Court declares that the Communist leaders "were properly and constitutionally convicted for violation of the Smith Act." Douglas dissents, asserting in his opinion: "There was a time in England when the concept of constructive treason flourished. Men were punished not for raising a hand against the king but for thinking murderous thoughts about him. The Framers of the Constitution were alive to that abuse and took steps to see that the practice would not flourish here. Treason was defined to require overt acts--the evolution of a plot against the country into an actual project. The present case is not one of treason. But the analogy is close when the illegality is made to turn on intent, not on the nature of the act. We then start probing men's minds for motive and purpose; they become entangled in the law not for what they did but for what they thought; they get convicted not for what they said but for the purpose with which they said it."

* * *

MR. JUSTICE DOUGLAS, dissenting.

If this were a case where those who claimed protection under the First Amendment were teaching the techniques of sabotage, the assassination of the President, the filching of documents from public files, the planting of bombs, the art of street warfare, and the like, I would have no doubts. The freedom to speak is not absolute; the teaching of methods of terror and other seditious conduct should be beyond the pale along with obscenity and immorality. This case was argued as if those were the facts. The argument imported much seditious conduct into the record. That is easy and it has popular appeal, for the activities of Communists in plotting and scheming against the free world are common knowledge. But the fact is that no such evidence was introduced at the trial. There is a statute which makes a seditious conspiracy unlawful.[1] Petitioners, however, were not charged with a "conspiracy to overthrow" the Government. They were charged with a conspiracy to form a party and groups and assemblies of people who teach and advocate the overthrow of our Government by force or violence and with a conspiracy to advocate and teach its overthrow by force and violence.[2] It may well be that indoctrination in the techniques of terror to destroy the Government would be indictable under either statute. But the teaching which is condemned here is of a different character.

So far as the present record is concerned, what petitioners did was to organize people to teach and themselves teach the Marxist-Leninist doctrine contained chiefly in four books:[3] Stalin, Foundations of Leninism (1924); Marx and Engels, Manifesto of the Communist Party (1848); Lenin, The State and Revolution (1917); History of the Communist Party of the Soviet Union (B.) (1939).

Those books are to Soviet Communism what Mein Kampf was to Nazism. If they are understood, the ugliness of Communism is revealed, its deceit and cunning are exposed, the nature of its activities becomes apparent, and the chances of its success less likely. That is not, of course, the reason why petitioners chose these books for their classrooms. They are fervent Communists to whom these volumes are gospel. They preached the creed with the hope that some day it would be acted upon.

The opinion of the Court does not outlaw these texts nor condemn them to the fire, as the Communists do literature offensive to their creed. But if the books themselves are not outlawed, if they can lawfully remain on library shelves, by what reasoning does their use in a classroom become a crime? It would not be a crime under the Act to introduce these books to a class, though that would be teaching what the creed of violent overthrow of the Government is. The Act, as construed, requires the element of intent--that those who teach the creed believe in it. The crime then depends not on what is taught but on who the teacher is. That is to make freedom of speech turn not on what is said, but on the intent with which it is said. Once we start down that road we enter territory dangerous to the liberties of every citizen.

There was a time in England when the concept of constructive treason flourished. Men were punished not for raising a hand against the king but for thinking murderous thoughts about him. The Framers of the Constitution were alive to that abuse and took steps to see that the practice would not flourish here. Treason was defined to require overt acts--the evolution of a plot against the country into an actual project. The present case is not one of treason. But the analogy is close when the illegality is made to turn on intent, not on the nature of the act. We then start probing men's minds for motive and purpose; they become entangled in the law not for what they did but for what they thought; they get convicted not for what they said but for the purpose with which they said it.

Intent, of course, often makes the difference in the law. An act otherwise excusable or carrying minor penalties may grow to an abhorrent thing if the evil intent is present. We deal here, however, not with ordinary acts but with speech, to which the Constitution has given a special sanction.

The vice of treating speech as the equivalent of overt acts of a treasonable or seditious character is emphasized by a concurring opinion, which by invoking the law of conspiracy makes speech do service for deeds which are dangerous to society. The doctrine of conspiracy has served divers and oppressive purposes and in its broad reach can be made to do great evil. But never until today has anyone seriously thought that the ancient law of conspiracy could constitutionally be used to turn speech into seditious conduct. Yet that is precisely what is suggested. I repeat that we deal here with speech alone, not with speech plus acts of sabotage or unlawful conduct. Not a single seditious act is charged in the indictment. To make a lawful speech unlawful because two men conceive it is to raise the law of conspiracy to appalling proportions. That course is to make a radical break with the past and to violate one of the cardinal principles of our constitutional scheme.

Free speech has occupied an exalted position because of the high service it has given our society. Its protection is essential to the very existence of a democracy. The airing of ideas releases pressures which otherwise might become destructive. When ideas compete in the market for acceptance, full and free discussion exposes the false and they gain few adherents. Full and free discussion even of ideas we hate encourages the testing of our own prejudices and preconceptions. Full and free discussion keeps a society from becoming stagnant and unprepared for the stresses and strains that work to tear all civilizations apart.

Full and free discussion has indeed been the first article of our faith. We have founded our political system on it. It has been the safeguard of every religious, political, philosophical, economic, and racial group amongst us. We have counted on it to keep us from embracing what is cheap and false; we have trusted the common sense of our people to choose the doctrine true to our genius and to reject the rest. This has been the one single outstanding tenet that has made our institutions the symbol of freedom and equality. We have deemed it more costly to liberty to suppress a despised minority than to let them vent their spleen. We have above all else feared the political censor. We have wanted a land where our people can be exposed to all the diverse creeds and cultures of the world.

There comes a time when even speech loses its constitutional immunity. Speech innocuous one year may at another time fan such destructive flames that it must be halted in the interests of the safety of the Republic. That is the meaning of the clear and present danger test. When conditions are so critical that there will be no time to avoid the evil that the speech threatens, it is time to call a halt. Otherwise, free speech which is the strength of the Nation will be the cause of its destruction.

Yet free speech is the rule, not the exception. The restraint to be constitutional must be based on more than fear, on more than passionate opposition against the speech, on more than a revolted dislike for its contents. There must be some immediate injury to society that is likely if speech is allowed. The classic statement of these conditions was made by Mr. Justice Brandeis in his concurring opinion in Whitney v. California, 274 U.S. 357, 376-377,

> Fear of serious injury cannot alone justify suppression of free speech and assembly. Men feared witches and burnt women. It is the function of speech to free men from the bondage of irrational fears. To justify suppression of free speech there must be reasonable ground to fear that serious evil will result if free speech is practiced. There must be reasonable ground to believe that the danger apprehended is imminent. There must

> be reasonable ground to believe that the evil to be prevented is a serious one. Every denunciation of existing law tends in some measure to increase the probability that there will be violation of it. Condonation of a breach enhances the probability. Expressions of approval add to the probability. Propagation of the criminal state of mind by teaching syndicalism increases it. Advocacy of law-breaking heightens it still further. But even advocacy of violation, however reprehensible morally, is not a justification for denying free speech where the advocacy falls short of incitement and there is nothing to indicate that the advocacy would be immediately acted on. The wide difference between advocacy and incitement, between preparation and attempt, between assembling and conspiracy, must be borne in mind. In order to support a finding of clear and present danger it must be shown either that immediate serious violence was to be expected or was advocated, or that the past conduct furnished reason to believe that such advocacy was then contemplated.
>
> Those who won our independence by revolution were not cowards. They did not fear political change. They did not exalt order at the cost of liberty. To courageous, self-reliant men, with confidence in the power of free and fearless reasoning applied through the processes of popular government, no danger flowing from speech can be deemed clear and present, unless the incidence of the evil apprehended is so imminent that it may befall before there is opportunity for full discussion. <u>If there be time to expose through discussion the falsehood and fallacies, to avert the evil by the processes of education, the remedy to be applied is more speech, not enforced silence.</u> (Italics added.)

I had assumed that the question of the clear and present danger, being so critical an issue in the case, would be a matter for submission to the jury. It was squarely held in Pierce v. United States, 252 U.S. 239, 244, to be a jury question. Mr. Justice Pitney, speaking for the Court, said, "Whether the statement contained in the pamphlet had a natural tendency to produce the forbidden consequences, as alleged, was a question to be determined not upon demurrer but by the jury at the trial." That is the only time the Court has passed on the issue. None of our other decisions is contrary. Nothing said in any of the nonjury cases has detracted from that ruling.[4] The statement in Pierce v. United States, supra, states the law as it has been and as it should be. The Court, I think, errs when it treats the question as one of law.

Yet, whether the question is one for the Court or the jury, there should be evidence of record on the issue. This record, however, contains no evidence whatsoever showing that the acts charged, viz., the teaching of the Soviet theory of revolution with the hope that it will be realized, have created any clear and present danger to the Nation. The Court, however, rules to the contrary. It says, "The formation by petitioners of such a highly organized conspiracy, with rigidly disciplined members subject to call when the leaders, these petitioners, felt that the time had come for action, coupled with the inflammable nature of world conditions, similar uprisings in other countries, and the touch-and-go nature of our relations with countries with whom petitioners were in the very least ideologically attuned, convince us that their convictions were justified on this score."

That ruling is in my view not responsive to the issue in the case. We might as well say that the speech of petitioners is outlawed because Soviet Russia and her Red Army are a threat to world peace.

The nature of Communism as a force on the world scene would, of course, be relevant to the issue of clear and present danger of petitoners' advocacy within the United States. But the primary consideration is the strength and tactical position of petitioners and their converts in this country. On that there is no evidence in the record. If we are to take judicial notice of the threat of Communists within the nation, it should not be difficult to conclude that as a political party they are of little consequence. Communists in this country have never made a respectable or serious showing in any election. I would doubt that there is a village, let alone a city or county or state, which the Communists could carry. Communism in the world scene is no bogeyman; but Communism as a political faction or party in this country plainly is. Communism has been so throughly exposed in this country that it has been crippled as a political force. Free speech has destroyed it as an effective political party. It is inconceivable that those who went up and down this country preaching the doctrine of revolution which petitioners espouse would have any success. In days of trouble and confusion, when bread lines were long, when the unemployed walked the streets, when people were starving, the advocates of a short-cut by revolution might have a chance to gain adherents. But today there are no such conditions. The country is not in despair; the people know Soviet Communism; the doctrine of Soviet revolution is exposed in all of its ugliness and the American people want none of it.

How it can be said that there is a clear and present danger that this advocacy will succeed is, therefore, a mystry. Some nations less resilient than the United States, where illiteracy is high and where democratic traditions are only budding, might have to take drastic steps and jail these men for merely speaking their creed. But in America they are miserable merchants of unwanted ideas; their wares remain unsold. The fact that their ideas are abhorrent does not make them powerful.

The political impotence of the Communists in this country does not, of course, dispose of the problem. Their numbers; their positions in industry and government; the extent to which they have in fact infiltrated the police, the armed services, transportation, stevedoring, power plants, munitions works, and other critical places--these facts all bear on the likelihood that their advocacy of the Soviet theory of revolution will endanger the Republic. But the record is silent on these facts. If we are to proceed on the basis of judicial notice, it is impossible for me to say that the Communists in this country are so potent or so strategically deployed that they must be suppressed for their speech. I could not so hold unless I were willing to conclude that the activities in recent years of committees of Congress, of the Attorney General, of labor unions, of state legislatures, and of Loyalty Boards were so futile as to leave the country on the edge of grave peril. To believe that petitioners and their following are placed in such critical positions as to endanger the Nation is to believe the incredible. If is safe to say that the followers of the creed of Soviet Communism are known to the F.B.I.; that in case of war with Russia they will be picked up overnight as were all prospective saboteurs at the commencement of World War II; that the invisible army of petitioners is the best known, the most beset, and the least thriving of any fifth column in history. Only those held by fear and panic could think otherwise.

This is my view if we are to act on the basis of judicial notice. But the mere statement of the opposing views indicates how important it is that we know the facts before we act. Neither prejudice nor hate nor senseless fear should be the basis of this solemn act. Free speech--the glory of our system of government--should not be sacrificed on anything less than plain and objective proof of danger that the evil advocated is imminent. On this record no one can say that petitioners and their converts are in such a strategic position as to have even the slightest chance of achieving their aims.

The First Amendment provides that "Congress shall make no law ... abridging the freedom of speech." The Constitution provides no exception. This does not mean, however, that the Nation need hold its hand until it is in such weakened condition that there is no time to protect itself from incitement to revolution. Seditious conduct can always be punished. But the command of the First Amendment is so clear that we should not allow Congress to call a halt to free speech except in the extreme case of peril from the speech itself. The First Amendment makes confidence in the common sense of our people and in their maturity of judgment the great postulate of our democracy. Its philosophy is that violence is rarely, if ever, stopped by denying civil liberties to those advocating resort to force. The First Amendment reflects the philosophy of Jefferson "that it is time enough for the rightful purposes of civil government, for its officers to interfere when principles break out into overt acts against peace and good order."[5] The political censor has no place in our public debates. Unless and until extreme and necessitous circumstances are shown, our aim should be to keep speech unfettered and to allow the processes of law to be invoked only when the provocateurs among us move from speech to action.

Vishinsky wrote in 1938 in The Law of the Soviet State, "In our state, naturally, there is and can be no place for freedom of speech, press, and so on for the foes of socialism."

Our concern should be that we accept no such standard for the United States. Our faith should be that our people will never give support to these advocates of revolution, so long as we remain loyal to the purposes for which our Nation was founded.

## APPENDIX TO OPINION OF MR. JUSTICE DOUGLAS

There have been numerous First Amendment cases before the Court raising the issue of clear and present danger since Mr. Justice Holmes first formulated the test in Schenck v. United States, 249 U.S. 47, 52. Most of them, however, have not involved jury trials.

The cases which may be deemed at all relevant to our problem can be classified as follows:

CONVICTIONS FOR CONTEMPT OF COURT (NON-JURY): Near v. Minnesota, 283 U.S. 697; Bridges v. California, 314 U.S. 252; Thomas v. Collins, 323 U.S. 516; Pennekamp v. Florida, 328 U.S. 331; Craig v. Harney, 331 U.S. 367.

CONVICTIONS BY STATE COURTS SITTING WITHOUT JURIES, GENERALLY FOR VIOLATION OF LOCAL ORDINANCES: Lovell v. Griffin, 303 U.S. 444; Schneider v. State, 308 U.S. 147; Cantwell v. Connecticut, 310 U.S. 296; Marsh v. Alabama, 326 U.S. 501; Tucker v. Texas, 326 U.S. 517; Winters v. New York, 333 U.S. 507; Saia v. New York, 334 U.S. 558; Kovacs v. Cooper, 336 U.S. 77; Kunz v. New York, 340 U.S. 290; Feiner v. New York, 340 U.S. 315.

INJUNCTIONS AGAINST ENFORCEMENT OF STATE OR LOCAL LAWS (NON-JURY): Grosjean v. American Press Co., 297 U.S. 233; Hague v. C.I.O., 307 U.S. 496; Minersville School District v. Gobitis, 310 U.S. 586; West Virginia Board of Education v. Barnette, 319 U.S. 624.

ADMINISTRATIVE PROCEEDINGS (NON-JURY): Bridges v. Wixon, 326 U.S. 135; Schneiderman v. United States, 320 U.S. 118; American Communications Association v. Douds, 339 U.S. 382.

CASES TRIED BEFORE JURIES FOR VIOLATIONS OF STATE LAWS DIRECTED AGAINST ADVOCACY OF ANARCHY, CRIMINAL SYNDICALISM, ETC.: Gilbert v. Minnesota, 254 U.S. 325; Gitlow v. New York, 268 U.S. 652; Whitney v. California, 274 U.S. 357; Fiske v. Kansas, 274 U.S. 380; Stromberg v. California, 283 U.S. 359; De Jonge v. Oregon, 299 U.S. 353; Herndon v. Lowry, 301 U.S. 242; Taylor v. Mississippi, 319 U.S. 583; or for minor local offenses: Cox v. New Hampshire, 312 U.S. 569; Chaplinsky v. New Hampshire, 315 U.S. 568; Terminiello v. Chicago, 337 U.S. 1; Niemotko v. Maryland, 340 U.S. 268.

FEDERAL PROSECUTIONS BEFORE JURIES UNDER THE ESPIONAGE ACT OF 1917 FOLLOWING WORLD WAR I: Schenck v. United States, 249 U.S. 47; Frohwerk v. United States, 249 U.S. 204; Debs v. United States, 249 U.S. 211; Abrams v. United States, 250 U.S. 616; Schaefer v. United States, 251 U.S. 466; Pierce v. United States, 252 U.S. 239. Pierce v. United States ruled that the question of clear and present danger was for the jury. In the other cases in this group the question whether the issue was for the court or the jury was not raised or passed upon.

FEDERAL PROSECUTION BEFORE A JURY UNDER THE ESPIONAGE ACT OF 1917 FOLLOWING WORLD WAR II: Hartzel v. United States, 322 U.S. 680. The jury was instructed on clear and present danger in terms drawn from the language of Mr. Justice Holmes in Schenck v. United States, supra, p. 52. The Court reversed the conviction on the ground that there had not been sufficient evidence for submission of the case to the jury.

NOTES

1. 18 U.S.C. § 2384 provides: "If two or more persons in any State or Territory, or in any place subject to the jurisdiction of the United States, conspire to overthrow, put down, or to destroy by force the Government of the United States, or to levy war against them, or to oppose by force the authority thereof, or by force to prevent, hinder, or delay the execution of any law of the United States, or by force to seize, take, or possess any property of the United States contrary to the authority thereof, they shall each be fined not more than $5,000 or imprisoned not more than six years, or both."

2. 54 Stat. 671, 18 U.S.C. §§ 10, 11.

3. Other books taught were Stalin, Problems of Leninism, Strategy and Tactics of World Communism (H.R. Doc. No. 619, 80th Cong., 2d Sess.), and Program of the Communist International.

4. The cases which reached the Court are analyzed in the Appendix attached to this opinion, post, p. 591.

5. 12 Hening's Stat. (Virginia 1823), c. 34, p. 84. Whipple,

Our Ancient Liberties (1927), p. 95, states: "This idea that the limit on freedom of speech or press should be set only by an actual overt act was not new. It had been asserted by a long line of distinguished thinkers including John Locke, Montesquieu in his The Spirit of the Laws ('Words do not constitute an overt act'), the Rev. Phillip Furneaux, James Madison, and Thomas Jefferson."

Tenney v. Brandhove, 341 U. S. 367 (1951)

Brandhove, a critic of the California senate fact-finding Committee on Un-American Activities, refuses to give testimony at a hearing conducted by that committee and is cited for contempt in the state courts; the jury fails to return a verdict and the prosecution is dropped. Brandhove asks to be awarded $10, 000 "'for legal counsel, traveling, hotel accommodations, and other matters pertaining and necessary to his defense' in the contempt proceeding arising out of the committee hearings. The plaintiff also asked for punitive damages." The Court of Appeals for the Ninth Circuit holds that "the complaint stated a cause of action against the committee and its members." Brandhove alleges that the hearing was designed "to intimidate and silence" him and to deter and prevent him from effectively exercising his constitutional rights of free speech and to petition the legislature for redress of grievances...." The United States Supreme Court decides against Brandhove. Douglas, the sole dissenter, states in his opinion: "it is one thing to give great leeway to the legislative right of speech, debate, and investigation. But when a committee perverts its power, brings down on an individual the whole weight of government for an illegal or corrupt purpose, the reason for the immunity ends. It was indeed the purpose of this civil rights legislation to secure federal rights against invasion by officers and agents of the states."

* * *

MR. JUSTICE DOUGLAS, dissenting.

I agree with the opinion of the Court as a statement of general principles governing the liability of legislative committees and members of the legislatures. But I do not agree that all abuses of legislative committees are solely for the legislative body to police.

We are dealing here with a right protected by the Constitution--the right of free speech. The charge seems strained and difficult to sustain; but it is that a legislative committee brought the weight of its authority down on respondent for exercising his right of free speech. Reprisal for speaking is as much an abridgment as a prior restraint. If a committee departs so far from its domain to deprive a citizen of a right protected by the Constitution, I can think of no reason why it should be immune. Yet that is the extent of the liability sought to be imposed on petitioners under 8 U. S. C. § 43.[1]

It is speech and debate in the legislative department which our constitutional scheme makes privileged. Included, of course, are the actions of legislative committees that are authorized to conduct hearings or make investigations so as to lay the foundation for legislative action. But we are apparently holding today that the actions of those committees have no limits in the eyes of the law. May they depart with impunity from their legislative functions, sit as kangaroo courts, and try men for their loyalty and their political beliefs? May they substitute trial before committees for trial before juries? May they sit as a board of censors over industry, prepare their blacklists of citizens, and issue pronouncements as devasting as any bill of attainder?

No other public official has complete immunity for his actions. Even a policeman who exacts a confession by force and violence can be held criminally liable under the Civil Rights Act, as we ruled only the other day in Williams v. United States, 341 U. S. 97. Yet now we hold that no matter the extremes to which a legislative committee may go it is not answerable to an injured party under the civil rights legislation. That result is the necessary consequence of our ruling since the test of the statute, so far as material here, is whether a constitutional right has been impaired, not whether the domain of the committee was traditional. It is one thing to give great leeway to the legislative right of speech, debate, and investigation. But when a committee perverts its power, brings down on an individual the whole weight of government for an illegal or corrupt purpose, the reason for the immunity ends. It was indeed the purpose of this civil rights legislation to secure federal rights against invasion by officers and agents of the states. I see no reason why any officer of government should be higher than the Constitution from which all rights and privileges of an office obtain.

NOTE

1. "Every person who, under color of any statute, ordinance,

regulation, custom, or usage, of any State or Territory, subjects, or causes to be subjected, any citizen of the United States or other person within the jurisdiction thereof to the deprivation of any rights, privileges, or immunities secured by the Constitution and laws, shall be liable to the party injured in an action at law, suit in equity, or other proper proceeding for redress."

Beilan v. Board of Education, 357 U.S. 399 (1958)

A Philadelphia public school teacher refuses to answer questions relating to Communist affiliations and associations put to him by the Superintendent of Schools and is dismissed for "incompetency." The Supreme Court finds against the teacher, arguing that "the question asked of petitioner by his superintendent was relevant to the issue of petitioner's fitness and suitability to serve as a teacher." Douglas dissents, asserting: "If it be said that we deal not with guilt or innocence but with frankness, the answer is the same. There are areas where government may not probe. Private citizens, private clubs, private groups may make such deductions and reach such conclusions as they choose from the failure of a citizen to disclose his beliefs, his philosophy, his associates. But government has no business penalizing a citizen merely for his beliefs or associations. It is government action that we have here."

* * *

MR. JUSTICE DOUGLAS, with whom MR. JUSTICE BLACK concurs, dissenting. *

The holding of the Court that the teacher in the Beilan case and the subway conductor in the Lerner case could be discharged from their respective jobs because they stood silent when asked about their Communist affiliations cannot, with due deference, be squared with our constitutional principles.

Among the liberties of the citizens that are guaranteed by the Fourteenth Amendment are those contained in the First Amendment. Stromberg v. California, 283 U.S. 359; De Jonge v. Oregon, 299 U.S. 353; Murdock v. Pennsylvania, 319 U.S. 105; Everson v. Board of Education, 330 U.S. 1; Staub v. City of Baxley, 355 U.S. 313, 321. These include the right to believe what one chooses, the right to differ from his neighbor, the right to pick and choose the political philosophy that he likes best, the right to associate with whomever he chooses, the right to join the groups he prefers, the privilege of selecting his own path to salvation. The Court put the matter succinctly in Board of Education v. Barnette, 319 U.S. 624, 641-642:

> We can have intellectual individualism and the rich cultural diversities that we owe to exceptional minds only at the price of occasional eccentricity and abnormal attitudes. When they are so harmless to others or to the State as those we deal with here, the price is not too great. But freedom to differ is not limited to things that do not matter much. That would be a mere shadow of freedom. The test of its substance is the right to differ as to things that touch the heart of the existing order.
>
> If there is any fixed star in our constitutional constellation, it is that no official, high or petty, can prescribe what shall be orthodox in politics, nationalism, religion, or other matters of opinion or force citizens to confess by word or act their faith therein.

We deal here only with a matter of belief. We have no evidence in either case that the employee in question ever committed a crime, ever moved in treasonable opposition against this country. The only mark against them--if it can be called such--is a refusal to answer questions concerning Communist Party membership. This is said to give rise to doubts concerning the competence of the teacher in the Beilan case and doubts as to the trustworthiness and reliability of the subway conductor in the Lerner case.

Our legal system is premised on the theory that every person is innocent until he is proved guilty. In this country we have, however, been moving away from that concept. We have been generating the belief that anyone who remains silent when interrogated about his unpopular beliefs or affiliations is guilty. I would allow no inference of wrongdoing to flow from the invocation of any constitutional right. I would not let that principle bow to popular passions. For all we know we are dealing here with citizens who are wholly innocent of any wrongful action. That must indeed be our premise. When we make the contrary assumption, we part radically with our tradition.

If it be said that we deal not with guilt or innocence but with frankness, the answer is the same. There are areas where government may not probe. Private citizens, private clubs, private groups may make such deductions and reach such conclusions as they choose from the failure of a citizen to disclose his beliefs, his philosophy, his associates. But government has no business penalizing a citizen merely for his beliefs or associations. It is government action that we have here. It is government action that the Fourteenth and First Amendments protect against. We emphasized in N.A.A.C.P. v. Alabama, decided this day, post, p. 449, that freedom to associate is one of those liberties protected against governmental action and that freedom from "compelled disclosure of affiliation with groups engaged in advocacy" is vital to that constitutional right. We gave protection in the N.A.A.C.P. case against governmental probing into political activities and associations of one dissident group of people. We should do the same here.

If we break with tradition and let the government penalize these citizens for their beliefs and associations, the most we can assume for their failure to answer is that they were Communists. Yet, as we said in Wieman v. Updegraff, 344 U.S. 183, 190, membership in the Communist Party "may be innocent." The member may have thought that the Communist movement would develop in the parliamentary tradition here, or he may not have been aware of any unlawful aim, or knowing it, may have embraced only the socialist philosophy of the group, not any political tactics of violence and terror. Many join associations, societies, and fraternities with less than full endorsement of all their aims.

We compound error in these decisions. We not only impute wrongdoing to those who invoke their constitutional rights. We go further and impute the worst possible motives to them.

As Judge Fuld said in dissent in the Lerner case, "It is a delusion to think that the nation's security is advanced by the sacrifice of the individual's basic liberties. The fears and doubts of the moment may loom large, but we lose more than we gain if we counter with a resort to alien procedures or with a denial of essential constitutional guarantees." 2 N.Y. 2d 355, 378, 141 N.E. 2d 533, 546.

Our initial error in all this business (see Dennis v. United States, 341 U.S. 494) was our disregard of the basic principle that government can concern itself only with the actions of men, not with their opinions or beliefs. As Thomas Jefferson said in 1779:

> "... the opinions of men are not the object of civil government, nor under its jurisdiction; ... it is time enough for the rightful purposes of civil government for its officers to interfere when principles break out into overt acts against peace and good order." [1]

The fitness of a subway conductor for his job depends on his health, his promptness, his record for reliability, not on his politics or philosophy of life. The fitness of a teacher for her job turns on her devotion to that priesthood, her education, and her performance in the library, in the laboratory, and the classroom, not on her political beliefs. Anyone who plots against the government and moves in treasonable opposition to it can be punished. Government rightly can concern itself with the actions of people. But it's time we called a halt to government's penalizing people for their beliefs. To repeat, individuals and private groups can make any judgments they want. But the realm of belief--as opposed to action--is one which the First Amendment places beyond the long arm of government.

A teacher who is organizing a Communist cell in a schoolhouse or a subway conductor who is preparing the transportation system for sabotage would plainly be unfit for his job. But we have no such evidence in the records before us. As my BROTHER BRENNAN points out, to jump to those conclusions on these records is to short-cut procedural due process.

In sum, we have here only a bare refusal to testify; and the Court holds that sufficient to show that these employees are unfit to hold their public posts. That makes qualification for public office turn solely on a matter of belief--a notion very much at war with the Bill of Rights.

When we make the belief of the citizen the basis of government action, we move toward the concept of <u>total security</u>. Yet <u>total security</u> is possible only in a totalitarian regime[2]--the kind of system we profess to combat.

## NOTES

*[Note: This opinion applies also to No. 165, <u>Lerner v. Casey, post,</u> p. 468.]

1. 2 Papers of Thomas Jefferson (Boyd ed. 1950) 546.

2. In an analogous situation, Judge Pope stated the problem for the Court of Appeals in Parker v. Lester, 227 F. 2d 708, 721:

"It cannot be said that in view of the large problem of protecting the national security against sabotage and other acts of subversion we can sacrifice and disregard the individual interest of these merchant seamen because they are comparatively few in number. It is not a simple case of sacrificing the interests of a few to the welfare of the many. In weighing the considerations of which we are mindful here, we must recognize that if these regulations may be sustained, similar regulations may be made effective in respect to other groups as to whom Congress may next choose to express its legislative fears. No doubt merchant seamen are in a sensitive position in that the opportunities for serious sabotage are numerous. If it can be said that a merchant seaman notwithstanding his being on board might sink the ship loaded with munitions for Korea, it is plain that many persons other than seamen would be just as susceptible to security doubts. The enginemen and trainmen hauling the cargo to the docks, railroad track and bridge inspectors, switchmen and dispatchers, have a multitude of opportunities for destruction. Dangerous persons might infiltrate the shipping rooms of factories where the munitions are being packed for shipment to Korea with opportunities for inserting bombs appropriately timed for explosion on board ship. All persons who are in factories making munitions and material for the armed forces have opportunities for sabotage, and the same may be said of all operators of transportation facilities, not to mention workers upon the docks....

"It may be possible that we have reached an age when our system of constitutional freedom and individual rights cannot hold its own against those who, under totalitarian discipline are prepared to infiltrate not only our public services, but our civilian employments as well. In the event of war we may have to anticipate Black Tom explosions on every waterfront, poison in our water systems, and sand in all important industrial machines. But the time has not come when we have to abandon a system of liberty for one modeled on that of the Communists: Such a system was not that ordained by the framers of our Constitution. It is the latter we are sworn to uphold."

## <u>Wilkinson v. United States,</u> 365 U.S. 399 (1961)

The Supreme Court upholds the conviction of Wilkinson, who had been cited for contempt of Congress for refusing to answer "Are you now a member of the Communist Party?" put to him by the House Un-American Activities Committee. Douglas dissents, stating in his opinion: "If it is 'Un-American' to criticize, impeach, and berate the Committee and to seek to have it abolished, then the Committee acted within the scope of its authority. But we take a dangerous leap when we reach the conclusion that criticism of the Committee was within the scope of the resolution.

"Criticism of government finds sanctury in several portions of the First Amendment. It is part of the right of free speech. It embraces freedom of the press. Can editors be summoned before the committee and be made to account for their editorials denouncing the committee, its tactics, its practices, its policies? If petitioner can be questioned concerning his opposition to the Committee, then I see no reason why editors are immune."

* * *

MR. JUSTICE DOUGLAS, with whom THE CHIEF JUSTICE and MR. JUSTICE BLACK concur, dissenting.

When petitioner was summoned before a subcommittee of the House Committee on Un-American Activities in Atlanta, Georgia, the Staff Director for the Committee made the following statement to him:

> It is the information of the committee or the suggestion of the committee that in anticipation of the hearings here in Atlanta, Georgia, you were sent to this area by the Communist Party for the purpose of developing a hostile sentiment to this committee and to its work for the purpose of undertaking to bring pressure upon the United States Congress to preclude these particular hearings. Indeed it is the fact that you were not even subpenaed for these particular hearings until we learned

> that you were in town for that very purpose and that you were not subpenaed to appear before this committee until you had actually registered in the hotel here in Atlanta.
>
> Now, sir, if you will tell this committee whether or not, while you are under oath, you are now a Communist, we intend to pursue that area of inquiry and undertake to solicit from you information respecting your activities as a Communist on behalf of the Communist Party, which is tied up directly with the Kremlin; your activities from the standpoint of propaganda; your activities from the standpoint of undertaking to destroy the Federal Bureau of Investigation and the Committee on Un-American Activities, because indeed this committee issued a report entitled 'Operation Abolition,' in which we told something, the information we then possessed, respecting the efforts of the Emergency Civil Liberties Committee, of which you are the guiding light, to destroy the F. B. I. and discredit the director of the F. B. I. and to undertake to hamstring the work of this Committee on Un-American Activities.
>
> So if you will answer that principal question, I intend to pursue the other questions with you to solicit information which would be of interest--which will be of vital necessity, indeed--to this committee in undertaking to develop legislation to protect the United States of America under whose flag you, sir, have protection.
>
> Now please answer the question: Are you now a member of the Communist Party?

Petitoner answered, "I am refusing to answer any questions of this committee."

After a further explanation he was directed to answer. He replied:

> I have the utmost respect for the broad powers which the Congress of the United States must have to carry on its investigations for legislative purposes. However, the United States Supreme Court has held that, broad as these powers may be, the Congress cannot investigate into an area where it cannot legislate, and this committee tends, by its mandate and by its practices, to investigate

> into precisely those areas of free speech, religion, peaceful association and assembly, and the press, wherein it cannot legislate and therefore it cannot investigate.[1]

The Committee[2] is authorized by the Resolution governing it to make investigations of "the extent, character, and objects of un-American propaganda activities in the United States."

If it is "un-American" to criticize, impeach, and berate the Committee and to seek to have it abolished, then the Committee acted within the scope of its authority in asking the questions. But we take a dangerous leap when we reach the conclusion that criticism of the Committee was within the scope of the Resolution.

Criticism of government finds sanctuary in several portions of the First Amendment. It is part of the right of free speech. It embraces freedom of the press. Can editors be summoned before the Committee and be made to account for their editorials denouncing the Committee, its tactics, its practices, its policies? If petitioner can be questioned concerning his opposition to the Committee, then I see no reason why editors are immune. The list of editors will be long as is evident from the editorial protests against the Committee's activities,[3] including its recent film, Operation Abolition.[4]

The First Amendment rights involved here are more than freedom of speech and press. Bringing people together in peaceable assemblies is in the same category. De Jonge v. Oregon, 299 U.S. 353. "The right of peaceable assembly is a right cognate to those of free speech and free press and is equally fundamental." Id., at 364. The right to petition "for a redress of grievances" is also part of the First Amendment; it too is fundamental to "the very idea of a government, republican in form." United States v. Cruikshank, 92 U.S. 542, 552. Chief Justice Hughes, speaking for the Court in the De Jonge case involving communist activities no more nor less lawful than those charged here, said:

> The greater the importance of safeguarding the community from incitements to the overthrow of our institutions by force and violence, the more imperative is the need to preserve inviolate the constitutional rights of free speech, free press and

> free assembly in order to maintain the opportunity for free political discussion, to the end that government may be responsive to the will of the people and that changes, if desired, may be obtained by peaceful means. Therein lies the security of the Republic, the very foundation of constitutional government. [De Jonge v. Oregon, supra, at 365.]

These are reasons why I would construe the Resolution narrowly so as to exclude criticism of the Committee. We have customarily done just that, insisting that if "an inquiry of dubious limits" is to be found in an Act or Resolution, Congress should unequivocally authorize it. United States v. Rumley, 345 U.S. 41, 46; United States v. Harris, 347 U.S. 612; Watkins v. United States, 354 U.S. 178, 198.

The indictment charged only the failure to answer the one question, "Are you now a member of the Communist Party?" That question in other contexts might well have been appropriate. We have here, however, an investigation whose central aim was finding out what criticism a citizen was making of the Government. That was the gist of the case presented to the jury.[5]

We cannot allow this man to go to prison for 12 months unless we hold that an investigation of those who criticize the Un-American Activities Committee was both authorized and constitutional. I cannot read the Resolution as authorizing that kind of investigation without assuming that the Congress intended to flout the First Amendment.

## NOTES

1. The Washington Post on January 4, 1961, made a similar criticism of the House Committee on Un-American Activities:

   "The Committee often functions as a kind of public pillory to punish men by publicity for offenses which the Constitution forbids Congress to make punishable by law. It 'exposes' men who express opinions or indulge in associaitons of which the Committee disapproves, carelessly calling them--or allowing witnesses under the cloak of congressional immunity to call them--Communists or Communist-sympathizers or Communist dupes.

   "The Committee, as a consequence of this conduct,

sometimes operates as a serious restraint on freedom of expression and freedom of association. It makes Americans fearful of uttering opinions for which they may be called to account by the Committee and fearful of joining organizations which the Committee may consider subversive."

2. The ultimate mandate of the parent Committee at the time of the subcommittee hearing was to be found in paragraph 17 (b), Rule XI, Rules of the House of Representatives, H. Res. 5, 85th Cong., 1st Sess., 60 Stat. 828. It provides: "The Committee on Un-American Activities, as a whole or by subcommittee, is authorized to make from time to time investigations of (i) the extent, character, and objects of un-American propaganda activities in the United States, (ii) the diffusion within the United States of subversive and un-American propaganda that is instigated from foreign countries or of a domestic origin and attacks the principle of the form of government as guaranteed by our Constitution, and (iii) all other questions in relation thereto that would aid Congress in any necessary remedial legislation." The record in this case also contains the mandate of the subcommittee (see note 5, infra), but the terms of the parent Committee's mandate are of course controlling. Of the purposes of the Committee, only the investigation of "un-American propaganda" activities seems even arguably to authorize the questions asked and the inquiry pursued in this case.

3. See note 1, supra.

4. The Washington Post said editorially on December 28, 1960:

"In his letters printed elsewhere in this newspaper today, Rep. Francis Walter asserts that the film Operation Abolition 'contains absolutely no distortions' and that the staff member who had admitted it contained such defects 'had not himself used the word "distortions."' In a television show over KCOP-TV, Los Angeles, a teaching assistant at the University of California referred to distortions in the film. William Wheeler, an investigator for the House Un-American Activities Committee, taking part in the program asked, 'What are you trying to prove by this?' The following exchange then took place:

"Mr. White: That the film has inaccuracies and distortions.

"Mr. Wheeler: I've admitted that.

"Mr. White: You've admitted that?

"Mr. Wheeler: Certainly.

"Mr. Walter offers some carefully selected quotes from the San Francisco press to refute this newspaper's assertion that the San Francisco police 'reacted with altogether needless ferocity.' Like the film Operation Abolition itself, he omits all the material showing the other side of the picture. For instance, San Francisco Chronicle reporter George Draper wrote:

" 'I did not see any of the kids actually fighting with the police. Their resistance was more passive. They would simply go limp and be manhandled out of the building.... I saw one slightly built lad being carried by two husky officers. One held the boy's shirt, the other had him by the feet. He was struggling, but he was no match for the two bigger men. Then from nowhere appeared a third officer. He ran up to the slender boy firmly held by the other two officers and clubbed him three times on the head. You could hear the hollow smack of the club striking. The boy went limp and was carried out.'

"Nor does Mr. Walter mention the report of another eyewitness, Mel Wax, a special correspondent of the New York Post.

" 'Never, in 20 years as a reporter, have I seen such brutality.... San Francisco police hurled women down the staircase, spines bumping on each marble stair.'

"To Mr. Walter, it is an admitted but 'decidedly minor' distortion in the film that Harry Bridges was represented as being on the scene just before the rioting broke out when, in point of fact, he did not arrive until after it was all over. 'Honest' this error may have been; but it was more than unfortunate. For it contributed considerably to the deceptive and distorted message of the film that the student demonstration was inspired and led by Communists.

"Communists may have tried to claim the credit which Mr. Walter accords them. Unquestionably the affair got out of hand, and no one condones the rowdiness that ensued. But the truth is that the demonstration was inspired by distaste for the Un-American Activities Committee. And it was led by students who intended nothing more than an orderly protest--an inalienable political right in the United States."

5. At the trial committee counsel was cross-examined as follows:

"Q. Mr. Arens, you stated before the committee that Mr. Wilkinson had come to Atlanta to stir up hostility to the committee, that he was doing everything he could to prevent these hearings from being held in Atlanta?

"A. Yes, sir.

"Q. And that you did not subpoena him until you discovered that he had arrived here for that purpose?

"A. That's correct, sir.

"Q. Now, you state that within the three general categories under which the committee was holding hearings here of colonization in the textile industry, entry and dissemination of foreign propaganda and Communist party propaganda activity in the South, you are stating that Mr. Wilkinson stirring up hostility to the House Committee on Un-American Activities comes within the category of Communist party propaganda activity which justified the House Committee to subpoena him and question him, is that correct? I just want to understand your position.

"A. Yes, in general I agree with you, yes."

Braden v. United States, 365 U.S. 431 (1961)

The Court upholds the conviction of Braden, who had refused to answer questions put to him by the House Committee on Un-American Activities. Justice Douglas dissents, stating in his opinion: "One would be wholly warranted in saying ... that a Committee's undisclosed information or unsupported surmise would not justify an investigation into matters that on their face seemed well within the First Amendment. If Watkins and Sweezy decided anything, they decided that before inroads in the First Amendment domain may be made, some demonstrable connection with Communism must first be established and the matter be plainly shown to be within the scope of the Committee's authority. Otherwise the Committee may roam at will, requiring any individual to disclose his association with any group or with any publication which is unpopular with the Committee and which it can discredit by calling it communistic."

* * *

MR. JUSTICE DOUGLAS, with whom THE CHIEF JUSTICE, MR. JUSTICE BLACK and MR. JUSTICE BRENNAN concur, dissenting.

At the bottom of this case are this Court's decisions in Pennsylvania v. Nelson, 350 U.S. 497, holding that Congress did not entrust to the States protection of the Federal Government against sedition, and Brown v. Board of Education, 347 U.S. 483, holding that racial segregation of students in public schools is unconstitutional. I had supposed until today that one could agree or disagree with those decisions without being hounded for his belief and sent to jail for concluding that his belief was beyond the reach of government.

On June 17, 1957, we decided Watkins v. United States, 354 U.S. 178, defining and curtailing the authority of Congressional Committees who sought the aid of the courts in holding witnesses in contempt.[1] We said in a six-to-one decision that "when First Amendment rights are threatened, the delegation of power to the committee must be clearly revealed in its charter" (id., at 198); that "there is no congressional power to expose for the sake of exposure" (id., at 200); that the meaning of "un-American" in the Resolution defining the Committee's authority is so vague that it is "difficult to imagine a less explicit authorizing resolution" (id., at 202); that before a witness chooses between answering or not answering he is entitled "to have knowledge of the subject to which the interrogation is deemed pertinent" (id., at 208-209); that in that case the Resolution and the statement of the Committee's chairman were "woefully inadequate to convey sufficient information as to the pertinency of the questions to the subject under inquiry." Id., 215.

Sweezy v. New Hampshire, 354 U.S. 234, decided the same day as the Watkins case, reversed a conviction arising out of a state investigation into "subversive activities" where a teacher was asked questions concerning his relation to Marxism. THE CHIEF JUSTICE in his opinion stated:

> Equally manifest as a fundamental principle of a democratic society is political freedom of the individual. Our form of government is built on the premise that every citizen shall have the right to engage in political expression and association. This right was enshrined in the First Amendment of the Bill of Rights. Exercise of these basic freedoms in America has traditionally been through the media of political associations. Any interference with the freedom of a party is simultaneously an interference with the freedom of its adherents. All political ideas cannot and should not be channeled into the programs of our two major parties. History has amply proved the virtue of political activity by minority, dissident groups, who innumerable times have been in the vanguard of democratic thought and whose programs were ultimately accepted. Mere unorthodoxy or dissent from the prevailing mores is not to be condemned. The absence of such voices would be a symptom of grave illness in our society." [Id., 250-251.]

The concurring opinion stated:

> Progress in the natural sciences is not remotely confined to findings made in the laboratory. Insights into the mysteries of nature are born of hypothesis and speculation. The more so is this true

> in the pursuit of understanding in the groping endeavors of what are called the social sciences, the concern of which is man and society. The problems that are the respective preoccupations of anthropology, economics, law, psychology, sociology and related areas of scholarship are merely departmentalized dealing, by way of manageable division of analysis, with interpenetrating aspects of holistic perplexities. For society's good--if understanding be an essential need of society--inquiries into these problems, speculations about them, stimulation in others of reflection upon them, must be left as unfettered as possible. Political power must abstain from intrusion into this activity of freedom, pursued in the interest of wise government and the people's well-being, except for reasons that are exigent and obviously compelling. [Id., 261-262.]

On June 8, 1959--two years after the Watkins and Sweezy decisions--we decided Barenblatt v. United States, 360 U.S. 109, where a divided Court gave only slight consideration to the type of pertinency claim that was raised in Watkins, Sweezy and the present case, in part because it could rely on the petitioner's failure to raise that objection before the Committee. See Barenblatt v. United States, supra, 123-125.

Petitioner, who was called as a witness by the Committee in July 1958, which was even before Barenblatt was decided, refused to answer, relying on the Watkins and Sweezy decisions "as they interpret the Constitution of the United States, protecting my right to private belief and association."

I think he was entitled to rely on them. The Act under which he stands convicted states that a witness is guilty if he "wilfully makes default, or who, having appeared, refuses to answer any question pertinent to the question under inquiry." 2 U.S.C. § 192. A refusal to answer was held in Sinclair v. United States, 279 U.S. 263, 299, not to be justified because one acted in good faith, the Court saying, "His mistaken view of the law is no defense." Yet no issue concerning the First Amendment was involved in the Sinclair case. When it is involved, as it is here, the propriety of the question in terms of pertinency should be narrowly resolved.

The Resolution under which the Committee on Un-American Activities acted in this case[2] is precisely the same as the one involved in Watkins v. United States, supra. We said concerning it, "It would be difficult to imagine a less explicit authorizing resolution. Who can define the meaning of 'un-American'? What is that single, solitary 'principle of the form of government as guaranteed by our Constitution'? ... At one time, perhaps, the resolution might have been read narrowly to confine the Committee to the subject of propaganda. The events that have transpired in the fifteen years before the interrogation of petitioner make such a construction impossible at this date." 354 U.S., at 202.

We emphasized the need, when First Amendment rights were implicated, to lay a foundation before probing that area. The authority of the Committee must then "be clearly revealed in its charter." Id., at 198. The "specific legislative need" must be disclosed. Id., at 205. The pertinency of the questions and the subject matter under inquiry must be made known "with the same degree of explicitness and clarity that the Due Process Clause requires in the expression of any element of a criminal offense." Id., at 209.

After Watkins anyone was entitled to rely on those propositions for protection of his First Amendment rights. The conditions and circumstances under which the questions were asked petitioner plainly did not satisfy the requirements specified in Watkins.

The setting of the six questions[3] which were asked petitioner and which he refused to answer shows nothing more than an exercise by him of First Amendment rights of speech and press and of petition to Congress. It was not shown that these activities were part of a matrix for the overthrow of government. It was not shown--unless the bare word of the Committee is taken as gospel--that these constitutional activities had any relation whatever to communism, subversion, or illegal activity of any sort or kind. It was not shown where and how the Committee was ever granted the right to investigate those who petition Congress for redress of grievances.

Petitioner and his wife were field secretaries of an organization known as the Southern Conference Education Fund. Prior to the committee hearing at Atlanta, Georgia, they wrote a letter [4] on the letterhead of the Southern Conference urging people to write their Congressmen and Senators to oppose three bills pending before the Congress which would, to use their words, "nullify" a decision of this Court "declaring state sedition laws inoperative." They added "We are especially concerned about this because we know from our own experience how such laws can be used against people working to bring about integration in the South. Most of these state statutes are broad and loosely worded, and to the officials of many of our Southern states integration is sedition. You can imagine what may happen if every little prosecutor in the South is turned loose with a state sedition law."

Also prior to the Committee hearing in Atlanta, a group of Negroes petitioned Congress against the proposed Atlanta investigation of the House Committee on Un-American Activities. That petition stated:

> We are informed that the Committee on Un-American Activities of the House of Representatives is planning to hold hearings in Atlanta, Georgia, at an early date.
>
> As Negroes residing in Southern states and the District of Columbia, all deeply involved in the struggle to secure full and equal rights for our people, we are very much concerned by this development.
>
> We are acutely aware of the fact that there is at the present time a shocking amount of un-American activity in our Southern states. To cite only a few examples, there are the bombings of the homes, schools, and houses of worship of not only Negroes but also of our Jewish citizens; the terror against Negroes in Dawson, Ga.; the continued refusal of boards of registrars in many Southern communities to allow Negroes to register and vote; and the activities of White Citizens Councils encouraging open defiance of the United States Supreme Court.
>
> However, there is nothing in the record of the House Committee on Un-American Activities to indicate that, if it comes South, it will investigate these things. On the contrary, all of its activities in recent years suggest that it is much more interested in harassing and labeling as 'subversive' any citizen who is inclined to be liberal or an independent thinker.
>
> For this reason, we are alarmed at the prospect of this committee coming South to follow the lead of Senator Eastland, as well as several state investigating committees, in trying to attach the 'subversive' label to any liberal white Southerner

> who dares to raise his voice in support of our democratic ideals.
>
> It was recently pointed out by four Negro leaders who met with President Eisenhower that one of our great needs in the South is to build lines of communication between Negro and white Southerners. Many people in the South are seeking to do this. But if white people who support integration are labeled 'subversive' by congressional committees, terror is spread among our white citizens and it becomes increasingly difficult to find white people who are willing to support our efforts for full citizenship. Southerners, white and Negro, who strive today for full democracy must work at best against tremendous odds. They need the support of every agency of our Federal Government. It is unthinkable that they should instead be harassed by committees of the United States Congress.
>
> We therefore urge you to use your influence to see that the House Committee on Un-American Activities stays out of the South--unless it can be persuaded to come to our region to help defend us against those subversives who oppose our Supreme Court, our Federal policy of civil rights for all, and our American ideals of equality and brotherhood.

Petitioner was charged by the Committee with preparing that petition; counsel for the Committee later stated that the purpose of the petition was "precluding or attempting to preclude or softening the very hearings which we proposed to have here." The Committee said that it was not concerned with integration. It said that "A number of names on that letter were names of those who had been closely associated with the Communist Party. Their interest and major part does not lie with honest integration. Their interest lies with the purposes of the Communist Party. And that is what we are looking into...."

Two of the questions which petitioner refused to answer pertained to the Southern Conference, the first one being "Did you participate in a meeting here at that time?" And the second one was "Who solicited quarters to be made available to the Southern Conference Educational Fund?"

Two other questions which petitioner refused to answer related to the Emergency Civil Liberties Committee. The first of these was "Are you connected with the Emergency Civil Liberties Committee?" The second one was "Did you and Harvey O'Connor in the course of your conferences there in Rhode Island, develop plans and strategy outlining work schedules for the Emergency Civil Liberties Committee?" The Committee counsel charged that Mr. O'Connor was "a hard-core member of the communist conspiracy, head of the Emergency Civil Liberties Committee."

A fifth question which petitioner refused to answer related to the letter I have previously mentioned [5] which he and his wife sent to the people urging them to write their Senators and Congressmen opposing three bills that would reinstate state sedition laws. The question relating to this letter was "Were you a member of the Communist Party the instant you affixed your signature to that letter?"

The sixth and final question which petitioner refused to answer concerned the Southern Newsletter. Counsel asked if petitioner had "anything to do" with that letter. Petitioner replied "I think you are now invading freedom of the press.... I object to your invasion of the freedom of the press, and I also decline to answer the questions on the same grounds. You are not only attacking integrationists, you are attacking the press."

There is nothing in the record to show that the Southern Conference or the Emergency Civil Liberties Committee or the Southern Newsletter had the remotest connection with the Communist Party. There is only the charge of the Committee that there was such a connection. That charge amounts to little more than innuendo. This is particularly clear with respect to the question relating to petitioner's membership in the Communist Party. Having drawn petitioner's attention to the letter he had written, [6] counsel for the Committee demanded to know if petitioner was a Communist "the instant you affixed your signature to that letter." No foundation at all had been laid for that question, and from the record no purpose for it appears, save the hope of the Committee to link communism with that letter which supported this Court's decision in Pennsylvania v. Nelson, supra. This Court, passing on the pertinency issue in Barenblatt v. United States, supra, 123-125, was careful to emphasize that Barenblatt "had heard the Subcommittee interrogate the witness Crowley along the same lines as he, petitioner, was evidently to be questioned, and had listened to Crowley's testimony identifying him as a former member of an alleged Communist student organization...." (Emphasis added.) No such foundation was ever laid here.

One would be wholly warranted in saying, I think, in light of the Watkins and Sweezy decisions that a Committee's undisclosed information or unsupported surmise would not justify an investigation into matters that on their face seemed well within the First Amendment.[7] If Watkins and Sweezy decided anything, they decided that before inroads in the First Amendment domain may be made, some demonstrable connection with communism must be first established and the matter be plainly shown to be within the scope of the Committee's authority. Otherwise the Committee may roam at will, requiring any individual to disclose his association with any group or with any publication which is unpopular with the Committee and which it can discredit by calling it communistic.

## NOTES

1. In that case the witness testified freely about himself but balked at talking about others:

"I am not going to plead the fifth amendment, but I refuse to answer certain questions that I believe are outside the proper scope of your committee's activities. I will answer any questions which this committee puts to me about myself. I will also answer questions about those persons whom I knew to be members of the Communist Party and whom I believe still are. I will not, however, answer any questions with respect to others with whom I associated in the past. I do not believe that any laws in this country requires me to testify about persons who may in the past have been Communist Party members or otherwise engaged in Communist Party activity but who to my best knowledge and belief have long since removed themselves from the Communist movement.

"I do not believe that such questions are relevant to the work of this committee nor do I believe that this committee has the right to undertake the public exposure of persons because of their past activities. I may be wrong, and the committee may have this power, but until and unless a court of law so holds and directs me to answer, I most firmly refuse to discuss the political activities of my past associates."

2. The Resolution provides in relevant part:

"The Committee on Un-American Activities, as a whole or by subcommittee, is authorized to make from time to time investigations of (1) the extent, character and objects of un-American propaganda activities in the United States, (2) the diffusion within the United States of subversive and un-American propaganda that is instigated from foreign countries or of a domestic origin and attacks the principle of the form of government as guaranteed by our Constitution, and (3) all other questions in relation thereto that would aid Congress in any necessary remedial legislation."

3. Petitioner was convicted on each of six counts of an indictment and sentenced to serve 12 months on each count, the sentences to run concurrently. Therefore if any one of the counts can be sustained an affirmance would be necessary. See Claassen v. United States, 142 U.S. 140, 147.

4. "Dear Friend:

"We are writing to you because of your interest in the Kentucky 'sedition' cases, which were thrown out of Court on the basis of a Supreme Court decision [Pennsylvania v. Nelson, supra] declaring state sedition laws inoperative.

"There are now pending in both houses of Congress bills that would nullify this decision. We understand that there is real danger that these bills will pass.

"We are especially concerned about this because we know from our own experience how such laws can be used against people working to bring about integration in the South. Most of these state statutes are broad and loosely worded, and to the officials of many of our Southern states integration is sedition. You can imagine what may happen if every little local prosecutor in the South is turned loose with a state sedition law.

"It is small comfort to realize that such cases would probably eventually be thrown out by the Supreme Court. Before such a case reaches the Supreme Court, the human beings involved have spent several years of their lives fighting off the attack, their time and talents have been diverted from the positive struggle for integration, and money needed for that struggle has been spent in a defensive battle.

"It should also be pointed out that these bills to validate state sedition laws are only a part of a sweeping attack on the U.S. Supreme Court. The real and ultimate target is the Court decisions outlawing segregation. Won't you write your two senators and your congressman asking them to oppose S. 654, S. 2646, and H.R. 977. Also ask them to stand firm against all efforts to curb the Supreme Court. It is important that you write--and get others to write--immediately as the bills may come up at any time.

"Cordially yours,
"CARL AND ANNE BRADEN,
"Field Secretaries."

5. Supra, note 4.

6. See supra, note 4.

7. "The consequences that flow from this situation are manifold. In the first place, a reviewing court is unable to make the kind of judgment made by the Court in United States v. Rumley, supra. The Committee is allowed, in essence, to define its own authority, to choose the direction and focus of its activities. In deciding what to do with the power that has been conferred upon them, members of the Committee may act pursuant to motives that seem to them to be the highest. Their decisions, nevertheless, can lead to ruthless exposure of private lives in order to gather data that is neither desired by the Congress nor useful to it. Yet it is impossible in this circumstance, with constitutional freedoms in jeopardy, to declare that the Committee has ranged beyond the area committed to it by its parent assembly because the boundaries are so nebulous." 354 U.S., at 204.

## Scales v. United States, 367 U.S. 203 (1961)

In a 5-4 decision, the Supreme Court upholds the conviction, under the Smith Act, of an "active" member of the Communist Party who had knowledge of the Party's teachings advocating violent overthrow of the United States Government by force and violence as speedily as circumstances would permit. Douglas dissents, declaring: "Of course, government can move against those who take up arms against it. Of course, the constituted authority has the right of self-preservation. But we deal in this prosecution of Scales only with the legality of ideas and beliefs, not with overt acts. The Court speaks of the prevention of 'dangerous behavior' by punishing those 'who work to bring about that behavior.' That formula returns man to the dark days when government determined what behavior was 'dangerous' and then policed the dissidents for tell-tale signs of advocacy."

* * *

MR. JUSTICE DOUGLAS, dissenting.

When we allow petitioner to be sentenced to prison for six years for being a "member" of the Communist Party, we make a sharp break with traditional concepts of First Amendment rights and make serious Mark Twain's lighthearted comment that "It is by the goodness of God that in our country we have those three unspeakably precious things: freedom of speech, freedom of conscience, and the prudence never to practice either of them."[1]

Even the Alien and Sedition Laws--shameful reminders of an early chapter in intolerance--never went so far as we go today. They were aimed at conspiracy and advocacy of insurrection and at the publication of "false, scandalous and malicious" writing against the Government, 1 Stat. 596. The Government then sought control over the press "in order to strike at one of the chief sources of disaffection and sedition." Miller, Crisis in Freedom (1951), p. 56. There is here no charge of conspiracy, no charge of any overt act to overthrow the Government by force and violence, no charge of any other criminal act. The charge is being a "member" of the Communist Party, "well-knowing" that it advocated the overthrow of the Government by force and violence, "said defendant intending to bring about such overthrow by force and violence as speedily as circumstances would permit." That falls far short of a charge of conspiracy. Conspiracy rests not in intention alone but in an agreement with one or more others to promote an unlawful project. United States v. Falcone, 311 U.S. 205, 210; Direct Sales Co. v. United States, 319 U.S. 703, 713. No charge of any kind or sort of agreement hitherto embraced in the concept of a conspiracy is made here.

We legalize today guilt by association, sending a man to prison when he committed no unlawful act. Today's break with tradition is a serious one. It borrows from the totalitarian philosophy. As stated by O'Brian, National Security and Individual Freedom (1955), pp. 27-28:

> The Smith Act of 1940 made it unlawful for any person to be or to become a member of or affiliate with any society, group, or assembly which teaches, advocates, or encourages the overthrow or destruction of any government in the United States by force or violence. These statutes [the Smith Act together with a 1920 amendment to the Immigration Law, Act of June 5, 1920, 41 Stat. 1008], therefore, imported into our law the alien doctrine of guilt by association, which up to this time had been regarded as abhorrent and which had never been recognized either by the courts or by the Department of Justice, even during the perils and excitements of the First World War.

The case is not saved by showing that petitioner was an active member. None of the activity constitutes a crime. The record contains evidence that Scales was the Chairman of the North and South Carolina Districts of the Communist Party. He recruited new members into the Party, and promoted the advanced education of selected young Party members in the theory of communism to be undertaken at secret schools. He was a director of one such school. He explained the principles of the Party to an FBI agent who posed as someone interested in joining the Party, and furnished him literature, including articles which criticized in vivid language the American "aggression" in Korea and described American "atrocities" committed on Korean citizens. He once remarked that the Party was setting up underground means of communication, and in 1951 he himself "went underground." At the school of which Scales was director, students were told (by someone else) that one of the Party's weaknesses was in failing to place people in key industrial positions. One witness told of a meeting arranged by Scales at which the staff of the school urged him to remain in his position in an industrial plant rather than return to college. In Scales' presence, students at the school were once shown how to kill a person with a pencil, a device which, it was said, might come in handy on a picket line. Other evidence showed Scales to have made several statements or distributed literature containing implicating passages. Among them were comments to the effect that the Party line was that the Negroes in the South and the working classes should be used to foment a violent revolution; that a Communist government could not be voted into power in this country because the Government controlled communication media, newspapers, the military, and the educational systems, and that force was the only way to achieve the revolution; that if a depression were to come the Communist America would be closer at hand than predicted by William Z. Foster; that the revolution would come within a generation; that it would be easier in the United States than in Russia to effectuate the revolution because of assistance and advice from Russian Communists. Petitioner at different times said or distributed literature which said that the goals of communism could only be achieved by violent revolution that would have to start internally with the working classes.

Not one single illegal act is charged to petitioner. That is why the essence of the crime covered by the indictment is merely belief [2]--belief in the proletarian revolution, belief in Communist creed.

Spinoza summed up in a sentence much of the history of the struggle of man to think and speak what he believes:

> Laws which decree what every one must believe, and forbid utterance against this or that opinion, have too often been enacted to confirm or enlarge the power of those who dared not suffer free inquiry to be made, and have by a perversion of authority turned the superstition of the mob into violence against opponents. [Tractatus Theologico-Politicus (London 1862) p. 349.]

"The thought of man shall not be tried, for the devil himself knoweth not the thought of man," said Chief Justice

Brian in Y.B. Pasch, 17 Edw. IV, f. 2, pl. 2. The crime of belief--presently prosecuted--is a carryback to the old law of treason where men were punished for compassing the death of the King. That law, which had been employed for "suppression of political opposition or the expression of ideas or beliefs distasteful to those in power," Hurst, Historic Background of the Treason Clause, 6 Fed. B.J. 305, 307, was rejected here, and the treason clause of our Constitution was "most praised for the reason that it prevented the use of treason trials as an instrument of political faction." Id., 307. Sedition or treason in the realm of politics and heresy in the ecclesiastical field had long centered on beliefs as the abhorrent criminal act. The struggle on this side of the Atlantic was to get rid of that concept and to punish men not for what they thought but for overt acts against the peace of the Nation. Cramer v. United States, 325 U.S. 1, 28-30. Montesquieu, who was a force in the thinking of those times (id., 15, n. 21), proclaimed against punishing thoughts or words:

> There was a law passed in England under Henry VIII, by which whoever predicted the king's death was declared guilty of high treason. This law was extremely vague; the terror of despotic power is so great that it recoils upon those who exercise it. In the king's last illness, the physicians would not venture to say he was in danger; and surely they acted very right.... Marsyas dreamed that he had cut Dionysius's throat. Dionysius put him to death, pretending that he would never have dreamed of such a thing by night if he had not thought of it by day. This was a most tyrannical action: for though it had been the subject of his thoughts, yet he had made no attempt towards it. The laws do not take upon them to punish any other than overt acts. [The Spirit of Laws (1949), Vol. 1, pp. 192-193.]
>
> Words do not constitute an overt act; they remain only in idea. [Id., 193.]

These were the notions that led to the restrictive definition of treason, presently contained in Art. III, § 3, of the Constitution, which requires overt acts. Cramer v. United States, supra; Haupt v. United States, 330 U.S. 631, 645 (concurring opinion); Hurst, Treason in the United States, 58 Harv. L. Rev. 395. Our long and painful experience with the law of treason, wholly apart from the First Amendment, should be enough warning that we as free people should not venture again into the field of prosecuting beliefs.

That was the philosophy behind Board of Education v. Barnette, 319 U.S. 624, 641-642:

> We can have intellectual individualism and the rich cultural diversities that we owe to exceptional minds only at the price of occasional eccentricity and abnormal attitudes. When they are so harmless to others or to the State as those we deal with here, the price is not too great. But freedom to differ is not limited to things that do not matter much. That would be a mere shadow of freedom. The test of its substance is the right to differ as to things that touch the heart of the existing order.
>
> If there is any fixed star in our constitutional constellation, it is that no official, high or petty, can prescribe what shall be orthodox in politics, nationalism, religion, or other matters of opinion or force citizens to confess by word or act their faith therein. If there are any circumstances which permit an exception, they do not now occur to us.

Nothing but beliefs is on trial in this case. They are unpopular and to most of us revolting. But they are nonetheless ideas or dogmas or faiths within the broad framework of the First Amendment. See Barenblatt v. United States, 360 U.S. 109, 145-152 (dissent). The creed truer to our faith was stated by the Bar Committee headed by Charles E. Hughes which in 1920 protested the refusal of the New York Assembly to seat five members of the Socialist Party: [3]

> ... it is of the essence of the institutions of liberty that it be recognized that guilt is personal and cannot be attributed to the holding of opinion or to mere intent in the absence of overt acts....

Belief in the principle of revolution is deep in our traditions. The Declaration of Independence[4] proclaims it:

> whenever any Form of Government becomes destructive of these Ends, it is the Right of the People to alter or to abolish it, and to institute new Government, laying its Foundation on such Principles, and organizing its Powers in such Form, as to them shall seem most likely to effect their Safety and Happiness.

This right of revolution has been and is a part of the fabric of our institutions.[5] Last century when Russia invaded Hungary and subdued her, Louis Kossuth came here to enlist American support. On January 8, 1852, Lincoln spoke in sympathy of the Hungarian cause and was a member of a committee which on January 9, 1852, submitted Resolutions in Behalf of Hungarian Freedom. Among these resolutions was one that read:

> That it is the right of any people, sufficiently numerous for national independence, to throw off, to revolutionize, their existing form of government, and to establish such other in its stead as they may choose. [Basler, Vol. II, The Collected Works of Abraham Lincoln (1953), p. 115.]

On January 12, 1848, Lincoln in an address before the United States House of Representatives stated: "Any people anywhere, being inclined and having the power, have the right to rise up, and shake off the existing government, and form a new one that suits them better. This is a most valuable, --a most sacred right--a right, which we hope and believe, is to liberate the world." Id., Vol. I, p. 438.

Of course, government can move against those who take up arms against it. Of course, the constituted authority has the right of self-preservation. But we deal in this prosecution of Scales only with the legality of ideas and beliefs, not with overt acts. The Court speaks of the prevention of "dangerous behavior" by punishing those "who work to bring about that behavior." That formula returns man to the dark days when government determined what behavior was "dangerous" and then policed the dissidents for tell-tale signs of advocacy. What is "dangerous behavior" that must be suppressed in its talkstage has had a vivid history even on this continent. The British colonial philosophy was summed up by Sir William Berkeley, who served from 1641 to 1677 as Virginia's Governor: "... I thank God, there are no free schools nor printing, and I hope we shall not have these hundred years; for learning has brought disobedience, and heresy, and sects into the world, and printing has divulged them, and libels against the best government. God keep us from both!" 2 Hening's Stat. Va. 1660-1682, p. 517. The history is familiar; much of it is reviewed in Chafee, The Blessings of Liberty (1956). He states in one paragraph what I think is the Jeffersonian conception of the First Amendment rights involved in the present case:

> We must choose between freedom and fear --we cannot have both. If the citizens of the United States persist in being afraid, the real rulers of this country will be fanatics fired with a zeal to save grown men from objectionable ideas by putting them under the care of official nursemaids. [Id., 156.]

In recent years we have been departing, I think, from the theory of government expressed in the First Amendment. We have too often been "balancing" the right of speech and association against other values in society to see if we, the judges, feel that a particular need is more important than those guaranteed by the Bill of Rights. Dennis v. United States, 341 U.S. 494, 508-509; Communications Assn. v. Douds, 339 U.S. 382, 399-400; N.A.A.C.P. v. Alabama, 357 U.S. 449, 463-466; Uphaus v. Wyman, 360 U.S. 72, 78-79; Barenblatt v. United States, 360 U.S. 109, 126-134; Bates v. Little Rock, 361 U.S. 516, 524; Shelton v. Tucker, 364 U.S. 479; Wilkinson v. United States, 365 U.S. 399; Braden v. United States, 365 U.S. 431; Konigsberg v. State Bar, 366 U.S. 36; In re Anastaplo, 366 U.S. 82. This approach, which treats the commands of the First Amendment as "no more than admonitions of moderation" (see Hand, The Spirit of Liberty (1960 ed.), p. 278), runs counter to our prior decisions. See Lovell v. Griffin, 303 U.S. 444, 450; Murdock v. Pennsylvania, 319 U.S. 105, 108; Board of Education v. Barnette, 319 U.S. 624, 639.

It also runs counter to Madison's views of the First Amendment as we are advised by his eminent biographer, Irving Brant:

> When Madison, wrote, 'Congress shall make no law' infringing these rights, he did not expect the Supreme Court to decide, on balance, whether Congress could or could not make a law infringing them. It was true, he observed in presenting his proposals, that state legislative bodies had violated many of the most valuable articles in bills of rights. But that furnished no basis for judging the effectiveness of the proposed amendments:
>
> If they are incorporated into the Constitution, independent tribunals of justice will consider themselves in a peculiar manner the guardians of those rights; they will be an impenetrable bulwark against every assumption of power in the Legislative or Executive; they will be naturally led to

> resist every encroachment upon rights expressly stipulated for in the Constitution by the declaration of rights.
>
> This statement by Madison, along with all the rest of his speech, is so devastating to the 'balance theory' that efforts have been and are being made to discredit its authenticity. The Annals of Congress, it is said, is not an official document, but a compilation of stenographic reports (by a shorthand reporter admitted to the floor for that purpose) published in the press and containing numerous errors. That is true, although the chief complaint was that partially caught sentences were meaningless. In general, that which was clearly reported was truly reported. In the case of this all-important speech, Madison spoke from notes, and the notes, in his handwriting are in the Library of Congress. They parallel the speech from end to end, scantily, but leaving no doubt of the fundamental faithfulness of the report. [The Madison Heritage, 35 N.Y.U. L. Rev. 882, 899-900.]

Brant goes on to relate how Madison opposed a resolution of censure against societies creating the political turmoil that was behind the Whiskey Rebellion. Id., p. 900. He expressed in the House the view that opinions are not objects of legislation. 'If we advert to the nature of Republican Government, we shall find that the censorial power is in the people over the Government, and not in the Government over the people." Id., p. 900.

The trend of history, as Jefferson noted, has been against the rights of man. He wrote that "The natural progress of things is for liberty to yield and government to gain ground."[6] The formula he prepared for a society where ideas flourished was not punishment of the unorthodox but education and enlightenment of the masses. Jefferson wrote to Madison on December 20, 1787:[7]

> I own, I am not a friend to a very energetic government. It is always oppressive. It places the governors indeed more at their ease, at the expense of the people. The late rebellion in Massachusetts has given more alarm, than I think it should have done. Calculate that one rebellion in thirteen States in the course of eleven years, is but one for each State in a century and a half. No country should be

> so long without one. Nor will any degree of power in the hands of government, prevent insurrections. In England, where the hand of power is heavier than with us, there are seldom half a dozen years without an insurrection. In France, where it is still heavier, but less despotic, as Montesquieu supposes, than in some other countries, and where there are always two or three hundred thousand men ready to crush insurrections, there have been three in the course of the three years I have been here, in every one of which greater numbers were engaged than in Massachusetts, and a great deal more blood was spilt. In Turkey, where the sole nod of the despot is death, insurrections are the events of every day. Compare again the ferocious depredations of their insurgents, with the order, the moderation and the almost self-extinguishment of ours. And say, finally, whether peace is best preserved by giving energy to the government, or information to the people. This last is the most certain, and the most legitimate engine of government. Educate and inform the whole mass of the people. Enable them to see that it is their interest to preserve peace and order, and they will preserve them. And it requires no very high degree of education to convince them of this. They are the only sure reliance for the preservation of our liberty.

This is the only philosophy consistent with the First Amendment. When belief in an idea is punished as it is today, we sacrifice those ideals and substitute an alien, totalitarian philosophy in their stead. [8]

"The most indifferent arguments," Bismarck said, "are good when one has a majority of bayonets." This is also true when one has the votes.

What we lose by majority vote today may be reclaimed at a future time when the fear of advocacy, dissent, and nonconformity no longer cast a shadow over us.

## APPENDIX TO OPINION OF MR. JUSTICE DOUGLAS

The constitutions of 15 States have, at one time or another, made specific provision for the right of revolution by reserving to the people the right to "alter, reform or abolish" the existing frame of government. See Pennsylvania Const. of 1873, Art. I § 2; Maryland Const. of 1867, Dec. of Rights, Art. I; Virginia Const. of 1902, Art. I, § 3; Alabama Const. of 1865, Art. I, § 2; Arkansas Const. of 1874, Art. II, § 1; Idaho Const. of 1889, Art. I, § 2; Kansas Const. of 1858, Art. I, § 2; Kentucky Const. of 1890, Bill of Rights, § 4; Ohio Const. of 1851, Art. I, § 2; Oregon Const. of 1857, Art. I, § 1; Tennessee Const. of 1870, Art. I, § 1; Texas Const. of 1876, Art. I, § 2; Vermont Const. of 1793, c. 1 Art. 7; West Virginia Const. of 1872, Art. 3, § 3; Wyoming Const. of 1889, Art. I, § 1. Some 24 other States have, or have had, slightly varying forms of the same provision. See New Hampshire Const., Pt. I, Art. 10; Massachusetts Const., Part of the First, Article VII; Connecticut Const., Article First, § 2; New Jersey Const., Art. I, § 2; Delaware Const., Preamble; North Carolina Const., Art. I, § 3; South Carolina Const., Art. 1, § 1; Rhode Island Const., Art. I, § 1; California Const., Art I, § 2; Colorado Const., Art. II, § 2; Florida Const., Dec. of Rights, § 2; Indiana Const., Art. I, § 1; Iowa Const., Art. I, § 2; Maine Const., Art. I, § 2; Michigan Const. of 1835, Art. I, § 2; Minnesota Const., Art. I, § 1; Mississippi Const., Art. 3, § 6; Missouri Const., Art. I, § 3; Montana Const., Art. III, § 2; Nevada Const., Art. I, § 2; North Dakota Const., Art. I, § 2; Oklahoma Const., Art. II, § 1; South Dakota Const., Art. VI, § 26; Utah Const., Art. I, § 2. The older constitutions often add a clause which shows the roots of these provisions in the right of revolution. "The doctrine of non-resistance against arbitrary power and oppression is absurd, slavish, and destructive of the good and happiness of mankind," the New Hampshire Const., Pt. I, Art. 10, recites. The same language may be found in Maryland Const., Dec. of Rights, Art. 6; Tennessee Const., Art. I, § 2.

These provisions have been considered by several state courts. It has been held that the general right of the people to alter or abolish the government does not deprive state courts from passing on the validity of constitutional amendments peacefully passed. Wells v. Bain, 75 Pa. St. 39, 46-49; Koehler & Lange v. Hill, 60 Iowa 543, 614-617, 15 N.W. 614-616; Bennett v. Jackson, 186 Ind. 533, 538-541, 116 N.E. 921, 922-923; Erwin v. Nolan, 280 Mo. 401, 406-407, 217 S.W. 837, 838-839. More recently, several state courts have had occasion to consider these provisions in connection with the persecution of Communists. See Commonwealth v. Widovich, 295 Pa. 311, 317-318, 145 A. 295, 297-298 (State Sedition Act); Nelson v. Wyman, 99 N.H.

33, 50-51, 105 A. 2d 756, 770-771 (legislative investigation); Braverman v. Bar Assn. of Balto., 209 Md. 328, 346-347, 121 A. 2d 473, 481-482 (disbarment of a lawyer convicted under the Smith Act). The last two of these decisions relied on language in the decision of this Court in Dennis v. United States, 341 U.S. 494, 501: "Whatever theoretical merit there may be to the argument that there is a 'right' to rebellion against dictatorial governments is without force where the existing structure of the government provides for peaceful and orderly change."

Yet the right of revolution has always meant more than this. "The words ...," said the court in Wells v. Bain, supra, 47, "embrace but three known recognized modes by which the whole people, the state, can give their consent to an alteration of an existing lawful frame of government, viz.:

"1. The mode provided in the existing constitution.
"2. A law, as the instrumental process of raising the body for revision and conveying to it the powers of the people.
"3. A revolution.

"The first two are peaceful means through which the consent of the people to alteration is obtained, and by which the existing government consents to be displaced without revolution. The government gives its consent, either by pursuing the mode provided in the constitution, or by passing a law to call a convention. If consent be not so given by the existing government the remedy of the people is in the third mode--revolution."

This does not mean the helplessness of the established government in the face of armed resistance, for that government has the duty of maintaining existing institutions. Wells v. Bain, supra, 49. But it does mean that the right of revolution is ultimately reserved to the people themselves, whatever formal, but useless, remedies the existing government may offer. This is shown in the history of our own revolution. Legislatures and governments have the right to protect themselves. They may judge as to the appropriate means of meeting force directed against them, but as to the propriety of the exercise of the ultimate right of revolution, there as John Locke says, "The people shall be judge." Second treatise on Civil Government, § 240. To forbid the teaching of the propriety of revolution, even where the teacher believes his own lesson, is to hinder the people in the free exercise of this great sovereign right. See Dennis v. United States, 341 U.S. 494, 581-586 (dissenting opinion).

Lincoln's full statement, made in 1848 and already referred to, reads:

> Any people anywhere, being inclined and having the power, have the right to rise up, and shake off the existing government, and form a new one that suits them better. This is a most valuable, --a most sacred right--a right, which we hope and believe, is to liberate the world. Nor is this right confined to cases in which the whole people of an existing government, may choose to exercise it. Any portion of such people that can, may revolutionize, and make their own, of so much of the teritory [sic] as they inhabit. More than this, a majority of any portion of such people may revolutionize, putting down a minority, intermingles with, or near about them, who may oppose their movement. Such minority, was precisely the case, of the tories of our own revolution. It is a quality of revolutions not to go by old lines, or old laws; but to break up both, and make new ones. [I Basler, The Collected Works of Abraham Lincoln (1953), pp. 438-439.]

## NOTES

1. Following the Equator (1903), Vol. I, p. 198.

2. The prototype of the present prosecution is found in Communist lands. The Communist Government in Czechoslovakia on October 6, 1948, promulgated a law, § 3 of which provided:

   "(1) Whoever publicly or before several people instigates against the Republic, against its independence, constitutional unity, territorial integrity or its people's democratic system [of government], its social or economic order, or against its national character as guaranteed by the Constitution, shall be punished for a minor crime by rigorous confinement for from three months to three years.

   "(2) The following shall be punished in like manner: Whoever intentionally or through gross negligence makes the dissemination of the instigative statement specified in Subsection 1 possible or easy."

3. N.Y.L. Doc., 143d Sess., 1920, Vol. 5, No. 30 p. 4.

4. "When honest men are impelled to withdraw their allegiance to the established law or custom of the community, still more when they are persuaded that such law or custom is too iniquitous to be longer tolerated, they seek for some principle more generally valid, some 'law' of higher authority, than the established law or custom of the community. To this higher law or more generally valid principle they then appeal in justification of actions which the community condemns as immoral or criminal. They formulate the law or principle in such a way that it is, or seems to them to be, rationally defensible. To them it is 'true' because it brings their actions into harmony with a rightly ordered universe, and enables them to think of themselves as having chosen the nobler part, as having withdrawn from a corrupt world in order to serve God or Humanity or a force that makes for the highest good." Becker, The Declaration of Independence (1942), pp. 277-278.

5. See the Appendix to this opinion, post, p. 275.

6. The Writings of Thomas Jefferson (Memorial ed. 1903) p. 37.

7. The Writings of Thomas Jefferson (Memorial ed. 1903) pp. 391-392.

8. Gellhorn, American Rights (1960), in commenting on Dennis v. United States, 341 U.S. 494, and Yates v. United States, 354 U.S. 298, states:

"The aftermath of the Yates case is interesting. By the end of 1956 convictions of Communist leaders under the Smith Act had numbered 114. Many of these cases were still pending in the appellate courts when the Yates decision was announced in June of 1957. On one ground or another, convictions were set aside and new trials were granted to many of these defendants. The Department of Justice itself dropped the prosecution of a considerable number, on the ground that they could not properly be convicted on the basis of the evidence now available. Most significantly of all, the cases against the nine remaining defendants in Yates, as to whom the Supreme Court had refused to dismiss the charges, were abandoned by the prosecution because there was insufficient evidence that they had advocated action as distinct from opinion. After all the clamor, after all the expressed alarm about the peril into which the United States was being plunged by this handful of misguided fanatics, the prosecution felt itself unable to show persuasively that the Communist spokesmen had engaged in the forbidden incitements to illegality.

"This should stimulate a sober second look at the surface attractions of programs of suppression and coercion. Occasionally the supporters of these programs are scoundrels who falsely parade themselves as upholders of democracy; but more often they are good and sincere men. Men genuinely devoted to worthy ends sometimes endorse efforts to force unanimity of sentiment, not because they consciously espouse authoritarianism, but because they hope thus to assure maximum support for the nation and its people. No matter how well intentioned they may be, however, those efforts themselves create a graver danger than they overcome. The perils sought to be suppressed are regularly overestimated. History shows in one example after another how excessive have been the fears of earlier generations, who shuddered at menaces that, with the benefit of hindsight, we now know were mere shadows. This in itself should induce the modern generation to view with prudent skepticism the recurrent alarms about the fatal potentialities of dissent. In any event, in a world torn between the merits of freedom and the blandishments of totalitarian power, the lovers of freedom cannot afford to sacrifice their moral superiority by adopting totalitarian methods in order to create a self-deluding sense of security. Suppression, once accepted as a way of life, is likely to spread. It reinforces the herd urge toward orthodoxies of all kinds--religious, economic, and moral as well as political." Pp. 82-83.

<u>Gibson v. Florida Legislative Investigating Committee,</u>
372 U.S. 539 (1963)

Gibson, the president of the Miami branch of the National Association for the Advancement of Colored People, was ordered to appear before a Florida legislative investigating committee, which had information that fourteen "Communists" had been associated with that N.A.A.C.P. branch. He refused to produce the membership records demanded by the committee and was cited for contempt. The United States Supreme Court found for Gibson, with Douglas writing a concurring opinion in which he declared: "The Florida court in this case said that a requirement of nondisclosure would provide an 'ideological asylum for those who would destroy by violence the very foundations upon which their governmental sanctuary stands.' 126 So. 2d 129, 132. But there is no showing here that the N.A.A.C.P. is engaged in any criminal activity of any kind whatsoever.... Whether it has members who have committed crimes is immaterial. One man's privacy may not be invaded because of another's perversity. If the files of the N.A.A.C.P. can be ransacked because some Communists may have joined it, then all walls of privacy are broken down.... By that reasoning the files of any society or club can be seized because members of a 'subversive' group had infiltrated it."

* * *

MR. JUSTICE DOUGLAS, concurring.

I join the opinion of the Court, because it is carefully written within the framework of our current decisions. But since the matters involved touch constitutional rights and since I see the Constitution in somewhat different dimensions than are reflected in our decisions, it seems appropriate to set out my views.

We deal here with the authority of a State to investigate people, their ideas, their activities. By virtue of the Fourteenth Amendment [1] the State is now subject to the same restrictions [2] in making the investigation as the First Amendment places on the Federal Government.

The need of a referee in our federal system has increased with the passage of time, not only in matters of commerce but in the field of civil rights as well. Today review of both federal and state action threatening individuals' rights is increasingly important if the Free Society envisioned by the Bill of Rights is to be our ideal. For in times of crisis, when ideologies clash, it is not easy to engender respect for the dignity of suspect minorities and for debate of unpopular issues. As the President of Yale University has stated:

> We have become too much a nation of lookers and listeners, a nation of spectators. Amidst the easy artificiality of our life, the plethora of substitutes for learning and thinking, the innumerable devices for avoiding or delegating personal responsibility for our opinions, even for having any opinions, the fine edge of our faith has been dulled, our creative powers atrophied. [A. Whitney Griswold, Baccalaureate Address Yale University, June 8, 1958 (Overbrook Press).[3]]

When the State or Federal Government is prohibited from dealing with a subject, it has no constitutional privilege to investigate it. An investigation to permit a legislature properly to perform its powers of internal management is of course allowed. See Barry v. Cunningham, 279 U.S. 597, 613. But otherwise the power to investigate is only an adjunct of the power to legislate--an auxiliary power "necessary and appropriate to that end." McGrain v. Daugherty, 273 U.S. 135, 175. Investigation to determine how constitutional laws are being administered marks one limitation. The other is an investigation to determine what constitutional laws should be passed. When the constitutional limits of lawmaking are passed, investigation is out of bounds, apart from the exception noted. See Kilbourn v. Thompson, 103 U.S. 168, 194-200; McGrain v. Daugherty, supra, 171-175. That is to say, investigations by a legislative committee which "could result in no valid legislation on the subject" are beyond the pale. Kilbourn v. Thompson, supra, p. 195. For it misses the whole point of our constitutional history to assume that "government," or any branch of government, somehow has rights and powers of its own apart from those necessarily attending the proper performance of its constitutional functions.

Joining a lawful organization, like attending a church, is an associational activity that comes within the purview of the First Amendment, which provides in relevant part: "Congress shall make no law ... abridging the freedom of speech, or of the press; or the right of the people, peaceably to assemble, and to petition the government for a redress of grievances." "Peaceably to assemble" as used in the First Amendment necessarily involves a coming together, whether regularly or spasmodically. Historically the right to assemble was secondary to the right to petition, the latter being the primary right.[4] But today, as the Court stated in De Jonge v. Oregon, 299 U.S. 353, 364, "The right of peaceable assembly is a right cognate to those of free speech and free press and is equally fundamental." Assembly, like speech, is indeed essential "in order to maintain the opportunity for free political discussion, to the end that government may be responsive to the will of the people and that changes, if desired, may be obtained by peaceful means." Id., p. 365. "The holding of meetings for peaceable political action cannot be proscribed." Ibid. A Free Society is made up of almost innumerable institutions through which views and opinions are expressed, opinion is mobilized, and social, economic, religious, educational, and political programs are formulated.[5]

Joining groups seems to be a passion with Americans.

Schlesinger, The Rise of the City (1933), reviews the zeal with which Americans in the last century became the world's greatest "joiners":

> "Now Americans turned with furious zeal to the creation of secret societies but to their own pattern. In the large cities some form of organized social commingling seemed called for to replace the spontaneous friendliness of small rural towns. Liberty and equality this generation was willing to take for granted, but fraternity filled a compelling human need. Moreover, the romantic opportunity to posture before a mystic brotherhood in all the glory of robe, plume and sword restored a sense of self-importance bruised by the anonymity of life amidst great crowds. If further inducement were needed, it was supplied by the provision made by most lodges for sickness and death benefits for their members.
>
> "As was to be expected, membership was greatest in the urbanized sections of the country notwithstanding the energy with which the Negroes of the South aped their white brethren and the increasing interest of Western farmers in lodge activities. By the end of the

> period there were over six million names on the rosters of fraternal bodies. America possessed more secret societies and a larger number of 'joiners' than all other nations." Id., pp. 288-290.

"It is not surprising, therefore, to find that at least five thousand national associations exist in the United States." Robison, Protection of Associations from Compulsory Disclosure of Membership, 58 Col. L. Rev. 614, 622.

A coming together is often necessary for communication--for those who listen as well as for those who speak. Demosthenes, it is said, went to the seashore and declaimed to the waves in order to correct a stammer. But normally a speaker implies an audience. Joining a group is often as vital to freedom of expression as utterance itself. Registering as a student in a school or joining a faculty is as vital to freedom of expression as joining a church is to the free exercise of religion. Joining a political party may be as critical to expression of one's views as hiring reporters is to the establishment of a free press. Some have thought that political and academic affiliations have a preferred position under the due process version of the First Amendment. See Sweezy v. New Hampshire, 354 U.S. 234, 261-267 (concurring opinion). But the associational rights protected by the First Amendment are in my view much broader and cover the entire spectrum in political ideology as well as in art, in journalism, in teaching, and in religion.

In my view, government is not only powerless to legislate with respect to membership in a lawful organization; it is also precluded from probing the intimacies of spiritual and intellectual relationships in the myriad of such societies and groups that exist in this country, regardless of the legislative purpose sought to be served. "[T]he provisions of the First Amendment ... of course reach and limit ... investigations." Barenblatt v. United States, 360 U.S. 109, 126. If that is not true, I see no barrier to investigation of newspapers, churches, political parties, clubs, societies, unions, and any other association for their political, economic, social, philosophical, or religious views. If, in its quest to determine whether existing laws are being enforced or new laws are needed, an investigating committee can ascertain whether known Communists or criminals are members of an organization not shown to be engaged in conduct properly subject to regulation, it is but a short and inexorable step to the conclusion that it may also probe to ascertain what effect they have had on the other members. For how much more "necessary and appropriate" this information is to the legislative purpose being pursued!

It is no answer to the conclusion that all such investigations are illegal to suggest that the committee is pursuing a lawful objective in the manner it has determined most appropriate. For, as Laurent Frantz, The First Amendment in the Balance, 71 Yale L.J. 1424, 1441, has so persuasively shown, "it does not follow that any objective can ever be weighed against an express limitation on the means available for its pursuit. The public interest in the suppression of crime, for example, cannot be weighed against a constitutional provision that accused persons may not be denied the right to counsel." When otherwise valid legislation is sought to be applied in an unconstitutional manner we do not sustain its application. See, e.g., Yick Wo v. Hopkins, 118 U.S. 356. A different test should not obtain for legislative investigations. "[A]ny constitutional limitation serves a significant function only insofar as it stands in the way of something which government thinks ought to be done. Nothing else needs to be prohibited." [6] Frantz, supra, at 1445.

For some of us a phase of the problem emerged in United States v. Rumely, 345 U.S. 41, 57-58 (concurring opinion), where several problems were posed. Can the Government demand of a publisher the names of the purchasers of his publications? Would not the spectre of a government agent then look over the shoulder of everyone who reads? Might not the purchase of a book or pamphlet today result in a subpoena tomorrow? Would not the fear of criticism go with every person into the bookstall? If the light of publicity may reach any student, any teacher, would not free inquiry be discouraged? For are there not always books and pamphlets that are critical of the administration or that preach an unpopular policy in domestic or foreign affairs or that are in disrepute in the orthodox school of thought? If the press and its readers were subject to the harassment of hearings, investigations, reports, and subpoenas, government would indeed hold a club over speech and over the press. Recognition of these dangers prompted our decision in Talley v. California, 362 U.S. 60, holding unconstitutional an ordinance requiring handbills to disclose the name and address of the distributor or printer. Plainly a legislative committee could not have obtained the same information from the petitioner in that case merely because it was seeking to determine whether Communists were behind the distribution as part of a massive propaganda campaign.

The problem was exposed again in Russell v. United States, 369 U.S. 749, where the press was being investigated. What I said there seems germane here. Since what an editor writes or thinks is none of the Government's business--except, of course, that Congress could punish the breach of a carefully drawn security law; see Near v. Minnesota, 283 U.S. 697, 715-716--it has no power to investigate the capacities, ideology, prejudices, or politics of those who write the news.

> It is said that Congress has the power to determine the extent of Communist infiltration so that it can know how much tighter the 'security' laws should be made. This proves too much. It would give Congress a roving power to inquire into fields in which it could not legislate. If Congress can investigate the press to find out if Communists have infiltrated it, it could also investigate the churches for the same reason. Are the pulpits being used to promote the Communist cause? Were any of the clergy ever members of the Communist Party? How about the governing board? How about those who assist the pastor and perhaps help prepare his sermons or do the research? Who comes to the confession and discloses that he or she once was a Communist?" [369 U.S., at 777.]

Bryant v. Zimmerman, 278 U.S. 63, 72, held that the Due Process Clause of the Fourteenth Amendment did not prevent a State from compelling a disclosure of the membership lists of the Ku Klux Klan. That decision was made in 1928 and it is unnecessary to decide now whether its vitality has survived such cases as NAACP v. Alabama, 357 U.S. 449; Bates v. Little Rock, 361 U.S. 516; and Louisiana v. NAACP, 366 U.S. 293, for we distinguished that case in NAACP v. Alabama, supra, at 465, saying, inter alia, "The decision was based on the particular character of the Klan's activities, involving acts of unlawful intimidation and violence." Moreover, the incorporation of the First Amendment into the Fourteenth had only recently been adumbrated (see Gitlow v. New York, 268 U.S. 652, 666) and the full exposition of the right of association that is part of the periphery of the First Amendment had not yet been made. Indeed Pierce v. Society of Sisters, 268 U.S. 510, which sustained the right of parents to avoid public schools and to put their children in parochial schools, rested in part on the property interest of the parochial schools. Id., pp. 534-535.

The right of association has become a part of the bundle of rights protected by the First Amendment (see, e. g., NAACP v. Alabama, supra), and the need for a pervasive right of privacy against government intrusion has been recognized, though not always given the recognition it deserves.[7] Unpopular groups (NAACP v. Alabama, supra) like popular ones are protected. Unpopular groups if forced to disclose their membership lists may suffer reprisals or other forms of public hostility. NAACP v. Alabama, supra, p. 462. But whether a group is popular or unpopular, the right of privacy implicit in the First Amendment creates an area into which the Government may not enter.

> Freedom of religion and freedom of speech guaranteed by the First Amendment give more than the privilege to worship, to write, to speak as one chooses; they give freedom not to do nor to act as the government chooses. The First Amendment in its respect for the conscience of the individual honors the sanctity of thought and belief. To think as one chooses, to believe what one wishes are important aspects of the constitutional right to be let alone. [Public Utilities Comm'n v. Pollak, 343 U.S. 451, 467-468 (dissenting opinion).]

There is no other course consistent with the Free Society envisioned by the First Amendment. For the views a citizen entertains, the beliefs he harbors, the utterances he makes, the ideology he embraces and the people he associates with are no concern of government.[8] That article of faith marks indeed the main difference between the Free Society which we espouse and the dictatorships both on the Left and on the Right.

As MR. JUSTICE BLACK said (dissenting) in Barenblatt v. United States, supra, 150-151:

> The fact is that once we allow any group which has some political aims or ideas to be driven from the ballot and from the battle for men's minds because some of its members are bad and some of its tenets are illegal, no group is safe. Today we deal with Communists or suspected Communists. In 1920, instead, the New York Assembly suspended duly elected legislators on the ground that, being Socialists, they were disloyal to the country's principles. In the 1830's the Masons were

> hunted as outlaws and subversives, and abolitionists were considered revolutionaries of the most dangerous kind in both North and South. Earlier still, at the time of the universally unlamented alien and sedition laws, Thomas Jefferson's party was attacked and its members were derisively called 'Jacobins.' Fisher Ames described the party as a 'French faction' guilty of 'subversion' and 'officered, regimented and formed to subordination.' Its members, he claimed, intended to 'take arms against the laws as soon as they dare.' History should teach us then, that in times of high emotional excitement minority parties and groups which advocate extremely unpopular social or governmental innovations will always be typed as criminal gangs and attempts will always be made to drive them out. It was knowledge of this fact, and of its great dangers, that caused the Founders of our land to enact the First Amendment as a guarantee that neither Congress nor the people would do anything to hinder or destroy the capacity of individuals and groups to seek converts and votes for any cause, however radical or unpalatable their principles might seem under the accepted notions of the time.

If a group is engaging in acts or a course of conduct that is criminal, it can be prosecuted, and it and its members can be investigated, save as the Self-Incrimination Clause of the Fifth Amendment sets up a barrier. In Louisiana v. NAACP, supra, a state statute requiring the N.A.A.C.P. to register and disclose its membership lists was involved. We denied enforcement of that law, saying that we are "in an area where, as Shelton v. Tucker, 364 U.S. 479, emphasized, any regulation must be highly selective in order to survive challenge under the First Amendment." 366 U.S., at 296. And we added:

> At one extreme is criminal conduct which cannot have shelter in the First Amendment. At the other extreme are regulatory measures which, no matter how sophisticated, cannot be employed in purpose or in effect to stifle, penalize, or curb the exercise of First Amendment rights. [Id., p. 297.]

The Florida court in this case said that a requirement of nondisclosure would provide an "ideological asylum for those who would destroy by violence the very foundations upon which their governmental sanctuary stands." 126 So. 2d 129, 132. But there is no showing here that the N.A.A.C.P. is engaged in any criminal activity of any kind whatsoever. The Florida Supreme Court in Graham v. Florida Legislati e Investigation Committee, 126 So. 2d 133, 136, conceded that the N. A. A. C. P. is "an organization perfectly legitimate but allegedly unpopular in the community." Whether it has members who have committed crimes is immaterial. One man's privacy may not be invaded because of another's perversity. If the files of the N.A.A.C.P. can be ransacked because some Communists may have joined it, then all walls of privacy are broken down. By that reasoning the records of the confessional can be ransacked because a "subversive" or a criminal was implicated. By that reasoning an entire church can be investigated because one member was an ideological stray or had once been a Communist or because the minister's sermon paralleled the party line. By that reasoning the files of any society or club can be seized because members of a "subversive" group had infiltrated it.

In sum, the State and the Federal Governments, by force of the First Amendment, are barred from investigating any person's faith or ideology by summoning him or by summoning officers or members of his society, church, or club.

Government can intervene only when belief, thought, or expression moves into the realm of action that is inimical to society. That was Jefferson's view. In his Bill for Establishing Religious Freedom he spoke primarily of religious liberty but in terms applicable to freedom of the mind in all of its aspects. It was his view that in the Free Society men's ideas and beliefs, their speech and advocacy are no proper concern of government. Only when they become brigaded with action can government move against them. Jefferson said: [9]

> ... that the opinions of men are not the object of civil government, nor under its jurisdiction; that to suffer the civil magistrate to intrude his powers into the field of opinion and to restrain the profession or propagation of principles on supposition of their ill tendency is a dangerous fallacy, which at once destroys all religious liberty, because he being of course judge of that tendency will make his opinions the rule of judgment, and approve or condemn the sentiments of others only as they shall

> square with or suffer from his own; that it is time enough for the rightful purposes of civil government for its officers to interfere when principles break out into overt acts against peace and good order; and finally, that truth is great and will prevail if left to herself; that she is the proper and sufficient antagonist to error, and has nothing to fear from the conflict unless by human interposition disarmed of her natural weapons, free argument and debate; errors ceasing to be dangerous when it is permitted freely to contradict them.

Madison too knew that tolerance for all ideas across the spectrum was the only true guarantee of freedom of the mind: [10]

> Whilst all authority in it will be derived from and dependent on the society, the society itself will be broken into so many parts, interests and classes of citizens, that the rights of individuals, or of the minority, will be in little danger from interested combinations of the majority. In a free government the security for civil rights must be the same as that for religious rights. It consists in the one case in the multiplicity of interests, and in the other in the multiplicity of sects. The degree of security in both cases will depend on the number of interests and sects....

Once the investigator has only the conscience of government as a guide, the conscience can become "ravenous," as Cromwell, bent on destroying Thomas More, said in Bolt, A Man For All Seasons (1960), p. 120. The First Amendment mirrors many episodes where men, harried and harassed by government, sought refuge in their conscience, as these lines of Thomas More show:

> MORE: And when we stand before God, and you are sent to Paradise for doing according to your conscience, and I am damned for not doing according to mine, will you come with me, for fellowship?
>
> CRANMER: So those of us whose names are there are damned, Sir Thomas?
>
> MORE: I don't know, Your Grace. I have no window to look into another man's conscience. I condemn no one.

> CRANMER: Then the matter is capable of question?
>
> MORE: Certainly.
>
> CRANMER: But that you owe obedience to your King is not capable of question. So weigh a doubt against a certainty--and sign.
>
> MORE: Some men think the Earth is round, others think it flat; it is a matter capable of question. But if it is flat, will the King's command make it round? And if it is round, will the King's command flatten it? No, I will not sign. [Id., pp. 132-133.]

Where government is the Big Brother,[11] privacy gives way to surveillance. But our commitment is otherwise. By the First Amendment we have staked our security on freedom to promote a multiplicity of ideas, to associate at will with kindred spirits, and to defy governmental intrusion into these precincts.[12]

NOTES

1. See Brennan, The Bill of Rights and the States, 36 N.Y. U.L. Rev. 761, 770-778.

2. Some have believed that these restraints as applied to the States through the Due Process Clause of the Fourteenth Amendment are less restrictive on them than they are on the Federal Government. That is the view of my Brother HARLAN. See Roth v. United States, 354 U.S. 476, 501, 506; Smith v. California, 361 U.S. 147, 169. Mr. Justice Jackson expressed the same view in Beauharnais v. Illinois, 343 U.S. 250, 288. And compare the opinions of Justices Holmes and Brandeis in Gitlow v. New York, 268 U.S. 652, 672, and Whitney v. California, 274 U.S. 357, 372. But that view has not prevailed. The Court has indeed applied the same First Amendment requirements to the States as to the Federal Government.
   As stated by MR. JUSTICE BLACK in Speiser v. Randall, 357 U.S. 513, 530 (concurring opinion):
   "[T]he First Amendment ... of course is applicable in all its particulars to the States. See, e.g., Staub v. City of Baxley, 355 U.S. 313; Poulos v. New Hampshire, 345 U.S. 395, 396-397; Everson v. Board of Education, 330 U.S. 1, 8; Thomas v. Collins, 323

U. S. 516; Board of Education v. Barnette, 319 U. S. 624, 639; Douglas v. Jeannette, 319 U. S. 157, 162; Martin v. Struthers, 319 U. S. 141; Murdock v. Pennsylvania, 319 U. S. 105, 109; Chaplinsky v. New Hampshire, 315 U. S. 568, 571; Bridges v. California, 314 U. S. 252, 263; Cantwell v. Connecticut, 310 U. S. 296, 303; Schneider v. State, 308 U. S. 147, 160; Lovell v. Griffin, 303 U. S. 444, 450; De Jonge v. Oregon, 299 U. S. 353, 364; Gitlow v. New York, 268 U. S. 652, 666."

These cases are inconsistent with the view that First Amendment rights protected against state invasion by the Due Process Clause of the Fourteenth Amendment are a watered-down version of what the First Amendment guarantees.

3. See Reich, Mr. Justice Black and the Living Constitution, 76 Harv. L. Rev. 673, 727-750.

4. Corwin, The Constitution and What It Means Today (1958), p. 203; Arendt, On Revolution (1963), p. 25.

5. Jefferson's grand design included a division "into hundreds"--a viable ward system through which the people exercised their rights of sovereignty. Letter to John Tyler, May 26, 1810:

"I have indeed two great measures at heart, without which no republic can maintain itself in strength. 1. That of general education, to enable every man to judge for himself what will secure or endanger his freedom. 2. To divide every county into hundreds, of such size that all the children of each will be within reach of a central school in it. But this division looks to many other fundamental provisions. Every hundred, besides a school, should have a justice of the peace, a constable and a captain of militia. These officers, or some others within the hundred, should be a corporation to manage all its concerns, to take care of its roads, its poor, and its police by patrols, etc. (as the selectmen of the eastern townships). Every hundred should elect one or two jurors to serve where requisite, and all other elections should be made in the hundreds separately, and the votes of all the hundreds be brought together. Our present captaincies might be declared hundreds for the present, with a power to the courts to alter them occasionally. These little republics would be the main strength of the great one. We owe to them the vigor given to our revolution in its commencement in the Eastern States, and by them the Eastern States were enabled to repeal the embargo in opposition to the Middle, Southern and Western States, and their large and lubberly division into counties which can never be assembled. General orders are given out from a centre to the foreman of every hundred, as to the sergeants of an army, and the whole nation is thrown into energetic action, in the same direction in one instance and as one man, and becomes absolutely irresistible. Could I once see this I should consider it as the dawn of the salvation of the republic, and say with old Simeon, 'nunc dimittis Domine.' " 12 Writings of Thomas Jefferson (Mem. ed. 1904) 393-394.

And see letter to John Cartwright, June 5, 1824, 16 Jefferson, op. cit., supra, 42, 44-46; letter to Samuel Kercheval, July 12, 1816, 15 Jefferson, op. cit., supra, 32-44; and letter to Samuel Kercheval, September 5, 1816. Id., at 70-71.

6. "But the advocate of 'judicial restraint' will insist that where there is room for a reasonable difference of opinion between ... [the legislative body] and the Court as to whether certain action violates the first amendment, ... [the legislature's] view should take precedence. There are excellent reasons why it should not. First of all, 'Congress shall make no law ... ' is an obvious and express effort to restrain ... [legislative] power. If that restraint is to be effective, then ... [the legislature] is the least appropriate body in the world to be accorded the final word as to what it means. And, while I have no desire to re-wage the general battle for judicial review, the evidence is reasonably clear that the first amendment was proposed with the express expectation and intention that the courts would enforce it." Id., at 1447-1448.

7. See generally Beaney, The Constitutional Right to Privacy in the Supreme Court, 1962 Supreme Court Review, 212; Dykstra, The Right Most Valued by Civilized Man, 6 Utah L. Rev. 305; Robison, Protection of Associations from Compulsory Disclosure of Membership, 58 Col. L. Rev. 614; Frantz, The First Amendment in the Balance, 71 Yale L.J. 1424.

A part of the philosophical basis of this right has its roots in the common law. As Warren and Brandeis, The Right to Privacy, 4 Harv. L. Rev. 193, 196, stated:

"The intensity and complexity of life, attendant upon advancing civilization, have rendered necessary some retreat from the world, and man, under the refining influence of culture, has become more sensitive to publicity, so that solitude and privacy have become more essential to the individual; but modern enterprise and invention have, through invasions upon his privacy, subjected him to mental pain and distress, far greater than could be inflicted by mere bodily injury."

See also Olmstead v. United States, 277 U.S. 438, 471, 472-479 (dissenting opinion, Brandeis, J.); Poe v. Ullman, 367 U.S. 497, 509, 515-522 (dissenting opinion).

Whether the problem involves the right of an individual to be let alone in the sanctuary of his home or his right to associate with others for the attainment of lawful purposes, the individual's interest in being free from governmental interference is the same, and, except for the limited situation where there is "probable cause" for believing that he is involved in a crime, the government's disability is equally complete.

8. As to problems raised when disclosure of members of a political organization which represents a foreign government is required, see Communist Party v. Control Board, 367 U.S. 1.

9. The Works of Thomas Jefferson (Fed. ed. 1904), Vol. 2, pp. 440-441.

10. Federalist, No. 51.

11. "Outside, even through the shut window pane, the world looked cold. Down in the street little eddies of wind were whirling dust and torn paper into spirals, and though the sun was shining and the sky a harsh blue, there seemed to be no color in anything except the posters that were plastered everywhere. The black-mustachio'd face gazed down from every commanding corner. There was one on the house front immediately opposite. BIG BROTHER IS WATCHING YOU, the caption said, while the dark eyes looked deep into Winston's own. Down at street level another poster, torn at one corner, flapped fitfully in the wind, alternately covering and uncovering the single word INGSOC. In the far distance a helicopter skimmed down between the roofs, hovered for an instant like a blue-bottle,

and darted away again with a curving flight. It was the Police Patrol, snooping into people's windows. The patrols did not matter, however. Only the Thought Police mattered." Orwell, Nineteen Eighty-Four (1949), 4.

12. "Those who won our independence believed that the final end of the State was to make men free to develop their faculties; and that in its government the deliberative forces should prevail over the arbitrary. They valued liberty both as an end and as a means. They believed liberty to be the secret of happiness and courage to be the secret of liberty. They believed that freedom to think as you will and to speak as you think are means indispensable to the discovery and spread of political truth; that without free speech and assembly discussion would be futile; that with them, discussion affords ordinarily adequate protection against the dissemination of noxious doctrine; that the greatest menace to freedom is an inert people; that public discussion is a political duty; and that this should be a fundamental principle of the American government...."

"Those who won our independence by revolution were not cowards. They did not fear political change. They did not exalt order at the cost of liberty. To courageous, self-reliant men, with confidence in the power of free and fearless reasoning applied through the processes of popular government, no danger flowing from speech can be deemed clear and present, unless the incidence of the evil apprehended is so imminent that it may befall before there is opportunity for full discussion. If there be time to expose through discussion the falsehood and fallacies, to avert the evil by the processes of education, the remedy to be applied is more speech, not enforced silence. Only an emergency can justify repression. Such must be the rule if authority is to be reconciled with freedom...." Whitney v. California, 274 U.S. 357, 375, 377 (concurring opinion of Mr. Justice Brandeis).

Lamont v. Postmaster General, 381 U.S. 301 (1965)

The Supreme Court finds unconstitutional a United States Post Office statute that required persons desiring to have delivered to them foreign "Communist political propaganda" addressed to them to return a card to the Post Office indicating that they wanted to receive the materials; if a card was not returned within twenty days it was assumed that the addressee did not want to receive the materials. Justice Douglas delivered the opinion of the Court, saying: "We rest on the narrow ground that the addressee in order to receive his mail must request in writing that it be delivered. This amounts in our judgment to an unconstitutional abridgment of the addressee's First Amendment rights. The addressee carries an affirmative obligation which we do not think the Government may impose on him. This requirement is almost certain to have a deterrent effect, especially as respects those who have sensitive positions. Their livelihood may be dependent on a security clearance. Public officials, like schoolteachers who have no tenure, might think they would invite disaster if they read what the Federal Government says contains the seeds of treason. Apart from them, any addressee is likely to feel some inhibition in sending for literature which federal officials have condemned as 'communist political propaganda.' The regime of this Act is at war with the 'uninhibited, robust, and wide-open' debate and discussion that are contemplated by the First Amendment."

* * *

MR. JUSTICE DOUGLAS delivered the opinion of the Court.

These appeals present the same question: is § 305 (a) of the Postal Service and Federal Employees Salary Act of 1962, 76 Stat. 840, constitutional as construed and applied? The statute provides in part:

> Mail matter, except sealed letters, which originates or which is printed or otherwise prepared in a foreign country and which is determined

> by the Secretary of the Treasury pursuant to rules and regulations to be promulgated by him to be 'communist political propaganda,' shall be detained by the Postmaster General upon its arrival for delivery in the United States, or upon its subsequent deposit in the United States domestic mails, and the addressee shall be notified that such matter has been received and will be delivered only upon the addressee's request, except that such detention shall not be required in the case of any matter which is furnished pursuant to subscription or which is otherwise ascertained by the Postmaster General to be desired by the addressee. [39 U.S.C. 4008 (a).]

The statute defines "communist political propaganda" as political propaganda (as that term is defined in §1 (j) of the Foreign Agents Registration Act of 1938 [1]) which is issued by or on behalf of any country with respect to which there is in effect a suspension or withdrawl of tariff concessions or from which foreign assistance is withheld pursuant to certain specified statutes. 39 U.S.C. §4008 (b). The statute contains an exemption from its provisions for mail addressed to government agencies and educational institutions, or officials thereof, and for mail sent pursuant to a reciprocal cultural international agreement. 39 U.S.C. § 4008 (c).

To implement the statute the Post Office maintains 10 or 11 screening points through which is routed all unsealed mail from the designated foreign countries. At these points the nonexempt mail is examined by Customs authorities. When it is determined that a piece of mail is "communist political propaganda," the addressee is mailed a notice identifying the mail being detained and advising that it will be destroyed unless the addressee requests delivery by returning an attached reply card within 20 days.

Prior to March 1, 1965, the reply card contained a space in which the addressee could request delivery of any "similar publication" in the future. A list of the persons thus manifesting a desire to receive "communist political propaganda" was maintained by the Post Office. The Government in its brief informs us that the keeping of this list was terminated, effective March 15, 1965. Thus, under the new practice, a notice is sent and must be returned for each individual piece of mail desired. The only standing instruction which it is now possible to leave with the Post Office is <u>not</u> to deliver any "communist political propaganda." [2] And the Solicitor General advises us that the Post Office Department "intends to retain its assumption that those who do not return the card want neither the identified publication nor any similar one arriving subsequently."

No. 491 arose out of the Post Office's detention in 1963 of a copy of the Peking Review # 12 addressed to appellant, Dr. Corliss Lamont, who is engaged in the publishing and distributing of pamphlets. Lamont did not respond to the notice of detention which was sent to him but instead instituted this suit to enjoin enforcement of the statute, alleging that it infringed his rights under the First and Fifth Amendments. The Post Office thereupon notified Lamont that it considered his institution of the suit to be an expression of his desire to receive "communist political propaganda" and therefore none of his mail would be detained. Lamont amended his complaint to challenge on constitutional grounds the placement of his name on the list of those desiring to receive "communist political propaganda." The majority of the three-judge District Court nonetheless dismissed the complaint as moot, 229 F. Supp. 913, because Lamont would now receive his mail unimpeded. Insofar as the list was concerned, the majority thought that any legally significant harm to Lamont as a result of being listed was merely a speculative possibility, and so on this score the controversy was not yet ripe for adjudication. Lamont appealed from the dismissal, and we noted probable jurisdiction. 379 U.S. 926.

Like Lamont, appellee Heilberg in No. 848, when his mail was detained, refused to return the reply card and instead filed a complaint in the District Court for an injunction against enforcement of the statute. The Post Office reacted to this complaint in the same manner as it had to Lamont's complaint, but the District Court declined to hold that Heilberg's action was thereby mooted. Instead the District Court reached the merits and unanimously held that the statute was unconstitutional under the First Amendment. 236 F. Supp. 405. The Government appealed and we noted probable jurisdiction. 379 U.S. 997.

There is no longer even a colorable question of mootness in these cases, for the new procedure, as described above, requires the postal authorities to send a separate notice for each item as it is received and the addressee to make a separate request for each item. Under the new system, we are told, there can be no list of persons who have manifested a desire to receive "communist political propaganda" and whose mail will therefore go through relatively unimpeded. The Government concedes that the changed procedure entirely precludes any claim of mootness and leaves for our consideration the sole question of the constitutionality of the statute.

We conclude that the Act as construed and applied is unconstitutional because it requires an official act (viz., returning the reply card) as a limitation on the unfettered exercise of the addressee's First Amendment rights. As stated by Mr. Justice Holmes in Milwaukee Pub. Co. v. Burleson, 255 U.S. 407, 437 (dissenting): "The United States may give up the Post Office when it sees fit, but while it carries it on the use of the mails is almost as much a part of free speech as the right to use our tongues...." [3]

We struck down in Murdock v. Pennsylvania, 319 U. S. 105, a flat license tax on the exercise of First Amendment rights. A registration requirement imposed on a labor union organizer before making a speech met the same fate in Thomas v. Collins, 323 U.S. 516. A municipal licensing system for those distributing literature was held invalid in Lovell v. Griffin, 303 U.S. 444. We recently reviewed in Harman v. Forssenius, 380 U.S. 528, an attempt by a State to impose a burden on the exercise of a right under the Twenty-fourth Amendment. There, a registration was required by all federal electors who did not pay the state poll tax. We stated:

> For federal elections, the poll tax is abolished absolutely as a prerequisite to voting, and no equivalent or milder substitute may be imposed. Any material requirement imposed upon the federal voter solely because of his refusal to waive the constitutional immunity subverts the effectiveness of the Twenty-fourth Amendment and must fall under its ban. [Id., p. 542.]

Here the Congress--expressly restrained by the First Amendment from "abridging" freedom of speech and of press--is the actor. The Act sets administrative officials astride the flow of mail to inspect it, appraise it, write the addressee about it, and await a response before dispatching the mail. Just as the licensing or taxing authorities in the Lovell, Thomas, and Murdock cases sought to control the flow of ideas to the public, so here federal agencies regulate the flow of mail. We do not have here, any more than we had in Hannegan v. Esquire, Inc., 327 U.S. 146, any question concerning the extent to which Congress may classify the mail and fix the charges for its carriage. Nor do we reach the question whether the standard here applied could pass constitutional muster. Nor do we deal with the right of Customs to inspect material from abroad for contraband. We rest on the narrow ground that the addressee in order to receive his mail must request in writing that it be delivered. This amounts in our judgment to an unconstitutional abridgment of the addressee's First Amendment rights. The addressee carries an affirmative obligation which we do not think the Government may impose on him. This requirement is almost certain to have a deterrent effect, especially as respects those who have sensitive positions. Their livelihood may be dependent on a security clearance. Public officials, like schoolteachers who have no tenure, might think they would invite disaster if they read what the Federal Government says contains the seeds of treason. Apart from them, any addressee is likely to feel some inhibition in sending for literature which federal officials have condemned as "communist political propaganda." The regime of this Act is at war with the "uninhibited, robust, and wide-open" debate and discussion that are contemplated by the First Amendment. New York Times Co. v. Sullivan, 376 U.S. 254, 270.

We reverse the judgment in No. 491 and affirm that in No. 848.

It is so ordered.

NOTES

1. "The term 'political propaganda' includes any oral, visual, graphic, written, pictorial, or other communication or expression by any person (1) which is reasonably adapted to, or which the person disseminating the same believes will, or which he intends to, prevail upon, indoctrinate, convert, induce, or in any other way influence a recipient or any section of the public within the United States with reference to the political or public interests, policies, or relations of a government of a foreign country or a foreign political party or with reference to the foreign policies of the United States or promote in the United States racial, religious, or social dissensions, or (2) which advocates, advises, instigates, or promotes any racial, social, political, or religious disorder, civil riot, or other conflict involving the use of force or violence in any other American republic or the overthrow of any government or

political subdivision of any other American republic by any means involving the use of force or violence." 22 U.S.C. § 611 (j).

2. A Post Office regulation permits a patron to refuse delivery of any piece of mail (39 CFR §44.1 (a)) or to request in writing a withholding from delivery for a period not to exceed two years of specifically described items of certain mail, including "foreign printed matter." Ibid. And see Schwartz, The Mail Must Not Go Through, 11 U.C.L.A. L. Rev. 805, 847.

3. "Whatever may have been the voluntary nature of the postal system in the period of its establishment, it is now the main artery through which the business, social, and personal affairs of the people are conducted and upon which depends in a greater degree than upon any other activity of government the promotion of the general welfare." Pike v. Walker, 73 App. D.C. 289, 291, 121 F. 2d 37, 39. And see Gellhorn, Individual Freedom and Governmental Restraints, p. 88 et seq. (1956).

Schneider v. Smith, 390 U.S. 17 (1968)

The Supreme Court decides that denying a merchant seaman a second assistant engineer position because he refused to submit to inquiries about his political ideas, beliefs, and associations is unconstitutional. Douglas delivers the opinion of the Court, saying that: "a saboteur on a merchant vessel may, of course, be dangerous. But no charge that appellant was a saboteur was made. Indeed, no conduct of appellant was at issue before the Commandant.... We are loath to conclude that Congress, in its grant of authority to the President to 'safeguard' vessels and waterfront facilities from 'sabotage or other subversive acts,' undertook to reach into the First Amendment area. The provision of the Act in question ..., speaks only in terms of actions, not ideas or beliefs or reading habits or social, educational, or political associations."

* * *

MR. JUSTICE DOUGLAS delivered the opinion of the Court.

Appellant, who has served on board American-flag commercial vessels in various capacities, is now qualified to act as a second assistant engineer on steam vessels. But between 1949 and 1964 he was employed in trades other than that of a merchant seaman. In October 1964 he applied to the Commandant of the Coast Guard for a validation of the permit or license which evidences his ability to act as a second assistant engineer.

Under the Magnuson Act, 64 Stat. 427, 50 U.S.C. § 191 (b), the President is authorized, if he finds that "the security of the United States is endangered by ... subversive activity," to issue rules and regulations "to safeguard against destruction, loss, or injury from sabotage or other subversive acts" all "vessels" in the territories or waters subject to the jurisdiction of the United States.[1]

President Truman promulgated Regulations, 33 CFR,

pt. 6, which gave the Commandant of the Coast Guard authority to grant or withhold validation of any permit or license evidencing the right of a seaman to serve on a merchant vessel of the United States. § 6.10-3. He is directed not to issue such validation unless he is satisfied that "the character and habits of life of such person are such as to authorize the belief that the presence of the individual on board would not be inimical to the security of the United States." § 6.10-1.

The questionnaire, which appellant in his application was required to submit, contained the following inquiry which he answered:

> ITEM 4. Do you now advocate, or have you ever advocated, the overthrow or alteration of the Government of the United States by force or violence or by unconstitutional means?
>
> ANSWER: No.

The questionnaire contained the following inquiries which related to his membership and participation in organizations which were on the special list of the Attorney General as authorized by Executive Order 10450; 18 Fed. Reg. 2489:

> ITEM 5. Have you ever submitted material for publication to any of the organizations listed in Item 6 below?
>
> ANSWER: No.
>
> ITEM 6. Are you now, or have you ever been, a member of, or affiliated or associated with in any way, any of the organizations set forth below?
>
> [There followed a list of more than 250 organizations.]
>
> ANSWER. Yes.
>
> If your answer is 'yes,' give full details in Item 7.
>
> ITEM 7. (Use this space to explain Items 1 through 6.... Attach a separate sheet if there is not enough space here.)
>
> ANSWER. I have been a member of many political & social organizations, including several named on this list.
>
> I cannot remember the names of most of them & could not be specific about any.
>
> To the best of my knowledge, I have not been a member or participated in the activities of any of these organizations for ten years.

Upon receiving the questionnaire returned by the appellant, the Commandant advised him that the information was not sufficient and that answers to further interrogatories were necessary. [2]

In reply, appellant, speaking through his counsel, admitted to the Commandant that he had been a member of the Communist Party as well as other organizations on the Attorney General's list and that he had subscribed to People's World. He said that he had joined the Party because of his personal philosophy and idealistic goals, but later quit it and the other organizations due to fundamental disagreement with Communist methods and techniques. But beyond that he said he would not answer because "it would be obnoxious to a truly free citizen to answer the kinds of questions under compulsion that you require." The Commandant declined to process the application further, relying upon 33 CFR § 121.05 (d) (2), which authorizes him to hold the application in abeyance if an applicant fails or refuses to furnish the additional information.

Appellant thereupon brought this action for declaratory relief that the provisions of the Magnuson Act in question and the Commandant's actions thereunder were unconstitutional, praying that the Commandant be directed to approve his application and that he be enjoined from interfering with appellant's employment upon vessels flying the American flag.

A three-judge court was convened and the complaint was dismissed. 263 F. Supp. 496. The case is here on appeal, 28 U.S.C. § 1253. We postponed the question of jurisdiction to the merits. 389 U.S. 810.

We agree, as does appellee, that the case was one to be heard by a three-judge court and that accordingly we have jurisdiction of this appeal. For appellant did raise the question as to whether the statute was unconstitutional because of vagueness and abridgment of First Amendment rights and also questioned whether the power to install a screening program was validly delegated. A three-judge court was accordingly proper. Baggett v. Bullitt, 377 U.S. 360; Zemel v. Rusk, 381 U.S. 1.

The Magnuson Act gives the President no express authority to set up a screening program for personnel on merchant vessels of the United States. As respects "any foreign-flag vessels" the power to control those who "go or remain on board" is clear. 50 U.S.C. § 191 (a). As respects personnel of our own merchant ships, the power exists under the Act only if it is found in the power to "safeguard" vessels and waterfront facilities against "sabotage or other subversive acts," that is, under § 191 (b). The Solicitor General argues that the power to exclude persons from vessels "clearly implies authority to establish a screening procedure for determining who shall be allowed on board." But that power to exclude is contained in § 191(a) which, as noted, applies to "foreign-flag vessels," while, as we have said, the issue tendered here must find footing in § 191 (b).[3]

We agree with the District Court that keeping our merchant marine free of saboteurs is within the purview of this Act. Our question is a much narrower one.

The Regulations prescribe the standards by which the Commandant is to judge the "character and habits of life" of the employee to determine whether his "presence ... on board" the vessel would be "inimical to the security of the United States":

> (a) Advocacy of the overthrow or alteration of the Government of the United States by unconstitutional means.
>
> (b) Commission of, or attempts or preparations to commit, an act of espionage, sabotage, sedition or treason, or conspiring with, or aiding or abetting another to commit such an act.
>
> (c) Performing, or attempting to perform, duties or otherwise acting so as to serve the interests of another government to the detriment of the United States.
>
> (d) Deliberate unauthorized disclosure of classified defense information.
>
> (e) Membership in, or affiliation or sympathetic association with, any foreign or domestic organization, association, movement, group, or combination of persons designated by the Attorney General pursuant to Executive Order 10450, as amended. [33 CFR § 121.03]

If we assume arguendo that the Act authorizes a type of screening program directed at "membership" or "sympathetic association," the problem raised by it and the Regulations would be kin to the one presented in Shelton v. Tucker, 364 U.S. 479, where a teacher to be hired by a public school of Arkansas had to submit an affidavit "listing all organizations to which he at the time belongs and to which he has belonged during the past five years." Id., at 481.

We held that an Act touching on First Amendment rights must be narrowly drawn so that the precise evil is exposed; that an unlimited and indiscriminate search of the employee's past which interferes with his associational freedom is unconstitutional. Id., at 487-490.

If we gave § 191 (b) the broad construction the Solicitor General urges, we would face here the kind of issue present in Shelton v. Tucker, supra, whether government can probe the reading habits, political philosophy, beliefs, and attitudes on social and economic issues of prospective seamen on our merchant vessels.

A saboteur on a merchant vessel may, of course, be dangerous. But no charge that appellant was a saboteur was made. Indeed, no conduct of appellant was at issue before the Commandant. The propositions tendered in the complaint were (1) plaintiff is now and always has been loyal to the United States; (2) he has not been active in any organization on the Attorney General's list for the past 10 years; (3) he has never committed any act of sabotage or espionage or any act inimical to the security of the United States. Those propositions were neither contested by the Commandant nor conceded. He took the position that admission of evidence on those propositions was "irrelevant and immaterial."

We are loath to conclude that Congress, in its grant of authority to the President to "safeguard" vessels and waterfront facilities from "sabotage or other subversive acts," undertook to reach into the First Amendment area. The provision of the Act in question, 50 U.S.C. § 191 (b), speaks only in terms of actions, not ideas or beliefs or reading habits or social, educational, or political associations.

The purpose of the Constitution and Bill of Rights, unlike more recent models promoting a welfare state, was to take government off the backs of people. The First Amendment's ban against Congress "abridging" freedom of speech, the right peaceably to assemble and to petition, and the "associational freedom" (Shelton v. Tucker, supra, at 490) that goes with those rights create a preserve where the views of the individual are made inviolate. This is the philosophy of Jefferson that "the opinions of men are not the object of civil government, nor under its jurisdiction.... [I]t is time enough for the rightful purposes of civil government for its officers to interfere when principles break out into overt acts against peace and good order...." [4]

No act of sabotage or espionage or any act inimical to the security of the United States is raised or charged in the present case.

In United States v. Rumely, 345 U.S. 41, the Court construed the statutory word "lobbying" to include only direct representation to Congress, its members, and its committees, not all activities tending to influence, encourage, promote, or retard legislation. Id., at 47. Such an interpretation of the statute, it was said, was "in the candid service of avoiding a serious constitutional doubt" (ibid.)--doubts that were serious "in view of the prohibition of the First Amendment." Id., at 46.

The holding in Rumely was not novel. It is part of the stream of authority which admonishes courts to construe statutes narrowly so as to avoid constitutional questions. [5]

The Court said in Rumely, "Whenever constitutional limits upon the investigative power of Congress have to be drawn by this Court, it ought only to be done after Congress has demonstrated its full awareness of what is at stake by unequivocally authorizing an inquiry of dubious limits. Experience admonishes us to tread warily in this domain." 345 U.S., at 46.

The present case involves investigation, not by Congress but by the Executive Branch, stemming from congressional delegation. When we read that delegation with an eye to First Amendment problems, we hesitate to conclude that Congress told the Executive to ferret out the ideological strays in the maritime industry. The words it used--"to safeguard ... from sabotage or other subversive acts"--refer to actions, not to ideas or beliefs. We would have to stretch those words beyond their normal meaning to give them the meaning the Solicitor General urges. Rumely, and its allied cases, teach just the opposite--that statutory words are to be read narrowly so as to avoid questions concerning the "associational freedom" that Shelton v. Tucker protected and concerning other rights within the purview of the First Amendment.

Reversed.

## NOTES

1. Section 191 provides in part:

"Whenever the President finds that the security of the United States is endangered by reason of actual or threatened war, or invasion, or insurrection, or subversive activity, or of disturbances or threatened disturbances of the international relations of the United States, the President is authorized to institute such measures and issue such rules and regulations--

"(a) to govern the anchorage and movement of any foreign-flag vessels in the territorial waters of the United States, to inspect such vessels at any time, to place guards thereon, and, if necessary in his opinion in order to secure such vessels from damage or injury, or to prevent damage or injury to any harbor or waters of the United States, or to secure the observance of rights and obligations of the United States, may take for such purposes full possession and control of such vessels and remove therefrom the officers and crew thereof, and all other persons not especially authorized by him to go or remain on board thereof;

"(b) to safeguard against destruction, loss, or injury from sabotage or other subversive acts, accidents, or other causes of similar nature, vessels, harbors, ports, and waterfront facilities in the United States, the Canal Zone, and all territory and water, continental or insular, subject to the jurisdiction of the United States."

2. "1. With respect to your statements above, furnish the following information, fully and honestly to the best of your ability:

"(a) List the names of the political and social organizations to which you belonged, and location.

"(b) Furnish approximate dates of membership.

"(c) Furnish full particulars concerning the extent of your activities and participation in the organizations (number and type of meetings/functions attended; positions or offices held; classes or schools attended; contributions made; etc.).

"(d) Your reason for discontinuing the membership.

"(e) Your present attitude toward the principles and objectives of the organizations.

"If your answer is 'YES' to the following Questions, <u>explain fully</u> in the space provided at the end of the Interrogatories:

"2. Are you now, or have you ever been, a member of or affiliated with, in any way, the Communist Party, its Subdivisions, Subsidiaries, of Affiliates?

"....................

(Answer 'Yes' or 'No.')

"3. Have you at any time been a subscriber to the People's World'?

".................... If your answer is 'Yes,'

(Answer 'Yes' or 'No.')

give dates.

4. 'Have you at any time engaged in any activities in behalf of the 'People's World'? ..................

(Answer 'Yes' or 'No.')

'If your answer is ''yes,'' furnish details.

"5. What is your present attitude toward the Communist Party?

"6. What is your present attitude toward the principles and objectives of Communism?

"7. What is your attitude toward the form of Government in the United States?"

3. It is true that Senator Magnuson when discussing this measure stated that it "will give the President the authority to invoke the same kind of security measures which were invoked in World War I and in World War II." 96 Cong. Rec. 10795. And from that the Solicitor General argues that the Act authorizes the broad sweeping personnel screening programs which were in force during World War II.

But this reference by Senator Magnuson apparently was to § 191 (a) which, as noted, covers "any foreign-flag vessels." When it came to § 191 (b) Senator Magnuson did not speak in terms of any screening program, but said:

"It [the bill] also has this purpose, which I think is a good one: As I have said before, the last stronghold of subversive activity in this country, in my opinion, or at least the last concentrated stronghold, has been around our waterfronts. It would be impossible for destruction to come to any great port of the United States, of which there are many, as the result of a ship coming into port with an atomic bomb or with biological or other destructive agency, without some liaison ashore. This would give authority to the President to instruct the FBI, in cooperation with the Coast Guard, the Navy, or any other appropriate governmental agency, to go to our water fronts and pick out people who might be subversives or security risks to this country. I think it goes a long way toward taking care of the domestic situation, as related to this subject, particularly in view of the large amount of talk we have had in the Senate within the past few days about Communists. The bill also protects that last loophole which is left, by which there might be some actual destruction along the shores of the United States." 96 Cong. Rec. 11321.

4. A Bill for Establishing Religious Freedom, Jeffersonian Cyclopedia 976 (1900).

5. United States v. Delaware & H. Co., 213 U.S. 366, 407-408; United States v. Harriss, 347 U.S. 612, 618, n. 6; International Machinists v. Street, 367 U.S. 740, 749; Lynch v. Overholser, 369 U.S. 705, 710-711; United States v. National Dairy Corp., 372 U.S. 29, 32.

## Laird v. Tatum, 408 U.S. 1 (1972)

The Supreme Court decides that Army surveillance of peaceful and lawful civilian political activity is not unconstitutional. Douglas dissents, stating in his opinion: "Surveillance of civilians is none of the Army's constitutional business and Congress has not undertaken to entrust it with any such function. The fact that since this litigation started the Army's surveillance may have been cut back is not an end of the matter.... The Constitution was designed to keep government off the backs of the people. The Bill of Rights was added to keep the precincts of belief and expression, of the press, of political and social activities free from surveillance. The Bill of Rights was designed to keep agents of government and official eavesdroppers away from assemblies of people. The aim was to allow men to be free and independent and to assert their rights against government. There can be no influence more paralyzing of that objective than Army surveillance. When an intelligence officer looks over every nonconformist's shoulder in the library, or walks invisibly by his side in a picket line, or infiltrates his club, the America once extolled as the voice of liberty heard around the world no longer is cast in the image which Jefferson and Madison designed...."

* * *

MR. JUSTICE DOUGLAS, with whom MR. JUSTICE MARSHALL concurs, dissenting.

I

If Congress had passed a law authorizing the armed services to establish surveillance over the civilian population, a most serious constitutional problem would be presented. There is, however, no law authorizing surveillance over civilians, which in this case the Pentagon concededly has undertaken. The question is whether such authority may be implied. One can search the Constitution in vain for any such authority.

The start of the problem is the constitutional distinction between the "militia" and the Armed Forces. By Art. I, § 8, of the Constitution the militia is specifically confined to precise duties: "to execute the Laws of the Union, suppress Insurrections and repel Invasions."

This obviously means that the "militia" cannot be sent overseas to fight wars. It is purely a domestic arm of the governors of the several States,[1] save as it may be called under Art. I, § 8, of the Constitution into the federal service. Whether the "militia" could be given powers comparable to those granted the FBI is a question not now raised, for we deal here not with the "militia" but with the "armies." The Army, Navy, and Air Force are comprehended in the constitutional term "armies." Article I, § 8, provides that Congress may "raise and support Armies," and "provide and maintain a Navy," and make "Rules for the Government and Regulation of the land and naval Forces." And the Fifth Amendment excepts from the requirements of a presentment or indictment of a grand jury "cases arising in the land or naval forces, or in the Militia, when in actual service in time of War or public danger."

Acting under that authority, Congress has provided a code governing the Armed Services. That code sets the procedural standards for the Government and regulation of the land and naval forces. It is difficult to imagine how those powers can be extended to military surveillance over civilian affairs.[2]

The most pointed and relevant decisions of the Court on the limitation of military authority concern the attempt of the military to try civilians. The first leading case was Ex parte Milligan, 4 Wall. 2, 124, where the Court noted that the conflict between "civil liberty" and "martial law" is "irreconcilable." The Court which made that announcement would have been horrified at the prospect of the military--absent a regime of martial law--establishing a regime of surveillance over civilians. The power of the military to establish such a system is obviously less than the power of Congress to authorize such surveillance. For the authority of Congress is restricted by its power to "raise" armies, Art. I, § 8; and, to repeat, its authority over the Armed Forces is stated in these terms, "To make Rules for the Government and Regulation of the land and naval Forces."

The Constitution contains many provisions guaranteeing

rights to persons. Those include the right to indictment by a grand jury and the right to trial by jury of one's peers. They include the procedural safeguards of the Sixth Amendment in criminal prosecutions; the protection against double jeopardy, cruel and unusual punishments--and, of course, the First Amendment. The alarm was sounded in the Constitutional Convention about the dangers of the armed services. Luther Martin of Maryland said, "when a government wishes to deprive its citizens of freedom, and reduce them to slavery, it generally makes use of a standing army." [3] That danger, we have held, exists not only in bold acts of usurpation of power but also in gradual encroachments. We held that court-martial jurisdiction cannot be extended to reach any person not a member of the Armed Forces at the times both of the offense and of the trial, which eliminates discharged soldiers. Toth v. Quarles, 350 U.S. 11. Neither civilian employees of the Armed Forces overseas, McElroy v. Guagliardo, 361 U.S. 281; Grishman v. Hagan, 361 U.S. 278, nor civilian dependents of military personnel accompanying them overseas, Kinsella v. Singleton, 361 U.S. 234; Reid v. Covert, 354 U.S. 1, may be tried by court-martial. And even as respects those in the Armed Forces we have held that an offense must be "service connected" to be tried by court-martial rather than by a civilian tribunal. O'Callahan v. Parker, 395 U.S. 258, 272.

The upshot is that the Armed Services--as distinguished from the "militia"--are not regulatory agencies or bureaus that may be created as Congress desires and granted such powers as seem necessary and proper. The authority to provide rules "governing" the Armed Services means the grant of authority to the Armed Services to govern themselves, not the authority to govern civilians. Even when "martial law" is declared, as it often has been, its appropriateness is subject to judicial review, Sterling v. Constantin, 287 U.S. 378, 401, 403-404. [4]

Our tradition reflects a desire for civilian supremacy and subordiantion of military power. The tradition goes back to the Declaration of Independence, in which it was recited that the King "has affected to render the Military independent of and superior to the Civil power." Thus, we have the "militia" restricted to domestic use, the restriction of appropriations to the "armies" to two years, Art. I, §8, and the grant of command over the armies and the militia when called into actual service of the United States to the President, our chief civilian officer. The tradition of civilian control over the Armed Forces was stated by Chief Justice Warren: [5]

> The military establishment is, of course, a necessary organ of government; but the reach of its power must be carefully limited lest the delicate balance between freedom and order be upset. The maintenance of the balance is made more difficult by the fact that while the military serves the vital function of preserving the existence of the nation, it is, at the same time, the one element of government that exercises a type of authority not easily assimilated in a free society....
>
> In times of peace, the factors leading to an extraordinary deference to claims of military necessity have naturally not been as weighty. This has been true even in the all too imperfect peace that has been our lot for the past fifteen years--and quite rightly so, in my judgment. It is instructive to recall that our Nation at the time of the Constitutional Convention was also faced with formidable problems. The English, the French, the Spanish, and various tribes of hostile Indians were all ready and eager to subvert or occupy the fledging Republic. Nevertheless, in that environment, our Founding Fathers conceived a Constitution and Bill of Rights replete with provisions indicating their determination to protect human rights. There was no call for a garrison state in those times of precarious peace. We should heed no such call now. If we were to fail in these days to enforce the freedom that until now has been the American citizen's birthright, we would be abandoning for the foreseeable future the constitutional balance of powers and rights in whose name we arm.

Thus, we have until today consistently adhered to the belief that

> [i]t is an unbending rule of law, that the exercise of military power, where the rights of the citizen are concerned, shall never be pushed beyond what the exigency requires. [Raymond v. Thomas, 91 U.S. 712, 716.

It was in that tradition that Youngstown Sheet & Tube Co. v. Sawyer, 343 U.S. 579, was decided, in which President Truman's seizure of the steel mills in the so-called Korean War was held unconstitutional. As stated by Justice Black:

> The order cannot properly be sustained as an exercise of the President's military power as Commander in Chief of the Armed Forces. The Government attempts to do so by citing a number of cases upholding broad powers in military commanders engaged in day-to-day fighting in a theater of war. Such cases need not concern us here. Even though 'theater of war' be an expanding concept, we cannot with faithfulness to our constitutional system hold that the Commander in Chief of the Armed Forces has the ultimate power as such to take possession of private property in order to keep labor disputes from stopping production. This is a job for the Nation's lawmakers, not for its military authorities. [Id., at 587.]

Madison expressed the fear of military dominance: [6]

> The veteran legions of Rome were an overmatch for the undisciplined valor of all other nations, and rendered her the mistress of the world.
>
> Not the less true is it, that the liberties of Rome proved the final victim to her military triumphs; and that the liberties of Europe, as far as they ever existed, have, with few exceptions, been the price of her military establishments. A standing force, therefore, is a dangerous, at the same time that it may be a necessary provision. On the smallest scale it has its inconveniences. On an extensive scale its consequences may be fatal. On any scale it is an object of laudable circumspection and precaution. A wise nation will combine all these considerations; and, whilst it does not rashly preclude itself from any resource which may become essential to its safety, will exert all its prudence in diminishing both the necessity and the danger of resorting to one which may be inauspicious to its liberties.
>
> The clearest marks of this prudence are stamped on the proposed Constitution. The Union itself, which it cements and secures, destroys every pretext for a military establishment which could be dangerous. America united, with a handful of troops, or without a single soldier, exhibits a more forbidding posture to foreign ambition than America disunited, with a hundred thousand veterans ready for combat.

As Chief Justice Warren has observed, the safeguards in the main body of the Constitution did not satisfy the people on their fear and concern of military dominance: [7]

> They were reluctant to ratify the Constitution without further assurances, and thus we find in the Bill of Rights Amendments 2 and 3, specifically authorizing a decentralized militia, guaranteeing the right of the people to keep and bear arms, and prohibiting the quartering of troops in any house in time of peace without the consent of the owner. Other Amendments guarantee the right of the people to assemble, to be secure in their homes against unreasonable searches and seizures, and in criminal cases to be accorded a speedy and public trial by an impartial jury after indictment in the district and state wherein the crime was committed. The only exceptions made to these civilian trial procedures are for cases arising in the land and naval forces. Although there is undoubtedly room for argument based on the frequently conflicting sources of history, it is not unreasonable to believe that our Founders' determination to guarantee the preeminence of civil over military power was an important element that prompted adoption of the Constitutional Amendments we call the Bill of Rights.

The action in turning the "armies" loose on surveillance of civilians was a gross repudiation of our traditions. The military, though important to us, is subservient and restricted purely to military missions. It even took an Act of Congress to allow a member of the Joint Chiefs of Staff to address the Congress; [8] and that small step did not go unnoticed but was in fact viewed with alarm by those respectful of the civilian tradition. Walter Lippmann has written that during World War II, he was asked to convey a message to Winston Churchill, while the latter was in Washington together with his chiefs of staff. It was desired that Churchill should permit his chiefs of staff to testify before Congress as to the proper strategy for waging the war. Lippmann explains, however, that he "never finished the message. For the old lion let out a roar demanding to know why I was so ignorant of the British way of doing things that I could dare to suggest that a British general should address a parliamentary body.

> As I remember it, what he said was 'I am the Minister of Defense and I, not the generals,

> will state the policy of His Majesty's government. [The Intervention of the General, Washington Post, Apr. 27, 1967, Sec. A, p. 21 col. 1. 9]

The act of turning the military loose on civilians even if sanctioned by an Act of Congress, which it has not been, would raise serious and profound constitutional questions. Standing as it does only on brute power and Pentagon policy, it must be repudiated as a usurpation dangerous to the civil liberties on which free men are dependent. For, as Senator Sam Ervin has said, "this claim of an inherent executive branch power of investigation and surveillance on the basis of people's beliefs and attitudes may be more of a threat to our internal security than any enemies beyond our borders." Privacy and Government Investigations, 1971 U. Ill. L.F. 137, 153.

II

The claim that respondents have no standing to challenge the Army's surveillance of them and the other members of the class they seek to represent is too transparent for serious argument. The surveillance of the Army over the civilian sector--a part of society hitherto immune from its control--is a serious charge. It is alleged that the Army maintains files on the membership, ideology, programs, and practices of virtually every activist political group in the country, including groups such as the Southern Christian Leadership Conference, Clergy and Laymen United Against the War in Vietnam, the American Civil Liberties Union, Women's Strike for Peace, and the National Association for the Advancement of Colored People. The Army uses undercover agents to infiltrate these civilian groups and to reach into confidential files of students and other groups. The Army moves as a secret group among civilian audiences, using cameras and electronic ears for surveillance. The data it collects are distributed to civilian officials in state, federal, and local governments and to each military intelligence unit and troop command under the Army's jurisdiction (both here and abroad); and these data are stored in one or more data banks.

Those are the allegations; and the charge is that the purpose and effect of the system of surveillance is to harass and intimidate the respondents and to deter them from exercising their rights of political expression, protest, and dissent "by invading their privacy, damaging their reputations, adversely affecting their employment and their opportunities for employment, and in other ways." Their fear is that "permanent reports of their activities will be maintained in the Army's data bank, and their 'profiles' will appear in the so-called 'Blacklist' and that all of this information will be released to numerous federal and state agencies upon request."

Judge Wilkey, speaking for the Court of Appeals, properly inferred that this Army surveillance "exercises a present inhibiting effect on their full expression and utilization of their First Amendment rights." 144 U.S. App. D.C. 72, 79, 444 F. 2d 947, 954. That is the test. The "deterrent effect" on First Amendment rights by government oversight marks an unconstitutional intrusion, Lamont v. Postmaster General, 381 U.S. 301, 307. Or, as stated by MR. JUSTICE BRENNAN, "inhibition as well as prohibition against the exercise of precious First Amendment rights is a power denied to government." Id., at 309. When refusal of the Court to pass on the constitutionality of an Act under the normal consideration of forbearance "would itself have an inhibitory effect on freedom of speech" then the Court will act. United States v. Raines, 362 U.S. 17, 22.

As stated by the Supreme Court of New Jersey, "there is good reason to permit the strong to speak for the weak or the timid in First Amendment matters." Anderson v. Sills, 56 N.J. 210, 220, 265 A. 2d 678, 684 (1970).

One need not wait to sue until he loses his job or until his reputation is defamed. To withhold standing to sue until that time arrives would in practical effect immunize from judicial scrutiny all surveillance activities, regardless of their misuse and their deterrent effect. As stated in Flast v. Cohen, 392 U.S. 83, 101, "in terms of Article III limitations on federal court jurisdiction, the question of standing is related only to whether the dispute sought to be adjudicated will be presented in an adversary context and in a form historically viewed as capable of judicial resolution." Or, as we put it in Baker v. Carr, 369 U.S. 186, 204, the gist of the standing issue is whether the party seeking relief has "alleged such a personal stake in the outcome of the controversy as to assure that concrete adverseness which sharpens the presentation of issues upon which the court so largely depends for illumination of difficult constitutional questions."

The present controversy is not a remote, imaginary conflict. Respondents were targets of the Army's surveillance. First, the surveillance was not casual but massive and comprehensive. Second, the intelligence reports were regularly and widely circulated and were exchanged with reports of the FBI, state and municipal police departments, and the CIA. Third, the Army's surveillance was not collecting material in public records but staking out teams of agents, infiltrating undercover agents, creating command posts inside meetings, posing as press photographers and newsmen, posing as TV newsmen, posing as students, and shadowing public figures.

Finally, we know from the hearings conducted by Senator Ervin that the Army has misused or abused its reporting functions. Thus, Senator Ervin concluded that reports of the Army have been "taken from the Intelligence Command's highly inaccurate civil disturbance teletype and filed in Army dossiers on persons who have held, or were being considered for, security clearances, thus contaminating what are supposed to be investigative reports with unverified gossip and rumor. This practice directly jeopardized the employment and employment opportunities of persons seeking sensitive positions with the federal government or defense industry." [10]

Surveillance of civilians is none of the Army's constitutional business and Congress has not undertaken to entrust it with any such function. The fact that since this litigation started this Army's surveillance may have been cut back is not an end of the matter. Whether there has been an actual cutback or whether the announcements are merely a ruse can be determined only after a hearing in the District Court. We are advised by an amicus curiae brief filed by a group of former Army Intelligence Agents that Army surveillance of civilians is rooted in secret programs of long standing:

> Army intelligence has been maintaining an unauthorized watch over civilian political activity for nearly 30 years. Nor is this the first time that Army intelligence has, without notice to its civilian superiors, overstepped its mission. From 1917 to 1924, the Corps of Intelligence Police maintained a massive surveillance of civilian political activity which involved the use of hundreds of civilian informants, the infiltration of civilian organizations and the seizure of dissenters and unionists, sometimes without charges. That activity was opposed--then as now--by civilian officials on those occasions when they found out about it, but it continued unabated until post-war disarmament and economies finally eliminated the bureaucracy that conducted it. [Pp. 29-30.]

This case involves a cancer in our body politic. It is a measure of the disease which afflicts us. Army surveillance, like Army regimentation, is at war with the principles of the First Amendment. Those who already walk submissively will say there is no cause for alarm. But submissiveness is not our heritage. The First Amendment was designed to allow rebellion to remain as our heritage. The Constitution was designed to keep government off the backs of the people. The Bill of Rights was added to keep the precincts of belief and expression, of the press, of political and social activities free from surveillance. The Bill of Rights was designed to keep agents of government and official eavesdroppers away from assemblies of people. The aim was to allow men to be free and independent and to assert their rights against government. There can be no influence more paralyzing of that objective than Army surveillance. When an intelligence officer looks over every nonconformist's shoulder in the library, or walks invisibly by his side in a picket line, or infiltrates his club, the America once extolled as the voice of liberty heard around the world no longer is cast in the image which Jefferson and Madison designed, but more in the Russian image, depicted in Appendix III to this opinion.

## APPENDIX I TO OPINION OF DOUGLAS, J., DISSENTING

The narrowly circumscribed domestic role which Congress has by statute authorized the Army to play is clearly an insufficient basis for the wholesale civilian surveillance of which respondents complain. The entire domestic mission of the armed services is delimited by nine statutes.

Four define the Army's narrow role as a back-up for civilian authority where the latter has proved insufficient to cope with insurrection:

10 U. S. C. § 331:

"Whenever there is an insurrection in any State against its government, the President may, upon the request of its legislature or of its governor if the legislature cannot be convened, call into Federal service such of the militia of the other States, in the number requested by that State, and use such of the armed forces, as he considers necessary to suppress the insurrection."

10 U.S.C. § 332:

"Whenever the President considers that unlawful obstructions, combinations, or assemblages, or rebellion against the authority of the United States, make it impracticable to enforce the laws of the United States in any State or Territory by the ordinary course of judicial proceedings, he may call into Federal service such of the militia of any State, and use such of the armed forces, as he considers necessary to enforce those laws to suppress the rebellion."

10 U.S.C. § 333:

"The President, by using the militia or the armed forces, or both, or by any other means, shall take such measures as he considers necessary to suppress, in a State, any insurrection, domestic violence, unlawful combination, or conspiracy, if it--

"(1) so hinders the execution of the laws of that State, and of the United States within the State, that any part or class of its people is deprived of a right, privilege, immunity, or protection named in the Constitution and secured by law, and the constituted authorities of that State are unable, fail, or refuse to protect that right, privilege, or immunity, or to give that protection; or

"(2) opposes or obstructs the execution of the laws of the United States or impedes the course of justice under those laws.

"In any situation covered by clause (1), the State shall be considered to have denied the equal protection of the laws secured by the Constitution."

10 U.S.C. § 334:

"Whenever the President considers it necessary to use the militia or the armed forces under this chapter, he shall, by proclamation, immediately order the insurgents to disperse and retire peaceably to their abodes within a limited time."

Two statutes, passed as a result of Reconstruction Era military abuses, prohibit military interference in civilian elections:

18 U.S.C. § 592:

"Whoever, being an officer of the Army or Navy, or

other person in the civil, military, or naval service of the United States, orders, brings, keeps, or has under his authority or control any troops or armed men at any place where a general or special election is held, unless such force be necessary to repel armed enemies of the United States, shall be fined not more than $5,000 or imprisoned not more than five years, or both; and be disqualified from holding any office of honor, profit, or trust under the United States.

"This section shall not prevent any officer or member of the armed forces of the United States from exercising the right of suffrage in any election district to which he may belong, if otherwise qualified according to the laws of the State in which he offers to vote."

18 U.S.C. §593:

"Whoever, being an officer or member of the Armed Forces of the United States, prescribes or fixes or attempts to prescribe or fix, whether by proclamation, order or otherwise, the qualifications of voters at any election in any State; or

"Whoever, being such officer or member, prevents or attempts to prevent by force, threat, intimidation, advice or otherwise any qualified voter of any State from fully exercising the right of suffrage at any general or special election; or

"Whoever, being such officer or member, orders or compels or attempts to compel any election officer in any State to receive a vote from a person not legally qualified to vote; or

"Whoever, being such officer or member, imposes or attempts to impose any regulations for conducting any general or special election in a State, different from those prescribed by law; or

"Whoever, being such officer or member, interferes in any manner with an election officer's discharge of his duties--

"Shall be fined not more than $5,000 or imprisoned not more than five years, or both; and disqualified from holding any office of honor, profit or trust under the United States.

"This section shall not prevent any officer or member of the Armed Forces from exercising the right of suffrage in any district to which he may belong, if otherwise qualified according to the laws of the State of such district."

Another Resconstruction Era statute forbids the use of military troops as a posse comitatus:

18 U.S.C. §1385:

"Whoever, except in cases and under circumstances expressly authorized by the Constitution or Act of Congress, willfully uses any part of the Army or the Air Force as a posse comitatus or otherwise to execute the laws shall be fined not more than $10,000 or imprisoned not more than two years, or both."

Finally, there are two specialized statutes. It was thought necessary to pass an Act of Congress to give the armed services some limited power to control prostitution near military bases, and an Act of Congress was required to enable a member of the Joint Chiefs of Staff to testify before Congress:

18 U.S.C. §1384:

"Within such reasonable distance of any military or naval camp, station, fort, post, yard, base, cantonment, training or mobilization place as the Secretary of the Army, the Secretary of the Navy, the Secretary of the Air Force, or any two or all of them shall determine to be needful to the efficiency, health, and welfare of the Army, the Navy, or the Air Force, and shall designate and publish in general orders or bulletins, whoever engages in prostitution or aids or abets prostitution or procures or solicits for purposes of prostitution, or keeps or sets up a house of ill fame, brothel, or bawdy house, or receives any person for purposes of lewdness, assignation, or prostitution into any vehicle, conveyance, place, structure, or building, or permits any person to remain for the purpose of lewdness, assignation, or prostitution in any vehicle, conveyance, place, structure, or building or leases or rents or contracts to lease or rent any vehicle, conveyance, place, structure or building, or part thereof, knowing or with good reason to know that it is intended to be used for any of the purposes herein prohibited shall be fined not more than $1,000 or imprisoned not more than one year, or both.

"The Secretaries of the Army, Navy, and Air Force and the Federal Security Administrator shall take such steps as they deem necessary to suppress and prevent such violations thereof, and shall accept the cooperation of the authorities of States and their counties, districts, and other political subdivisions in carrying out the purpose of this section.

"This section shall not be construed as conferring on the personnel of the Departments of the Army, Navy, or Air Force or the Federal Security Agency any authority to make criminal investigations, searches, seizures, or arrests of civilians charged with violations of this section."

10 U.S.C. §141 (e):

"After first informing the Secretary of Defense, a member of the Joint Chiefs of Staff may make such recommendations to Congress relating to the Department of Defense as he may consider appropriate."

## APPENDIX II TO OPINION OF DOUGLAS, J., DISSENTING

Walter Lippman gave the following account of his conversation with Churchill:

> The President's bringing Gen. Westmoreland home in order to explain the war reminds me of an instructive afternoon spent during the Second World War. The country and the Congress were divided on the question of whether to strike first against Hitler or first against Japan. Churchill and Roosevelt had agreed on the policy of Hitler first. But there were large and powerful groups in the country, many of them former isolationists in the sense that they were anti-European, who wanted to concentrate American forces on winning the war against Japan. Even the American chiefs of staff were divided on this question of high strategy.
>
> Churchill had come to Washington, accompanied by the British chiefs of staff, to work out with President Roosevelt and the Administration the general plan of the global war. One morning I had a telephone call from Sen. Austin, who was a strong believer in the Churchill-Roosevelt line. He said in effect, 'I know you are seeing the Prime Minister this afternoon and I wish you would ask him to tell his chiefs of staff to come to Congress and testify in favor of our strategical policy.' Quite innocently I said I would do this, and when Churchill received me that afternoon I began by saying that I had a message from Sen. Austin. 'Would the Prime Minister instruct his chiefs of staff to go to the Senate Foreign Relations Committee....' I never finished the message. For the old lion let out a roar demanding to know why I was so ignorant of the British way of doing things that I could dare to suggest that a British general should address a parliamentary body.

> As I remember it, what he said was, 'I am the Minister of Defense and I, not the generals, will state the policy of His Majesty's government.'
>
> No one who ever aroused the wrath of Churchill is likely to forget it. I certainly have not forgotten it. I learned an indelible lesson about one of the elementary principles of democratic government. And therefore, I take a very sour view of a field commander being brought home by the President to educate the Congress and the American people.

Our military added political departments to their staffs. A Deputy Chief of Naval Operations, Military Policy Division, was first established in the Department of the Navy by President Truman in 1945. In the Office of Secretary of Defense that was done by President Truman in 1947, the appointee eventually becoming Assistant Secretary for International Security Affairs. A like office was established in 1961 in the Department of the Army by President Kennedy and another for the Air Force in 1957 by President Eisenhower. Thus, when the Pentagon entered a Washington, D.C., conference, its four "Secretaries of State" faced the real Secretary of State and more frequently than not talked or stared him down. The Pentagon's "Secretaries of State" usually spoke in unison; they were clear and decisive with no ifs, ands, or buts, and in policy conferences usually carried the day.

By 1968 the Pentagon was spending $34 million a year on non-military social and behavioral science research both at home and abroad. One related to "witchcraft, sorcery, magic, and other psychological phenomena" in the Congo. Another concerned the "political influence of university students in Latin America." Other projects related to the skill of Korean women as divers, snake venoms in the Middle East, and the like. Research projects were going on for the Pentagon in 40 countries in sociology, psychology, and behavioral sciences.

The Pentagon became so powerful that no President would dare crack down on it and try to regulate it.

The military approach to world affairs conditioned our thinking and our planning after World War II.

We did not realize that to millions of these people there was no difference between a Communist dictatorship and the dictatorship under which they presently lived. We did not realize that in some regions of Asia it was the Communist party that identified itself with the so-called reform programs, the other parties being mere instruments for keeping a ruling class in power. We did not realize that, in the eyes of millions of illiterates, the choice between democracy and communism was not the critical choice it would be for us.

We talked about "saving democracy." But the real question in Asia, the Middle East, Africa, and Latin America was whether democracy would ever be born.

We forgot that democracy in most lands is an empty word. We asked illiterate people living at the subsistence level to furnish staging grounds for a military operation whose outcome, in their eyes, had no relation to their own welfare. Those who rejected our overtures must be communists, we said. Those who did not approve our military plans must be secretly aligning with Russia, we thought.

So it was that in underdeveloped areas we became identified not with ideas of freedom, but with bombs, planes, and tanks. We thought less and less in terms of defeating communism with programs of political action, more and more in terms of defeating communism with military might. Our foreign aid mounted; but nearly 70% of it was military aid.

Our fears mounted as the cold war increased in intensity. These fears had many manifestations. The communist threat inside the country was magnified and exalted far beyond its realities. Irresponsible talk fanned the flames. Accusations were loosely made. Character assassinations were common. Suspicion took the place of goodwill. We needed to debate with impunity and explore to the edges of problems. We needed to search to the horizon for answers to perplexing problems. We needed confidence in each other. But in the 40's, 50's, and 60's suspicions grew. Innocent acts became telltale marks of disloyalty. The coincidence that an idea paralleled Soviet Russia's policy for a moment of time settled an aura of doubt around a person. The Intervention of the General, Washington Post, Apr. 27, 1967, Sec. A, p. 21, col. 1.

## APPENDIX III TO OPINION OF DOUGLAS, J., DISSENTING

Alexander I. Solzhenitsyn, the noted Soviet author, made the following statement March 30, 1972, concerning surveillance of him and his family (reported in the Washington Post, Apr. 3, 1972):

"A kind of forbidden, contaminated zone has been created around my family, and to this day, there are people in Ryazan [where Solzhenitsyn used to live] who were dismissed from their jobs for having visited my house a few years ago. A corresponding member of the Academy of Sciences, T. Timofeyev, who is director of a Moscow institute, became so scared when he found out that a mathematician working under him was my wife that he dismissed her with unseemly haste, although this was just after she had given birth and contrary to all laws...

"It happens that an informant [for his new book on the history of prerevolutionary Russia] may meet with me. We work an hour or two and as soon as he leaves my house, he will be closely followed, as if he were a state criminal, and they will investigate his background, and then go on to find out who this man meets, and then, in turn, who that [next] person is meeting.

"Of course they cannot do this with everyone. The state security people have their schedule, and their own profound reasoning. On some days, there is no surveillance at all, or only superficial surveillance. On other days, they hang around, for example when Heinrich Boll came to see me [he is a German writer who recently visited Moscow]. They will put a car in front of each of the two approaches [to the courtyard of the apartment house where he stays in Moscow] with three men in each car--and they don't work only one shift. Then off they go after my visitors, or they trail people who leave on foot.

"And if you consider that they listen around the clock to telephone conversations and conversations in my home, they analyze recording tapes and all correspondence, and then collect and compare all these data in some vast premises--and these people are not underlings--you cannot but be amazed that so many idlers in the prime of life and strength, who could be better occupied with productive work for the benefit of the fatherland, are busy with my friends and me, and keep inventing enemies."

NOTES

1. I have expressed my doubts whether the "militia" loses its constitutional role by an Act of Congress which incorporates it in the armed services. Drifka v. Brainard, 89 S. Ct. 434, 21 L. Ed. 2d 427.

2. See Appendix I to this opinion, infra, p. 29.

3. 3 M. Farrand, Records of the Federal Convention 209 (1911).

4. Even some actions of the Armed Services in regulating their own conduct may be properly subjected to judicial scrutiny. Those who are not yet in the Armed Services have the protection of the full panoply of the laws governing admission procedures, see, e.g., McKart v. United States, 395 U.S. 185; Oestereich v. Selective Service Board, 393 U.S. 233. Those in the service may use habeas corpus to test the jurisdiction of the Armed Services to try or detain them, see, e.g., Parisi v. Davidson, 405 U.S. 34; Noyd v. Bond, 395 U.S. 683, 696 n. 8; Reid v. Covert, 354 U.S. 1; Billings v. Truesdell, 321 U.S. 542. And, those in the Armed Services may seek the protection of civilian, rather than military, courts when charged with crimes not service connected, O'Callahan v. Parker, 395 U.S. 258.

5. The Bill of Rights and the Military, 37 N.Y.U.L. Rev. 181, 182, 193 (1962).

6. The Federalist No. 41.

7. N. 5, supra, at 185.

8. The National Security Act of 1947, amended by § 5 of the Act of Aug. 10. 1949. 63 Stat. 580, provided in § 202 (c) (6):

"No provision of this Act shall be so construed as to prevent a Secretary of a military department or a member of the Joint Chiefs of Staff from presenting to the Congress, on his own initiative, after first so informing the Secretary of Defense, any recommendation relating to the Department of Defense that he may deem proper." See H.R. Conf. Rep. No. 1142, 81st Cong., 1st Sess., 18. This provision is now codified as 10 U.S.C. § 141 (e).

9. The full account is contained in Appendix II, infra, at 33.

10. Hearings on Federal Data Banks, Computers and the Bill of Rights, before the Subcommittee on Constitutional Rights of the Senate Committee on the Judiciary, 92d Cong., 1st Sess. (1971).

# GROUP AND INDIVIDUAL LIBEL

## Beauharnais v. Illinois, 343 U.S. 250 (1952)

The Supreme Court upholds the conviction of Beauharnais, who had been found guilty in Illinois of distributing racist literature. Douglas dissents, declaring in his opinion: "Emotions sway speakers and audiences alike. Intemperate speech is a distinctive characteristic of man. Hotheads blow off and release destructive energy in the process. They shout and rave, exaggerating weaknesses, magnifying error, viewing with alarm. So it has been from the beginning; and so it will be throughout time. The Framers of the Constitution knew human nature as well as we do. They too had lived in dangerous days; they too knew the suffocating influence of orthodoxy and standardized thought. They weighed the complusions for restrained speech and thought against the abuses of liberty. They chose liberty. That should be our choice today no matter how distasteful to us the pamphlet of Beauharnais may be."

* * *

MR. JUSTICE DOUGLAS, dissenting.

Hitler and his Nazis showed how evil a conspiracy could be which was aimed at destroying a race by exposing it to contempt, derision, and obloquy. I would be willing to concede that such conduct directed at a race or group in this country could be made an indictable offense. For such a project would be more than the exercise of free speech. Like picketing, it would be free speech plus.

I would also be willing to concede that even without the element of conspiracy there might be times and occasions when the legislative or executive branch might call a halt to inflammatory talk, such as the shouting of "fire" in a school or a theatre.

My view is that if in any case other public interests are to override the plain command of the First Amendment, the peril of speech must be clear and present, leaving no room for argument, raising no doubts as to the necessity of curbing speech in order to prevent disaster.

The First Amendment is couched in absolute terms--freedom of speech shall not be abridged. Speech has therefore a preferred position[1] as contrasted to some other civil rights. For example, privacy, equally sacred to some, is protected by the Fourth Amendment only against unreasonable searches and seizures. There is room for regulation of the ways and means of invading privacy. No such leeway is granted the invasion of the right of free speech guaranteed by the First Amendment. Until recent years that had been the course and direction of constitutional law. Yet recently the Court in this and in other cases[2] has engrafted the right of regulation onto the First Amendment by placing in the hands of the legislative branch the right to regulate "within reasonable limits" the right of free speech. This to me is an ominous and alarming trend. The free trade in ideas which the Framers of the Constitution visualized disappears. In its place there is substituted a new orthodoxy--an orthodoxy that changes with the whims of the age or the day, an orthodoxy which the majority by solemn judgment proclaims to be essential to the safety, welfare, security, morality, or health of society. Free speech in the constitutional sense disappears. Limits are drawn--limits dictated by expediency, political opinion, prejudices or some other desideratum of legislative action.

An historic aspect of the issue of judicial supremacy was the extent to which legislative judgment would be supreme in the field of social legislation. The vague contours of the Due Process Clause were used to strike down laws deemed by the Court to be unwise and improvident.[3] That trend has been reversed. In matters relating to business, finance, industrial and labor conditions, health and the public welfare, great leeway is now granted the legislature,[4] for there is no guarantee in the Constitution that the status quo will be preserved against regulation by government. Freedom of speech, however, rests on a different constitutional basis. The First Amendment says that freedom of speech, freedom of press, and the free exercise of religion shall not be abridged. That is a negation of power on the part of each and every department of government. Free speech, free press, free exercise of religion are placed separate and apart; they are above and beyond the police power; they are not subject to regulation in the manner of factories, slums, apartment houses, production of oil, and the like.

The Court in this and in other cases places speech

under an expanding legislative control. Today a white man stands convicted for protesting in unseemly language against our decisions invalidating restrictive covenants. Tomorrow a Negro will be haled before a court for denouncing lynch law in heated terms. Farm laborers in the West who compete with field hands drifting up from Mexico; whites who feel the pressure of orientals; a minority which finds employment going to members of the dominant religious group--all of these are caught in the mesh of today's decision. Debate and argument even in the courtroom are not always calm and dispassionate. Emotions sway speakers and audiences alike. Intemperate speech is a distinctive characteristic of man. Hotheads blow off and release destructive energy in the process. They shout and rave, exaggerating weaknesses, magnifying error, viewing with alarm. So it has been from the beginning; and so it will be throughout time. The Framers of the Constitution knew human nature as well as we do. They too had lived in dangerous days; they too knew the suffocating influence of orthodoxy and standardized thought. They weighed the complusions for restrained speech and thought against the abuses of liberty. They chose liberty. That should be our choice today no matter how distasteful to us the pamphlet of Beauharnais may be. It is true that this is only one decision which may later be distinguished or confined to narrow limits. But it represents a philosophy at war with the First Amendment--a constitutional interpretation which puts free speech under the legislative thumb. It reflects an influence moving ever deeper into our society. It is notice to the legislatures that they have the power to control unpopular blocs. It is a warning to every minority that when the Constitution guarantees free speech it does not mean what it says.

NOTES

1. Murdock v. Pennsylvania, 319 U.S. 105, 115; Thomas v. Collins, 323 U.S. 516, 530; Saia v. New York, 334 U.S. 558, 561.

2. Dennis v. United States, 341 U.S. 494; Feiner v. New York, 340 U.S. 315. Cf. Breard v. Alexandria, 341 U.S. 622; American Communications Assn. v. Douds, 339 U.S. 382; Osman v. Douds, 339 U.S. 846.

3. Lochner v. New York, 198 U.S. 45; Coppage v. Kansas, 236 U.S. 1; Ribnik v. McBride, 277 U.S. 350.

4. Nebbia v. New York, 291 U.S. 502; West Coast Hotel Co. v. Parrish, 300 U.S. 379; Lincoln Union v. Northwestern Co., 335 U.S. 525; Day-Brite Lighting, Inc. v. Missouri, 342 U.S. 421.

Rosenblatt v. Baer, 383 U.S. 75 (1966)

The Supreme Court decides in a libel case that "an otherwise impersonal attack on governmental operations cannot be used to establish defamation of those administering such operations absent evidence that the implication of wrongdoing was read as specifically directed at the plaintiff, whether he is considered a public official or a member of a group responsible for governmental operations, and whether or not others were also implicated." Douglas states in his concurring opinion: "In my view the First Amendment would bar Congress from passing any libel law, the Alien and Sedition Act (1 Stat. 596) to the contrary notwithstanding."

* * *

MR. JUSTICE DOUGLAS, concurring.

In New York Times Co. v. Sullivan, 376 U.S. 254, we dealt with elected officials.[1] We now have the question as to how far its principles extend or how far down the hierarchy we should go.

The problems presented are considerable ones. Maybe the key man in a hierarchy is the night watchman responsible for thefts of state secrets. Those of us alive in the 1940's and 1950's witnessed the dreadful ordeal of people in the public service being pummelled by those inside and outside government, with charges that were false, abusive, and damaging to the extreme. Many of them, unlike the officials in New York Times who ran for election, rarely had opportunity for rejoinder.

Yet if free discussion of public issues is the guide, I see no way to draw lines that exclude the night watchman, the file clerk, the typist, or, for that matter, anyone on the public payroll. And how about those who contract to carry out governmental missions? Some of them are as much in the public domain as any so-called officeholder. And how about the dollar-a-year man, whose prototype was publicized in United States v. Mississippi Valley Generating Co., 364 U.S.

520?[2] And the industrialists who raise the price of a basic commodity? Are not steel and aluminum in the public domain? And the labor leader who combines trade unionism with bribery and racketeering? Surely the public importance of collective bargaining puts labor as well as management into the public arena so far as the present constitutional issue is concerned.[3]

The Court in Thornhill v. Alabama, 310 U.S. 88, 101-102, put the issue as follows:

> The freedom of speech and of the press guaranteed by the Constitution embraces at the least the liberty to discuss publicly and truthfully all matters of public concern without previous restraint or fear of subsequent punishment. The exigencies of the colonial period and the efforts to secure freedom from oppressive administration developed a broadened conception of these liberties as adequate to supply the public need for information and education with respect to the significant issues of the times.... Freedom of discussion, if it would fulfill its historic function in this nation, must embrace all issues about which information is needed or appropriate to enable the members of society to cope with the exigencies of their period.

If the term "public official" were a constitutional term, we would be stuck with it and have to give it content. But the term is our own; and so long as we are fashioning a rule of free discussion of public issues, I cannot relate it only to those who, by the Court's standard, are deemed to hold public office.

The question in final analysis is the extent to which the Due Process Clause of the Fourteenth Amendment has displaced the libel laws of the States. I do not suppose anyone would have thought in those terms at the time the Amendment was adopted. But constitutional law is not frozen as of a particular moment of time. It was indeed not until 1931 that this Court squarely held that the First Amendment was applicable to the States by reason of the Fourteenth (Stromberg v. California, 283 U.S. 359, 368-369)--New York Times being merely an application and extension of that principle. But since freedom of speech is now the guideline, do state libel laws have any place at all in our constitutional system, at least when it comes to public issues? If freedom of speech is the guide, why is it restricted to speech addressed to the larger public matters and not applicable to speech at the lower levels of science, the humanities, the professions, agriculture, and the like?

In my view the First Amendment would bar Congress from passing any libel law, the Alien and Sedition Act (1 Stat. 596) to the contrary notwithstanding. Some think that due process as applied to the States is a watered-down federal version as respects the guarantees in the Bill of Rights that are incorporated into the Fourteenth Amendment. See, e.g., Roth v. United States, 354 U.S. 476, 501 (separate opinion); Beauharnais v. Illinois, 343 U.S. 250, 287 (dissenting opinion). That has been the minority view, the majority maintaining that there is no difference. If there is no difference and if I am right in assuming Congress could not constitutionally pass a libel law, then the question is whether a public issue, not a public official, is involved. [4]

The case is therefore for me in a different posture than the one discussed by the Court. I would prefer to dismiss the writ as improvidently granted. [5] To facilitate our work, [6] however, I have decided to join Part II of the Court's opinion, as well as MR. JUSTICE BLACK'S separate opinion, and to concur in the judgment.

## NOTES

1. And cf. Farmers Union v. WDAY, 360 U.S. 525, holding that a radio station is not liable for defamatory statements made in a speech broadcast over such station under § 315 (a) of the Federal Communications Act of 1934 by a candidate for public office.

2. He in fact received no compensation from the Government, but was given $10 per day in lieu of subsistence, plus transportation expenses. See 364 U.S., at 533.

3. Cf. Linn v. United Plant Guard Workers, ante, p. 53, where the principle of New York Times Co. v. Sullivan, supra, is extended via the path of pre-emption, to the field of labor relations.

4. There is the view that the "most absolute construction of the First Amendment, as applied to the states by the

Fourteenth, would permit a line to be drawn between the spurious common law of seditious libel and the genuine common law of civil liability for defamation of private character." Brant, The Bill of Rights: Its Origin and Meaning 502-503 (1965). But that ipse dixit overlooks our decisions which, without defining the outer limits, establish that the First Amendment applies to both. Compare New York Times Co. v. Sullivan, supra, with Garrison v. Louisiana, 379 U.S. 64.

5. The complaint was drawn and the trial conducted in conformity with the defamation law as it existed prior to New York Times. Whether the complaint can be amended to conform to the theory of liability announced in New York Times is wholly a matter of state law. See N.H. Rev. Stat. Ann. § 514:9 (1955). Whether there can be a new trial is also wholly a matter of state law. See N.H. Rev. Stat. Ann. § 526:1 (1955). Whether respondent is a "public official" in the New York Times sense in not ascertainable from the record. We do not even know whether he took an oath of office. So far as we know, he may, have been a hybrid in the nature of an independent contractor. Moreover, the oral argument and the briefs were not squarely addressed to the larger and profoundly important questions stirred by this litigation.

6. Cf. Mr. Justice Rutledge in Screws v. United States, 325 U.S. 91, 113, 134.

## Time, Inc. v. Hill, 385 U.S. 374 (1967)

The Supreme Court reverses a lower court judgment that had awarded a Pennsylvania family $30,000 damages to be paid by Time, Inc., publishers of Life magazine, which had published an article in 1955 linking the play The Desperate Hours with the family's experience of being held hostage by three escaped convicts in 1952. "The complaint sought damages ... on allegations that the Life article was intended to, and did, give the impression that the play mirrored the Hill family's experience, which, to the knowledge of defendant ' ... was false and untrue.' " In his concurring opinion Douglas writes: "A fictionalized treatment of the event is, in my view, as much in the public domain as would be a watercolor of the assassination of a public official. It seems to me irrelevant to talk of any right to privacy in this context. Here a private person is catapulted into the news by events over which he had no control."

* * *

MR. JUSTICE DOUGLAS, concurring.

As intimated in my separate opinion in Rosenblatt v. Baer, 383 U.S. 75, 88, and in the opinion of my Brother BLACK in the same case, id., at 94, state action to abridge freedom of the press is barred by the First and Fourteenth Amendments where the discussion concerns matters in the public domain. The episode around which this book was written had been news of the day for some time. The most that can be said is that the novel, the play, and the magazine article revived that interest. A fictionalized treatment of the event is, in my view, as much in the public domain as would be a watercolor of the assassination of a public official. It seems to me irrelevant to talk of any right of privacy in this context. Here a private person is catapulted into the news by events over which he had no control. He and his activities are then in the public domain as fully as the matters at issue in New York Times Co. v. Sullivan, 376 U.S. 254. Such privacy as a person normally has ceases when his life has ceased to be private.

Once we narrow the ambit of the First Amendment, creative writing is imperiled and the "chilling effect" on free expression which we feared in Dombrowski v. Pfister, 380 U.S. 479, 487,[1] is almost sure to take place. That is, I fear, the result once we allow an exception for "knowing or reckless falsity." Such an elusive exception gives the jury, the finder of the facts, broad scope and almost unfettered discretion. A trial is a chancy thing, no matter what safeguards are provided. To let a jury on this record return a verdict or not as it chooses is to let First Amendment rights ride on capricious or whimsical circumstances, for emotions and prejudices often do carry the day. The exception for "knowing or reckless falsity" is therefore, in my view, an abridgment of speech that is barred by the First and Fourteenth Amendments. But as indicated in my Brother BLACK'S opinion I have joined the Court's opinion in order to make possible an adjudication that controls this litigation. Cf. Mr. Justice Rutledge, concurring, Screws v. United States, 325 U.S. 91, 113, 134.

NOTE

1. And see Baggett v. Bullitt, 377 U.S. 360; NAACP v. Button, 371 U.S. 415.

Gertz v. Robert Welch, Inc., 418 U.S. 323 (1974)

A John Birch Society publication labels an attorney a "Leninist" and a "communist fronter." The Supreme Court reverses a lower court decision that had held such language was not libelous, the Supreme Court arguing that Gertz, the attorney, was not a "public figure." Douglas dissents, declaring in his opinion: "I have stated before my view that the First Amendment would bar Congress from passing any libel law. This was the view held by Thomas Jefferson and it is one Congress has never challenged through enactment of a civil libel statute.... With the First Amendment made applicable to the States through the Fourteenth, I do not see how States have any more ability to 'accommodate' freedoms of speech or of the press than does Congress."

* * *

MR. JUSTICE DOUGLAS, dissenting.

The Court describes this case as a return to the struggle of "defin[ing] the proper accommodation between the law of defamation and the freedoms of speech and press protected by the First Amendment." It is indeed a struggle, once described by Mr. Justice Black as "the same quagmire" in which the Court "is now helplessly struggling in the field of obscenity." Curtis Publishing Co. v. Butts, 388 U.S. 130, 171 (concurring opinion). I would suggest that the struggle is a quite hopeless one, for, in light of the command of the First Amendment, no "accommodation" of its freedoms can be "proper" except those made by the Framers themselves.

Unlike the right of privacy which, by the terms of the Fourth Amendment, must be accommodated with reasonable searches and seizures and warrants issued by magistrates, the rights of free speech and of a free press were protected by the Framers in verbiage whose proscription seems clear. I have stated before my view that the First Amendment would bar Congress from passing any libel law.[1] This was the view held by Thomas Jefferson[2] and it is one Congress has never challenged through enactment of a civil libel statute. The sole congressional attempt at this variety of First Amendment muzzle was in the Sedition Act of 1798--a criminal libel act never tested in this Court and one which expired by its terms three years after enactment. As President, Thomas Jefferson pardoned those who were convicted under the Act, and fines levied in its prosecution were repaid by Act of Congress.[3] The general consensus was that the Act constituted a regrettable legislative exercise plainly in violation of the First Amendment.[4]

With the First Amendment made applicable to the States through the Fourteenth,[5] I do not see how States have any more ability to "accommodate" freedoms of speech or of the press than does Congress. This is true whether the form of the accommodation is civil or criminal since "[w]hat a State may not constitutionally bring about by means of a criminal statute is likewise beyond the reach of its civil law of libel." New York Times Co. v. Sullivan, 376 U. S. 254, 277. Like Congress, States are without power "to use a civil libel law or any other law to impose damages for merely discussing public affairs." Id., at 295 (Black, J., concurring).[6]

Continued recognition of the possibility of state libel suits for public discussion of public issues leaves the freedom of speech honored by the Fourteenth Amendment a diluted version of First Amendment protection. This view is only possible if one accepts the position that the First Amendment is applicable to the States only through the Due Process Clause of the Fourteenth, due process freedom of speech being only that freedom which this Court might deem to be "implicit in the concept of ordered liberty."[7] But the Court frequently has rested state free speech and free press decisions on the Fourteenth Amendment generally[8] rather than on the Due Process Clause alone. The Fourteenth Amendment speaks not only of due process but also of "privileges and immunities" of United States citizenship. I can conceive of no privilege or immunity with a higher claim to recognition against state abridgment than the freedoms of speech and of the press. In our federal system we are all subject to two governmental regimes, and freedoms of speech and of the press protected against the infringement of only one are quite illusory. The identity of the oppressor is, I would think, a matter of relative indifference to the oppressed.

There can be no doubt that a State impinges upon free and open discussion when it sanctions the imposition of damages for such discussion through its civil libel laws. Discussion of public affairs is often marked by highly charged emotions, and jurymen, not unlike us all, are subject to those emotions. It is indeed this very type of speech which is the reason for the First Amendment since speech which arouses little emotion is little in need of protection. The vehicle for publication in this case was the American Opinion, a most controversial periodical which disseminates the views of the John Birch Society, an organization which many deem to be quite offensive. The subject matter involved "Communist plots," "conspiracies against law enforcement agencies," and the killing of a private citizen by the police. With any such amalgam of controversial elements pressing upon the jury, a jury determination, unpredictable in the most neutral circumstances, becomes for those who venture to discuss heated issues, a virtual roll of the dice separating them from liability for often massive claims of damage.

It is only the hardy publisher who will engage in discussion in the face of such risk, and the Court's preoccupation with proliferating standards in the area of libel increases the risks. It matters little whether the standard be articulated as "malice" or "reckless disregard of the truth" or "negligence," for jury determinations by any of those criteria are virtually unreviewable. This Court, in its continuing delineation of variegated mantles of First Amendment protection, is, like the potential publisher, left with only speculation on how jury findings were influences by the effect the subject matter of the publication had upon the minds and viscera of the jury. The standard announced today leaves the States free to "define for themselves the appropriate standard of liability for a publisher or broadcaster" in the circumstances of this case. This of course leaves the simple negligence standard as an option, with the jury free to impose damages upon a finding that the publisher failed to act as "a reasonable man." With such continued erosion of First Amendment protection, I fear that it may well be the reasonable man who refrains from speaking.

Since in my view the First and Fourteenth Amendments prohibit the imposition of damages upon respondent for this discussion of public affairs, I would affirm the judgment below.

NOTES

1. See, e.g., Rosenblatt v. Baer, 383 U.S. 75, 90 (concurring).

2. In 1798 Jefferson stated:
"[The First Amendment] thereby guard[s] in the same sentence, and under the same words, the freedom of religion, of speech, and of the press: insomuch, that whatever violates either, throws down the sanctuary which covers the others, and that libels, falsehood, and defamation, equally with heresy and false religion, are withheld from the cognizance of federal tribunals.... " 8 The Works of Thomas Jefferson 464-465 (Ford ed. 1904) (emphasis added).

3. See, e.g., Act of July 4, 1840, c. 45, 6 Stat. 802, accompanied by H.R.Rep. No. 86, 26th Cong., 1st Sess. (1840).

4. Senator Calhoun in reporting to Congress assumed the invalidity of the Act to be a matter "which no one now doubts." Report with Senate Bill No. 122, S. Doc. No. 118, 24th Cong., 1st Sess., 3 (1836).

5. See Stromberg v. California, 283 U.S. 359, 368-369.

6. Since this case involves a discussion of public affairs, I need not decide at this point whether the First Amendment prohibits all libel actions. "An unconditional right to say what one pleases about public affairs is what I consider to be the minimum guarantee of the First Amendment." New York Times Co. v. Sullivan, 376 U.S. 254, 297 (Black, J., concurring) (emphasis added). But "public affairs" includes a great deal more than merely political affairs. Matters of science, economics, business, art, literature, etc., are all matters of interest to the general public. Indeed, any matter of sufficient general interest to prompt media coverage may be said to be a public affair. Certainly police killings, "Communist conspiracies," and the like qualify.

A more regressive view of free speech has surfaced but it has thus far gained no judicial acceptance. Solicitor General Bork has stated:
"Constitutional protection should be accorded only to speech that is explicitly political. There is no basis for judicial intervention to protect any other form of expression, be it scientific, literary or that variety of expression we call obscene or pornographic. Moreover, within that category of speech we ordinarly call political, there should be no constitutional obstruction to

laws making criminal any speech that advocates forcible overthrow of the government or the violation of any law." Bork, Neutral Principles and Some First Amendment Problems, 47 Ind. L. J. 1, 20 (1971).

According to this view, Congress, upon finding a painting aesthetically displeasing or a novel poorly written or a revolutionary new scientific theory unsound could constitutionally prohibit exhibition of the painting, distribution of the book or discussion of the theory. Congress might also proscribe the advocacy of the violation of any law, apparently without regard to the law's constitutionality. Thus, were Congress to pass a blatantly invalid law such as one prohibiting newspaper editorials critical of the Government, a publisher might be punished for advocating its violation. Similarly, the late Dr. Martin Luther King, Jr., could have been punished for advising blacks to peacefully sit in the front of buses or to ask for service in restaurants segregated by law.

7. See Palko v. Connecticut, 302 U.S. 319, 325. As Mr. Justice Black has noted, by this view the test becomes "whether the government has an interest in abridging the right involved and, if so, whether that interest is of sufficient importance, in the opinion of a majority of the Supreme Court, to justify the government's action in doing so. Such a doctrine can be used to justify almost any government suppression of First Amendment freedoms. As I have stated many times before, I cannot subscribe to this doctrine because I believe that the First Amendment's unequivocal command that there shall be no abridgement of the rights of free speech shows that the men who drafted our Bill of Rights did all the 'balancing' that was to be done in this field." H. Black, A Constitutional Faith 52 (1969).

8. See, e.g., Bridges v. California, 314 U.S. 252, 263 n. 6 (Black, J.); Murdock v. Pennsylvania, 319 U.S. 105, 108 (DOUGLAS, J.); Saia v. New York, 334 U. S. 558, 560 (DOUGLAS, J.); Talley v. California, 362 U.S. 60, 62 (Black, J.); DeGregory v. Attorney General of New Hampshire, 383 U.S. 825, 828 (DOUGLAS, J.); Elfbrandt v. Russell, 384 U.S. 11, 18 (DOUGLAS, J.); Mills v. Alabama, 384 U.S. 214, 218 (Black, J.); Mine Workers v. Illinois Bar Assn., 389 U.S. 217, 221-222, and n. 4 (Black, J.).

Letter Carriers v. Austin, 418 U.S. 264 (1974)

The Court decides that the listing of "scabs" in a union newsletter and the accompanying short "essay" by Jack London calling a scab a "traitor" are not libelous. Douglas concurs, stating in his opinion: "Since I do not think that discussion is free in the constitutional sense when it subjects the speaker to the penalty of libel judgments, in my view the ability of Congress or the Executive to formulate any labor policy penalizing those who might 'say naughty things during labor disputes' is precisely nil."

* * *

MR. JUSTICE DOUGLAS, concurring in the result.

As the Court states, this case calls upon us to determine the extent to which state libel laws may be used to penalize statements expressed in the course of a labor dispute. In this instance Virginia's libel laws were used to impose massive damages[1] upon a labor union for publicly expressing, during the heat of an organizational drive, its highly pejorative but not too surprising opinion of "scabs." I agree that this expression is protected and that the judgments below cannot stand. Unlike the Court, however, I do not view the task of reconciling the competing state and federal interests in this area as a difficult one, nor do I view the federal interest as merely a matter of federal labor policy. I think that such expression is constitutionally protected and I cannot agree that there might be situations "where the use of this writing or other similar rhetoric in a labor dispute could be actionable."

I agree with the Court that federal labor policy, as manifested both in the NLRA and in Executive Order 11491, favors uninhibited, robust and wide open debate in labor disputes. I disagree with the Court, however, on the reach of that policy. I think that the pre-emptive effect of federal labor regulation is such that States are prohibited from interfering with those federally regulated relations by arming disputants in labor controversies with an arsenal of defamation laws. See Linn v. Plant Guard Workers, 383 U.S. 53, 69 (Fortas, J., dissenting). Though referring to this state of affairs as federal labor policy, I expressly reject any implication that the policy could be otherwise were Congress or the Executive to reassess the underlying considerations and attempt to reformulate the policy.

We said in Thornhill v. Alabama, 310 U.S. 88, 102, that, "[i]n the circumstances of our times the dissemination of information concerning the facts of a labor dispute must be regarded as within that area of free discussion that is guaranteed by the Constitution."[2] Since I do not think that discussion is free in the constitutional sense when it subjects the speaker to the penalty of libel judgments, in my view the ability of Congress or the Executive to formulate any labor policy penalizing those who might "say naughty things during labor disputes"[3] is precisely nil. I believe the Framers did all the policy-making necessary in this area when they devised the constitutional framework which binds us all. As I stated in Gertz v. Robert Welch, Inc., post, at 356-357, the First Amendment would prohibit Congress from passing any libel law[4] and the limitation on labor policy formulation is but an example of the general restriction.

If the States were not limited to the same extent as the Federal Government in restraining discussion, the preemptive effect of federal labor regulations would be crucial. But I have always thought that the application of the First Amendment to the States through the Fourteenth[5] leaves the States as constitutionally impotent as the Federal Government in enforcing such restrictions. This conclusion is compelled if freedom of speech is regarded, as I think it must be, as a privilege or immunity of United States citizenship within the meaning of that term in the Fourteenth Amendment rather than some ephemeral right protected against state intrusion only to the extent a majority of this Court might view as "implicit in the concept of ordered liberty."[6] As I stated in my dissent to Gertz v. Robert Welch, Inc., post, at 358-359:

> [T]he Court frequently has rested state free speech and free press decisions on the Fourteenth Amendment generally rather than on the Due Process Clause alone. The Fourteenth Amendment speaks not only of due process but also of 'privileges and immunities' of United States citizenship. I can conceive of no privilege or immunity with a higher claim to recognition against state abridgement than the freedoms of speech and of the press.

Since labor disputes are " 'within that area of free

discussion that is guaranteed by the Constitution' " and since in my view the States and the Federal Government are equally bound to honor that guarantee, the fate of the libel award in this case is clear. "Discussion is not free ... within the meaning of our First Amendment, if that discussion may be penalized by judgments for damages in libel actions." Linn v. Plant Guard Workers, 383 U.S., at 68 (Black, J., dissenting). The extensive damages awarded in this case well illustrate that any protection short of a complete bar to suits for defamation will be cold comfort to those who enter the arena of free discussion in labor disputes. The imaginative vituperation which is commonplace in labor strife well exceeds the "normal" levels of hyperbole to which most members of the community may be accustomed. A jury determination in a libel suit, no matter what the standard of recovery, is as likely to be influenced by community attitudes toward unionization and the often colorful individuals involved in its promotion as by any real appreciation for the damage perceived as inflicted by any alleged falsehood.

Since I do not believe that the judgments below are consistent with either federal labor policy or with constitutionally protected free speech, I concur in their reversal.

## NOTES

1. The judgments in this case awarded damages of $165,000 but the total figure might be larger since at least one other suit arising out of the same publication has been held in abeyance pending the outcome of this appeal.

2. The view has been expressed that the First Amendment should accord protection only to explicitly political speech. See Bork, Neutral Principles and Some First Amendment Problems, 47 Ind. L.J. 1, 20 (1971). Decisions such as Thornhill, however, reject any such emasculative reading of the First Amendment. As Mr. Justice Black has said: "There is nothing in the language of the First Amendment to indicate that it protects only political speech, although to provide such protection was no doubt a strong reason for the Amendment's passage." H. Black, A Constitutional Faith 46 (1969). The importance of free discussion in all areas was well preceived in this country before our constitutional scheme was formulated. In a letter sent to the inhabitants of Quebec in 1774, the Continental Congress

spoke of "five great rights," stating in part: "The last right we shall mention, regards the freedom of the press. The importance of this consists, besides the advancement of truth, science, morality, and arts in general, in its diffusion of liberal sentiments on the administration of Government...." 1 Journals of the Continental Congress 1774-1789, p. 108 (Ford ed. 1904) (emphasis added).

3. See Linn v. Plant Guard Workers, 383 U.S. 53, 67 (Black, J., dissenting).

4. See also Rosenblatt v. Baer, 383 U.S. 75, 90 (concurring). In explaining the constitutional history which led him to the same conclusion, Mr. Justice Black said of the Framers: "They knew what history was behind them; they were familiar with the sad and useless tragedies of countless people who had had their tongues plucked out, their ears cut off or their hands chopped off, or even worse things done to them, because they dared to speak or write their opinions. They wanted to ordain in this country that the new central government should not tell the people what they should believe or say or publish." H. Black, A Constitutional Faith 46 (1969).

5. See, e.g., Stromberg v. California, 283 U.S. 359, 368-369; cases complied in Gertz v. Robert Welch, Inc., post, at 359 n. 8 (DOUGLAS, J., dissenting).

6. See Palko v. Connecticut, 302 U.S. 319.

"THE RIGHT TO HEAR, TO LISTEN, TO KNOW"

AND

THE RIGHTS NOT TO SPEAK AND NOT TO LISTEN

Public Utilities Comm'n v. Pollak, 343 U.S. 451 (1952)

The Supreme Court decides that the Public Utilities Commission of the District of Columbia order permitting the radio broadcasting of music, announcements, and advertisements on buses and streetcars constitutional. Douglas dissents, declaring in his opinion: "One who tunes in on an offensive program at home can turn it off or tune in another station, as he wishes. One who hears disquieting or unpleasant programs in public places, such as restaurants, can get up and leave. But the man on the streetcar has no choice but to sit and listen, or perhaps to sit and try not to listen."

* * *

MR. JUSTICE DOUGLAS, dissenting.

This is a case of first impression. There are no precedents to construe; no principles previously expounded to apply. We write on a clean slate.

The case comes down to the meaning of "liberty" as used in the Fifth Amendment. Liberty in the constitutional sense must mean more than freedom from unlawful government restraint; it must include privacy as well, if it is to be a repository of freedom. The right to be let alone is indeed the beginning of all freedom. Part of our claim to privacy is in the prohibition of the Fourth Amendment against unreasonable searches and seizures. It gives the guarantee that a man's home is his castle beyond invasion either by inquisitive or by officious people. A man loses that privacy of course when he goes upon the streets or enters public places. But even in his activities outside the home he has immunities from controls bearing on privacy. He may not be compelled against his will to attend a religious service; he may not be forced to make an affirmation or observe a ritual that violates his scruples; he may not be made to accept one religious, political, or philosophical creed as against another. Freedom of religion and freedom of speech guaranteed by the First Amendment give more than the privilege to worship, to write, to speak as one chooses; they give freedom not to do nor to act as the government chooses. The First Amendment in its respect for the conscience of the individual honors the sanctity of thought and belief. To think as one chooses, to believe what one wishes are important aspects of the constitutional right to be let alone.

If we remembered this lesson taught by the First Amendment, I do not believe we would construe "liberty" within the meaning of the Fifth Amendment as narrowly as the Court does. The present case involves a form of coercion to make people listen. The listeners are of course in a public place; they are on streetcars traveling to and from home. In one sense it can be said that those who ride the streetcars do so voluntarily. Yet in a practical sense they are forced to ride, since this mode of transportation is today essential for many thousands. Compulsion which comes from circumstances can be as real as compulsion which comes from a command.

The streetcar audience is a captive audience. It is there as a matter of necessity, not of choice. One who is in a public vehicle may not of course complain of the noise of the crowd and the babble of tongues. One who enters any public place sacrifices some of his privacy. My protest is against the invasion of his privacy over and beyond the risks of travel.

The government may use the radio (or television) on public vehicles for many purposes. Today it may use it for a cultural end. Tomorrow it may use it for political purposes. So far as the right of privacy is concerned the purpose makes no difference. The music selected by one bureaucrat may be as offensive to some as it is soothing to others. The news commentator chosen to report on the events of the day may give overtones to the news that please the bureau head but which rile the streetcar captive audience. The political philosophy which one radio speaker exudes may be thought by the official who makes up the streetcar programs to be best for the welfare of the people. But the man who listens to it on his way to work in the morning and on his way home at night may think it marks the destruction of the Republic.

One who tunes in on an offensive program at home can turn it off or tune in another station, as he wishes. One who hears disquieting or unpleasant programs in public places, such as restaurants, can get up and leave. But the man on the streetcar has no choice but to sit and listen, or perhaps to sit and to try not to listen.

When we force people to listen to another's ideas, we give the propagandist a powerful weapon. Today it is a business enterprise working out a radio program under the auspices of government. Tomorrow it may be a dominant political or religious group. Today the purpose is benign; there is no invidious cast to the programs. But the vice is inherent in the system. Once privacy is invaded, privacy is gone. Once a man is forced to submit to one type of radio program, he can be forced to submit to another. It may be but a short step from a cultural program to a political program.

If liberty is to flourish, government should never be allowed to force people to listen to any radio program. The right of privacy should include the right to pick and choose from competing entertainments, competing propaganda, competing philosophies. If people are let alone in those choices, the right of privacy will pay dividends in character and integrity. The strength of our system is in the dignity, the resourcefulness, and the independence of our people. Our confidence is in their ability as individuals to make the wisest choice. That system cannot flourish if regimentation takes hold. The right of privacy, today violated, is a powerful deterrent to any one who would control men's minds.

Engel v. Vitale, 370 U.S. 421 (1962)

The Supreme Court decides that "state officials may not compose an official state prayer and require that it be recited in the public schools of the state at the beginning of each school day--even if the prayer is denominationally neutral and pupils who wish to do so may remain silent or be excused from the room while the prayer is being recited." In his concurring opinion Douglas states: "The First Amendment leaves the Government in a position not of hostility to religion but of neutrality. The philosophy is that the atheist or agnostic--the nonbeliever--is entitled to go his own way. The philosophy is that if government interferes in matters spiritual, it will be a divisive force. The First Amendment teaches that government neutral in the field of religion better serves all religious interests."

* * *

MR. JUSTICE DOUGLAS, concurring.

It is customary in deciding a constitutional question to treat it in its narrowest form. Yet at times the setting of the question gives it a form and content which no abstract treatment could give. The point for decision is whether the Government can constitutionally finance a religious exercise. Our system at the federal and state levels is presently honeycombed with such financing.[1] Nevertheless, I think it is an unconstitutional undertaking whatever form it takes.

First, a word as to what this case does not involve.

Plainly, our Bill of Rights would not permit a State or the Federal Government to adopt an official prayer and penalize anyone who would not utter it. This, however, is not that case, for there is no element of compulsion or coercion in New York's regulation requiring that public schools be opened each day with the following prayer:

> Almighty God, we acknowledge our dependence upon Thee, and we beg Thy blessings upon us, our parents, our teachers and our Country.

The prayer is said upon the commencement of the school day, immediately following the pledge of allegiance to the flag. The prayer is said aloud in the presence of a teacher, who either leads the recitation or selects a student to do so. No student, however, is compelled to take part. The respondents have adopted a regulation which provides that "Neither teachers nor any school authority shall comment on participation or non-participation ... nor suggest or request that any posture or language be used or dress be worn or be not used or not worn." Provision is also made for excusing children, upon written request of a parent or guardian, from the saying of the prayer or from the room in which the prayer is said. A letter implementing and explaining this regulation has been sent to each taxpayer and parent in the school district. As I read this regulation, a child is free to stand or not stand, to recite or not recite, without fear of reprisal or even comment by the teacher or any other school official.

In short, the only one who need utter the prayer is the teacher; and no teacher is complaining of it. Students can stand mute or even leave the classroom, if they desire. [2]

McCollum v. Board of Education, 333 U.S. 203, does not decide this case. It involved the use of public school facilities for religious education of students. Students either had to attend religious instruction or "go to some other place in the school building for pursuit of their secular studies.... Reports of their presence or absence were to be made to their secular teachers." Id., at 209. The influence of the teaching staff was therefore brought to bear on the student body, to support the instilling of religious principles. In the present case, school facilities are used to say the prayer and the teaching staff is employed to lead the pupils in it. There is, however, no effort at indoctrination and no attempt at exposition. Prayers of course may be so long and of such a character as to amount to an attempt at the religious instruction that was denied the public schools by the McCollum case. But New York's prayer is of a character that does not involve any element of proselytizing as in the McCollum case.

The question presented by this case is therefore an extremely narrow one. It is whether New York oversteps the bounds when it finances a religious exercise.

What New York does on the opening of its public schools is what we do when we open court. Our Crier has from the beginning announced the convening of the Court and then added "God save the United States and this Honorable Court." That utterance is a supplication, a prayer in which we, the judges, are free to join, but which we need not recite any more than the students need recite the New York prayer.

What New York does on the opening of its public schools is what each House of Congress[3] does at the opening of each day's business.[4] Reverend Frederick B. Harris is Chaplain of the Senate; Reverend Bernard Braskamp is Chaplain of the House. Guest chaplains of various denominations also officiate.[5]

In New York the teacher who leads in prayer is on the public payroll; and the time she takes seems minuscule as compared with the salaries appropriated by state legislatures and Congress for chaplains to conduct prayers in the legislative halls. Only a bare fraction of the teacher's time is given to reciting this short 22-word prayer, about the same amount of time that our Crier spends announcing the opening of our sessions and offering a prayer for this Court. Yet for me the principle is the same, no matter how briefly the prayer is said, for in each of the instances given the person praying is a public official on the public payroll, performing a religious exercise in a governmental institution.[6] It is said that the element of coercion is inherent in the giving of this prayer. If that is true here, it is also true of the prayer with which this Court is convened, and of those that open the Congress. Few adults, let alone children, would leave our courtroom or the Senate or the House while those prayers are being given. Every such audience is in a sense a "captive" audience.

At the same time I cannot say that to authorize this prayer is to establish a religion in the strictly historic meaning of those words.[7] A religion is not established in the usual sense merely by letting those who choose to do so say the prayer that the public school teacher leads. Yet once government finances a religious exercise it inserts a divisive influence into our communities.[8] The New York Court said that the prayer given does not conform to all of the tenets of the Jewish, Unitarian, and Ethical Culture groups. One of the petitioners is an agnostic.

"We are a religious people whose institutions presuppose a Supreme Being." Zorach v. Clauson, 343 U.S. 306, 313. Under our Bill of Rights free play is given for making religion an active force in our lives.[9] But "if a religious leaven is to be worked into the affairs of our people, it is to be done by individuals and groups, not by the Government."

McGowan v. Maryland, 366 U.S. 420, 563 (dissenting opinion). By reason of the First Amendment government is commanded "to have no interest in theology or ritual" (id., at 564), for on those matters "government must be neutral." Ibid. The First Amendment leaves the Government in a position not of hostility to religion but of neutrality. The philosophy is that the atheist or agnostic--the nonbeliever--is entitled to go his own way. The philosophy is that if government interferes in matters spiritual, it will be a divisive force. The First Amendment teaches that a government neutral in the field of religion better serves all religious interests.

My problem today would be uncomplicated but for Everson v. Board of Education, 330 U.S. 1, 17, which allowed taxpayers' money to be used to pay "the bus fares of parochial school pupils as a part of a general program under which" the fares of pupils attending public and other schools were also paid. The Everson case seems in retrospect to be out of line with the First Amendment. Its result is appealing, as it allows aid to be given to needy children. Yet by the same token, public funds could be used to satisfy other needs of children in parochial schools--lunches, books, and tuition being obvious examples. Mr. Justice Rutledge stated in dissent what I think is durable First Amendment philosophy:

> The reasons underlying the Amendment's policy have not vanished with time or diminished in force. Now as when it was adopted the price of religious freedom is double. It is that the church and religion shall live both within and upon that freedom. There cannot be freedom of religion, safeguarded by the state, and intervention by the church or its agencies in the state's domain or dependency on its largesse. Madison's Remonstrance, Par. 6, 8. The great condition of religious liberty is that it be maintained free from sustenance, as also from other interferences, by the state. For when it comes to rest upon that secular foundation it vanishes with the resting. Id., Par. 7, 8. Public money devoted to payment of religious costs, educational or other, brings the quest for more. It brings too the struggle of sect against sect for the larger share or for any. Here one by numbers alone will benefit most, there another. That is precisely the history of societies which have had an established religion and dissident groups. Id., Par. 8, 11. It is the very thing Jefferson and Madison experienced and sought to guard against, whether in its blunt or in its more screened forms. Ibid.

> The end of such strife cannot be other than to destroy the cherished liberty. The dominating group will achieve the dominant benefit; or all will embroil the state in their dissensions. Id., Par. 11. [Id., pp. 53-54.]

With this prayer New York breaks with that tradition. I therefore join the Court in reversing the judgment.

## NOTES

1. "There are many 'aids' to religion in this country at all levels of government. To mention but a few at the federal level, one might begin by observing that the very First Congress which wrote the First Amendment provided for chaplains in both Houses and in the armed services. There is compulsory chapel at the service academies, and religious services are held in federal hospitals and prisons. The President issues religious proclamations. The Bible is used for the administration of oaths. N.Y.A. and W.P.A. funds were available to parochial schools during the depression. Veterans receiving money under the 'G.I.' Bill of 1944 could attend denominational schools, to which payments were made directly by the government. During World War II, federal money was contributed to denominational schools for the training of nurses. The benefits of the National School Lunch Act are available to students in private as well as public schools. The Hospital Survey and Construction Act of 1946 specifically made money available to non-public hospitals. The slogan 'In God We Trust' is used by the Treasury Department, and Congress recently added God to the pledge of allegiance. There is Bible-reading in the schools of the District of Columbia, and religious instruction is given in the District's National Training School for Boys. Religious organizations are exempt from the federal income tax and are granted postal privileges. Up to defined limits--15 per cent of the adjusted gross income of individuals and 5 per cent of the net income of corporations--contributions to religious organizations are deductible for federal income tax purposes. There are no limits to the deductibility of gifts and bequests to religious institutions made under the federal gift and estate tax laws. This list of federal 'aids' could easily be expanded, and of course there is a long list in each state." Fellman, The Limits of Freedom (1959), pp. 40-41.

2. West Point Cadets are required to attend chapel each Sunday. Reg., c. 21, § 2101. The same requirement obtains at the Naval Academy (Reg., c. 9 § 0901, (1), (a)), and at the Air Force Academy except First Classmen. Catalogue, 1962-1963, p. 110. And see Honeywell, Chaplains of the United States Army (1958); Jorgensen, The Service of Chaplains to Army Air Units, 1917-1946, Vol. I (1961).

3. The New York Legislature follows the same procedure. See e.g., Vol. 1, N.Y. Assembly Jour., 184th Sess., 1961, p. 8; Vol. 1, N.Y. Senate Jour., 184th Sess., 1961, p. 5.

4. Rules of the Senate provide that each calendar day's session shall open with prayer. See Rule III, Senate Manual, S. Doc. No. 2, 87th Cong., 1st Sess. The same is true of the Rules of the House. See Rule VII, Rules of the House of Representatives, H. R. Doc. No. 459, 86th Cong., 2d Sess. The Chaplains of the Senate and of the House receive $8,810 annually. See 75 Stat. 320, 324.

5. It would, I assume, make no difference in the present case if a different prayer were said every day or if the ministers of the community rotated, each giving his own prayer. For some of the petitioners in the present case profess no religion.

The Pledge of Allegiance, like the prayer, recognizes the existence of a Supreme Being. Since 1954 it has contained the words "one Nation under God, indivisible, with liberty and justice for all." 36 U.S.C. § 172. The House Report recommending the addition of the words "under God" stated that those words in no way run contrary to the First Amendment but recognize "only the guidance of God in our national affairs." H.R. Rep. No. 1693, 83d Cong., 2d Sess., p. 3. And see S. Rep. No. 1287, 83d Cong., 2d Sess. Senator Ferguson, who sponsored the measure in the Senate, pointed out that the words "In God We Trust" are over the entrance to the Senate Chamber. 100 Cong. Rec. 6348. He added:

"I have felt that the Pledge of Allegiance to the Flag which stands for the United States of America should recognize the Creator who we really believe is in control of the destinies of this great Republic.

"It is true that under the Constitution no power is lodged anywhere to establish a religion. This is not an attempt to establish a religion; it has nothing to do with anything of that kind. It relates to belief in God, in whom we sincerely repose our trust. We know that America cannot be defended by guns, planes, and ships alone. Appropriations and expenditures for defense will be of value only if the God under whom we live believes that we are in the right. We should at all times recognize God's province over the lives of our people and over this great Nation." Ibid. And see 100 Cong. Rec. 7757 et seq. for the debates in the House.

The Act of March 3, 1865, 13 Stat. 517, 518 authorized the phrase "In God We Trust" to be placed on coins. And see 17 Stat. 427. The first mandatory requirement for the use of that motto on coins was made by the Act of May 18, 1908, 35 Stat. 164. See H.R. Rep. No. 1106, 60th Cong., 1st Sess.; 42 Cong. Rec. 3384 et seq. The use of the motto on all currency and coins was directed by the Act of July 11, 1955, 69 Stat. 290. See H.R. Rep. No. 662, 84th Cong., 1st Sess.; S. Rep. No. 637, 84th Cong., 1st Sess. Moreover, by the Joint Resolution of July 30, 1956, our national motto was declared to be "In God We Trust." 70 Stat. 732. In reporting the Joint Resolution, the Senate Judiciary Committee stated:

"Further official recognition of this motto was given by the adoption of the Star-Spangled Banner as our national anthem. One stanza of our national anthem is as follows:

" 'O, thus be it ever when freemen shall stand
Between their lov'd home and the war's desolation!
Blest with vict'ry and peace may the heav'n rescued land
Praise the power that hath made and preserved us a nation!
Then conquer we must when our cause it is just,
And this be our motto--"In God is our trust."
And the Star-Spangled Banner in triumph shall wave
O'er the land of the free and the home of the brave.'

"In view of these words in our national anthem, it is clear that 'In God we trust' has a strong claim as our national motto." S. Rep. No. 2703, 84th Cong., 2d Sess., p. 2.

6. The fact that taxpayers do not have standing in the federal courts to raise the issue (Frothingham v. Mellon, 262 U.S. 447) is of course no justification for drawing

a line between what is done in New York on the one hand and on the other what we do and what Congress does in this matter of prayer.

7. The Court analogizes the present case to those involving the traditional Established Church. We once had an Established Church, the Anglican. All baptisms and marriages had to take place there. That church was supported by taxation. In these and other ways the Anglican Church was favored over the others. The First Amendment put an end to placing any one church in a preferred position. It ended support of any church or all churches by taxation. It went further and prevented secular sanction to any religious ceremony, dogma, or rite. Thus, it prevents civil penalties from being applied against recalcitrants or nonconformists.

8. Some communities have a Christmas tree purchased with the taxpayers' money. The tree is sometimes decorated with the words "Peace on earth, goodwill to men." At other times the authorities draw from a different version of the Bible which says "Peace on earth to men of goodwill." Christmas, I suppose, is still a religious celebration, not merely a day put on the calendar for the benefit of merchants.

9. Religion was once deemed to be a function of the public school system. The Northwest Ordinance, which antedated the First Amendment, provided in Article III that "Religion, morality, and knowledge being necessary to good government and the happiness of mankind, schools and the means of education shall forever be encouraged."

## Kleindienst v. Mandel, 408 U.S. 753 (1972)

The Supreme Court upholds the right of the Attorney General to refuse a temporary visa to a Belgian Marxist journalist and theoretician who had been invited by American scholars to speak at academic conferences in the United States, the refusal based on a law barring persons who advocate or publish "the economic, international, and governmental doctrines of world Communism." Douglas dissents, asserting in his opinion: "We should assume that where propagation of ideas is permissible as being within our constitutional framework, the Congress did not undertake to make the Attorney General a censor. For as stated by Justice Jackson in Thomas v. Collins ... 'the very purpose of the First Amendment is to foreclose public authority from assuming a guardianship of the public mind through regulating the press, speech, and religion. In this field every person must be his own watchman for truth, because the forefathers did not trust any government to separate the true from the false for us.' "

* * *

MR. JUSTICE DOUGLAS, dissenting.

Under The Chinese Exclusion Case, 130 U.S. 581, rendered in 1889, there could be no doubt but that Congress would have the power to exclude any class of aliens from these shores. The accent at the time was on race. Mr. Justice Field, writing for the Court, said: "If, therefore, the government of the United States, through its legislative department, considers the presence of foreigners of a different race in this country, who will not assimilate with us, to be dangerous to its peace and security, their exclusion is not to be stayed because at the time there are no actual hostilities with the nation of which the foreigners are subject." Id., at 606.

An ideological test, not a racial one, is used here. But neither, in my view, is permissible, as I have indicated on other occasions.[1] Yet a narrower question is raised here.

Under the present Act aliens who advocate or teach "the economic, international, and governmental doctrines of world communism" are ineligible to receive visas "[e]xcept as otherwise provided in this Act."[2] The "except" provision is contained in another part of the same section[3] and states that an inadmissable alien "may, after approval by the Attorney General of a recommendation by the Secretary of State or by the consular officer" be admitted "temporarily despite his inadmissibility."

Dr. Ernest Mandel, who is described as "an orthodox Marxist of the Trotskyist school," has been admitted to this country twice before--once as a working journalist in 1962 and once as a lecturer in 1968. The present case involves his third application, made in 1969, to attend a conference at Stanford University on Technology and the Third World. He was also invited to attend other conferences, one at MIT, and to address several universities, Princeton, Amherst, the New School, Columbia, and Vassar. This time the Department of Justice refused to grant a waiver recommended by the State Department; and it claims that it need not state its reasons, that the power of the Attorney General is unfettered.

Dr. Mandel is not the sole complainant. Joining him are the other appellees who represent the various audiences which Dr. Mandel would be meeting were a visa to issue. While Dr. Mandel, an alien who seeks admission, has no First Amendment rights while outside the Nation, the other appellees are on a different footing. The First Amendment involves not only the right to speak and publish but also the right to hear, to learn, to know. Martin v. City of Struthers, 319 U.S. 141, 143; Stanley v. Georgia, 394 U.S. 557, 564.

Can the Attorney General under the broad discretion entrusted in him decide

that one who maintains that the earth is round can be excluded?

that no one who believes in the Darwinian theory shall be admitted?

that those who promote a Rule of Law to settle international difference rather than a Rule of Force may be barred?

that a genetic biologist who lectures on the way to create life by one sex alone is beyond the pale?

that an exponent of plate tectonics can be barred?

that one should be excluded who taught that Jesus when he arose from the Sepulcher, went east (not up) and became a teacher at Hemis Monastery in the Himalayas?

I put the issue that bluntly because national security is not involved. Nor is the infiltration of saboteurs. The Attorney General stands astride our international terminals that bring people here to bar those whose ideas are not acceptable to him. Even assuming, arguendo, that those on the outside seeking admission have no standing to complain, those who hope to benefit from the traveler's lectures do.

Thought control is not within the competence of any branch of government. Those who live here may need exposure to the ideas of people of many faiths and many creeds to further their education. We should construe the Act generously by that First Amendment standard, saying that once the State Department has concluded that our foreign relations permit or require the admission of a foreign traveler, the Attorney General is left only problems of national security, importation of heroin, or other like matters within his competence.

We should assume that where propagation of ideas is permissible as being within our constitutional framework, the Congress did not undertake to make the Attorney General a censor. For as stated by Justice Jackson in Thomas v. Collins, 323 U.S. 516, 545 (concurring), "[t]he very purpose of the First Amendment is to foreclose public authority from assuming a guardianship of the public mind through regulating the press, speech, and religion. In this field every person must be his own watchman for truth, because the forefathers did not trust any government to separate the true from the false for us."

In Brandenburg v. Ohio, 395 U.S. 444 (which overruled Whitney v. California, 274 U.S. 357), we held that the First Amendment does not permit a State "to forbid or proscribe advocacy of the use of force or of law violation except where such advocacy is directed to inciting or producing imminent lawless action and is likely to incite or produce such action." Id., at 447. That case involved propagation of the views of the Ku Klux Klan. The present case involves teaching the communist creed.[4] But, as we held in Noto v. United States, 367 U.S. 290, 297-298:

> [T]he mere abstract teaching of Communist theory, including the teaching of the moral propriety or even moral necessity for a resort to force and violence, is not the same as preparing a group for violent action and steeling it to such action.

As a matter of statutory construction, I conclude that Congress never undertook to entrust the Attorney General with the discretion to pick and choose among the ideological offerings which alien lecturers tender from our platforms, allowing those palatable to him and disallowing others.[5] The discretion entrusted to him concerns matters commonly within the competence of the Department of Justice--national security, importation of drugs, and the like.

I would affirm the judgment of the three-judge District Court.

NOTES

1. See Harisiades v. Shaughnessy, 342 U.S. 580, 598 (dissenting opinion); Galvan v. Press, 347 U.S. 522, 533 (dissenting opinion).

2. § 212 (a) (28) (G) (v) of the Immigration and Nationality Act of 1952, 66 Stat. 185, 8 U.S.C. § 1182 (a) (28) (G) (v).

3. § 212 (d) (3) (A), 8 U.S.C. § 1182 (d) (3) (A).

4. The Court recognizes the legitimacy of appellees' First Amendment claim, ante, at 762-765. It argues, however, that inasmuch as the Attorney General gave a "facially legitimate and bona fide" reason to refuse Dr. Mandel a waiver of ineligibility, the Court should not "look behind the exercise of that discretion, nor test it by balancing its justification against [appellees'] First Amendment interests...." First, so far as the record reveals, there is absolutely no support for the Attorney General's claim that Dr. Mandel consciously abused his visa privileges in 1968. Indeed, the State Department itself concedes that he "was apparently not informed [in 1962 and 1968] that a visa was issued only after obtaining a waiver of ineligibility and therefore may not have been aware of the conditions and limitations attached to the visa issuance." (Emphasis supplied.) App. 22. Second, the activities which the Attorney General labeled "flagrant abuses" of Dr. Mandel's opportunity to speak in the United States appear merely to have been his speaking at more universities than his visa application indicated. Indeed, he spoke at more than 30 universities in the United States and

Canada, including Harvard, the University of California at Berkeley, Swarthmore, Notre Dame, Antioch, Michigan, three appearances at Columbia, two at the University of Pennsylvania, and the keynote address at the 1968 Socialist Scholars Conference held at Rutgers. App. 25. It would be difficult to invent a more trivial reason for denying the academic community the chance to exchange views with an internationally respected scholar.

5. As indicated in S. Rep. No. 1137, 82d Cong., 2d Sess., 12, the discretion vested in the Attorney General was to be exercised "for emergent reasons or for reasons deemed strictly in the public interest." Ideological controls are not congenial to our First Amendment traditions and therefore should not be inferred.

Lehman v. City of Shaker Heights, 418 U.S. 298 (1974)

"This case," says the Supreme Court, "presents the question whether a city which operates a public rapid transit system and sells advertising space for car cards on its vehicles is required by the First and Fourteenth Amendments to accept paid political advertising on behalf of a candidate for public office." The Court decides that the city's refusal to make available advertising space for the candidate did not violate the candidate's free speech or equal protection rights. Douglas concurs, declaring in his opinion: "In asking us to force the system to accept his message as a vindication of his constitutional rights, the petitioner overlooks the constitutional rights of the commuters. While petitioner clearly has a right to express his views to those who wish to listen, he has no right to force his message upon an audience incapable of declining to receive it. In my view the right of the commuters to be free from forced intrusions on their privacy precludes the city from transforming its vehicles of public transportation into forums for the dissemination of ideas upon this captive audience."

* * *

MR. JUSTICE DOUGLAS, concurring in the judgment.

Petitioner, a candidate for state office, attempted to purchase space for paid political advertising on vehicles of the Shaker Heights Rapid Transit System, a system owned and operated by the city of Shaker Heights, Ohio. Metromedia, Inc., the exclusive advertising agent for the system, refused petitioner the space on the basis of a contract with the system prohibiting the acceptance of political advertisements. Petitioner unsuccessfully sought injunctive relief in the state courts to restrain the city and Metromedia from refusing his advertising.

The petitioner contends that, by selling advertising space, the city has turned its buses into free speech forums and the city is now prohibited by the First Amendment, applicable to the States through the Fourteenth,[1] from refusing space for political advertisements.

My Brother BRENNAN would find that "[a] forum for communication was voluntarily established when the city installed the physical facilities for the advertisements and, by contract with Metromedia, created the necessary administrative machinery for regulating access to that forum." Post, at 314. If the streetcar or bus were a forum for communication akin to that of streets or public parks, considerable problems would be presented. "The privilege of a citizen of the United States to use the streets and parks for communication of views on national questions may be regulated in the interest of all ... but it must not, in the guise of regulation, be abridged or denied." Hague v. CIO, 307 U.S. 496, 515-516. But a streetcar or bus is plainly not a park or sidewalk or other meeting place for discussion, any more than is a highway. It is only a way to get to work or back home. The fact that it is owned and operated by the city does not without more make it a forum.

Bus and streetcar placards are in the category of highway billboards which have long been used to display an array of commercial and political messages. But this particular form of communication has been significantly curtailed by state regulation adopted pursuant to the Highway Beautification Act of 1965, 23 U.S.C. §131, which conditions certain federal highway funds upon strict regulation of highway advertising. Ohio is among the States which have sought to protect the interests of their motorists[2] by enacting regulations pursuant to the Act. Ohio Rev. Code Ann. §5516.01 et seq. (Supp. 1973). The fact that land on which a billboard rests is municipal land does not curtail or enhance such regulatory schemes.

If a bus is a forum it is more akin to a newspaper than to a park. Yet if a bus is treated as a newspaper, then, as we hold this date, Miami Herald Publishing Co. v. Tornillo, ante, p. 241, the owner cannot be forced to include in his offerings news or other items which outsiders may desire but which the owner abhors. Newspaper cases are cited to support petitioner's claim. The First Amendment, however, draws no distinction between press privately owned, and press owned otherwise. And if we are to turn a bus or streetcar into either a newspaper or a park, we take great liberties with people who because of necessity become commuters and at the same time captive viewers or listeners.

In asking us to force the system to accept his message as a vindication of his constitutional rights, the petitioner overlooks the constitutional rights of the commuters. While petitioner clearly has a right to express his views to those who wish to listen, he has no right to force his message upon an audience incapable of declining to receive it. In my view the right of the commuters to be free from forced intrusions on their privacy precludes the city from transforming its vehicles of public transportation into forums for the dissemination of ideas upon this captive audience.

Buses are not recreational vehicles used for Sunday chautauquas as a public park might be used on holidays for such a purpose; they are a practical necessity for millions in our urban centers. I have already stated this view in my dissent in Public Utilities Comm'n v. Pollak, 343 U.S. 451, 469, involving the challenge by some passengers to the practice of broadcasting radio programs over loudspeakers in buses and streetcars: "One who tunes in on an offensive program at home can turn it off or tune in another station, as he wishes. One who hears disquieting or unpleasant programs in public places, such as restaurants, can get up and leave. But the man on the streetcar has no choice but to sit and listen, or perhaps to sit and to try not to listen." There is no difference when the message is visual, not auricular. In each the viewer or listener is captive.

I agree with Mr. Justice Brandeis who, quoting from a Utah State Court decision,[3] said that the visual message in streetcars is no different, for "'[a]dvertisements of this sort are constantly before the eyes of observers on the streets and in street cars to be seen without the exercise of choice or volition on their part. Other forms of advertising are ordinarily seen as a matter of choice on the part of the observer.... In the case of newspapers and magazines, there must be some seeking by the one who is to see and read the advertisement. The radio can be turned off, but not so the billboard or street car placard.'" Packer Corp. v. Utah, 285 U.S. 105, 110.

I do not view the content of the message as relevant either to petitioner's right to express it or to the commuters' right to be free from it. Commercial advertisements may be as offensive and intrusive to captive audiences as any political message. But the validity of the commercial advertising program is not before us since we are not faced with one complaining of an invasion of privacy through forced exposure to commercial ads. Since I do not believe that petitioner has any constitutional right to spread his message before this captive audience, I concur in the Court's judgment.

## NOTES

1. The Court has frequently rested state free speech and free press decisions on the Fourteenth Amendment generally, rather than on the Due Process Clause alone. See, e.g., Bridges v. California, 314 U.S. 252, 263 n. 6; Saia v. New York, 334 U.S. 558, 560; Elfbrandt v. Russell, 384 U.S. 11, 18; Mills v. Alabama, 384 U.S. 214, 218.

2. In a survey of motorists in Ohio, 71% expressed the opinion that billboards should be banned from the interstate highway system. Hearings on S. 1467 before the Subcommittee on Roads of the Senate Committee on Public Works, 90th Cong., 1st Sess., 43-44 (1967).

3. 77 Utah 500, 515, 297 P. 1013, 1019 (1931).

## APPENDIX

Freedom of Speech Cases Decided by the United States Supreme Court During the Tenure of Justice William O. Douglas, 1939-1975

### 1939-1949

Bridges v. Wixon, 326 U.S. 135 (1945)
Cantwell v. Connecticut, 310 U.S. 296 (1940)
Chaplinsky v. New Hampshire, 315 U.S. 568 (1942)
Cox v. New Hampshire, 312 U.S. 569 (1941)
Craig v. Harney, 331 U.S. 367 (1947)
Douglas v. City of Jeannette, 319 U.S. 157 (1943)
Follett v. Town of McCormick, 321 U.S. 573 (1944)
Hannegan v. Esquire, 327 U.S. 146 (1946)
Hartzel v. United States, 322 U.S. 680 (1944)
In re Summers, 325 U.S. 561 (1945)
Jones v. Opelika, 316 U.S. 584 (1942)
Keegan v. United States, 325 U.S. 478 (1945)
Kovacs v. Cooper, 336 U.S. 77 (1949)
Largent v. Texas, 318 U.S. 418 (1943)
Marsh v. Alabama, 326 U.S. 501 (1946)
Milkwagon Drivers Union v. Meadowmoor Dairies, 312 U.S. 287 (1941)
Murdock v. Pennsylvania, 319 U.S. 105 (1943)
Musser v. Utah, 333 U.S. 95 (1948)
Nye v. United States, 313 U.S. 33 (1941)
Prince v. Massachusetts, 321 U.S. 159 (1944)
Saia v. New York, 334 U.S. 558 (1948)
Schneider v. State, 308 U.S. 147 (1939)
Schneiderman v. United States, 320 U.S. 118 (1943)
Terminiello v. Chicago, 337 U.S. 1 (1949)
Thomas v. Collins, 323 U.S. 516 (1945)
Thornhill v. Alabama, 310 U.S. 88 (1940)
United Public Workers v. Mitchell, 330 U.S. 75 (1947)
United States v. Ballard, 322 U.S. 78 (1944)
United States v. C.I.O., 335 U.S. 106 (1948)
West Virginia Bd. of Education v. Barnette, 319 U.S. 624 (1943)
Winters v. New York, 333 U.S. 507 (1948)

## 1950-1959

Adler v. Board of Education, 342 U.S. 485 (1952)
American Communications Assn. v. Douds, 339 U.S. 382 (1950)
Bailey v. Richardson, 341 U.S. 918 (1951)
Barenblatt v. United States, 360 U.S. 109 (1959)
Barsky v. Board of Regents, 347 U.S. 442 (1954)
Beard v. City of Alexandria, 341 U.S. 622 (1951)
Beauharnais v. Illinois, 343 U.S. 250 (1952)
Beilan v. Board of Public Education, 357 U.S. 399 (1958)
Black v. Cutter Laboratories, 351 U.S. 292 (1956)
Burstyn v. Wilson, 343 U.S. 495 (1952)
Butler v. Michigan, 352 U.S. 380 (1957)
Cole v. Young, 351 U.S. 536 (1956)
Communist Party v. Subversive Activities Control Bd., 351 U.S. 115 (1956)
Dennis v. United States, 341 U.S. 494 (1951)
Emspak v. United States, 349 U.S. 190 (1955)
Feiner v. New York, 340 U.S. 315 (1951)
First Unitarian Church v. Los Angeles, 357 U.S. 545 (1958)
Flaxer v. United States, 358 U.S. 147 (1958)
Fowler v. Rhode Island, 345 U.S. 67 (1953)
Garner v. Board of Public Works, 341 U.S. 716 (1951)
Gerende v. Board of Supervisors, 341 U.S. 56 (1951)
Greene v. McElroy, 360 U.S. 474 (1959)
Harrison v. NAACP, 360 U.S. 167 (1959)
Joint Anti-Fascist Refugee Committee v. McGrath, 341 U.S. 123 (1951)
Kingsley Books, Inc. v. Brown, 354 U.S. 426 (1957)
Kunz v. New York, 340 U.S. 290 (1951)
Mesarosh v. United States, 352 U.S. 1 (1956)
NAACP v. Bennett, 360 U.S. 471 (1959)
Niemotko v. Maryland, 340 U.S. 268 (1951)
One, Inc. v. Olesen, 355 U.S. 371 (1958)
Osman v. Douds, 339 U.S. 846 (1950)
Peters v. Hobby, 349 U.S. 331 (1955)
Poulos v. New Hampshire, 345 U.S. 395 (1953)
Quinn v. United States, 349 U.S. 155 (1955)
Roth v. United States, 354 U.S. 476 (1957)
Sacher v. United States, 356 U.S. 576 (1958)
Schware v. Board of Examiners, 353 U.S. 232 (1957)
Scull v. Virginia, 359 U.S. 344 (1959)
Service v. Dulles, 354 U.S. 363 (1957)
Smith v. California, 361 U.S. 147 (1959)
Speiser v. Randall, 357 U.S. 513 (1958)

Staub v. City of Baxley, 355 U.S. 313 (1958)
Superior Films, Inc. v. Dept. of Education, 346 U.S. 587 (1954)
Sweezy v. New Hampshire, 354 U.S. 234 (1957)
United States v. Harriss, 347 U.S. 612 (1954)
United States v. Rumely, 345 U.S. 41 (1953)
United States v. United Automobile Workers, 352 U.S. 567 (1957)
Uphaus v. Wyman, 360 U.S. 72 (1959)
Vitarelli v. Seaton, 359 U.S. 535 (1959)
Watkins v. United States, 354 U.S. 178 (1957)
Wieman v. Updegraff, 344 U.S. 183 (1952)
Yates v. United States, 354 U.S. 298 (1957)

## 1960-1969

Adderley v. Florida, 385 U.S. 39 (1966)
Amalgamated Food Employees v. Logan Plaza, 391 U.S. 308 (1968)
American Committee for Protection of Foreign Born v. Subversive Activities Control Board, 380 U.S. 503 (1965)
Baggett v. Bullitt, 377 U.S. 360 (1964)
Bantam Books, Inc. v. Sullivan, 372 U.S. 58 (1963)
Braden v. United States, 365 U.S. 431 (1961)
Brandenburg v. Ohio, 395 U.S. 444 (1969)
Brown v. Louisiana, 383 U.S. 131 (1966)
Cafeteria and Restaurant Workers Union v. McElroy, 367 U.S. 886 (1961)
Cameron v. Johnson, 390 U.S. 611 (1968)
Carroll v. President and Commissioners of Princess Anne, 393 U.S. 175 (1968)
Cox v. Louisiana, 379 U.S. 536 (1965)
Cox v. Louisiana, 379 U.S. 559 (1965)
Cramp v. Board of Public Instruction, 368 U.S. 278 (1961)
DeGregory v. Attorney General, 383 U.S. 825 (1966)
Deutch v. United States, 367 U.S. 456 (1961)
Edwards v. South Carolina, 372 U.S. 229 (1963)
Elfbrandt v. Russell, 384 U.S. 11 (1966)
Engel v. Vitale, 370 U.S. 421 (1962)
Freedman v. Maryland, 380 U.S. 51 (1965)
Garner v. Louisiana, 368 U.S. 201 (1961)
Garrison v. Louisiana, 379 U.S. 64 (1964)
Gibson v. Florida Legislative Investigation Committee, 372 U.S. 539 (1963)
Ginsberg v. New York, 390 U.S. 629 (1968)
Ginzburg v. United States, 383 U.S. 463 (1966)

Gojack v. United States, 384 U.S. 702 (1966)
Greene v. United States, 376 U.S. 149 (1964)
Gregory v. Chicago, 394 U.S. 111 (1969)
Henry v. City of Rock Hill, 376 U.S. 776 (1964)
In re Anastaplo, 366 U.S. 82 (1961)
Jacobellis v. Ohio, 378 U.S. 184 (1964)
Keyishian v. Board of Regents, 385 U.S. 589 (1967)
Konigsberg v. State Bar of California, 366 U.S. 36 (1961)
Lamont v. Postmaster General, 381 U.S. 301 (1965)
Lee Art Theatre, Inc. v. Virginia, 392 U.S. 626 (1968)
Manual Enterprises v. Day, 370 U.S. 478 (1962)
Marcus v. Search Warrant, 367 U.S. 717 (1961)
Memoirs v. Massachusetts, 383 U.S. 413 (1966)
Mishkin v. New York, 383 U.S. 502 (1966)
NAACP v. Button, 371 U.S. 415 (1963)
New York Times v. Sullivan, 376 U.S. 254 (1964)
Noto v. United States, 367 U.S. 290 (1961)
O'Brien v. United States, 391 U.S. 367 (1967)
Pickering v. Board of Education, 391 U.S. 563 (1968)
A Quantity of Copies of Books v. Kansas, 378 U.S. 205 (1964)
Rabeck v. New York, 391 U.S. 462 (1968)
Redrup v. New York, 386 U.S. 767 (1967)
Rosenblatt v. Baer, 383 U.S. 75 (1966)
Russell v. United States, 369 U.S. 746 (1962)
St. Amant v. Thompson, 390 U.S. 727 (1968)
Scales v. United States, 367 U.S. 203 (1961)
Shelton v. Tucker, 364 U.S. 479 (1960)
Shuttlesworth v. City of Birmingham, 394 U.S. 147 (1969)
Silber v. United States, 370 U.S. 717 (1962)
Stanley v. Georgia, 394 U.S. 557 (1969)
Street v. New York, 394 U.S. 576 (1969)
Talley v. California, 362 U.S. 60 (1960)
Teitel Film Corp. v. Cusack, 390 U.S. 139 (1968)
Times Film Corp. v. Chicago, 365 U.S. 43 (1961)
Tinker v. De Moines Independent Community School District, 393 U.S. 503 (1969)
Torcaso v. Watkins, 367 U.S. 488 (1961)
United States v. O'Brien, 391 U.S. 367 (1968)
United States v. Robel, 389 U.S. 258 (1967)
Uphaus v. Wyman, 364 U.S. 388 (1960)
Veterans of Abraham Lincoln Brigade v. Subversive Activities Control Board, 380 U.S. 513 (1965)
W.E.B. Du Bois Clubs of America v. Clark, 389 U.S. 309 (1967)
Wheeldin v. Wheeler, 373 U.S. 647 (1963)
Whitehall v. Elkins, 389 U.S. 54 (1967)
Wilkinson v. United States, 365 U.S. 399 (1961)

## 1970-1975

Bachellar v. Maryland, 397 U.S. 564 (1970)
Baird v. State Bar of Arizona, 401 U.S. 1 (1971)
Blount v. Rizzi, 400 U.S. 410 (1971)
Board of Regents v. Roth, 408 U.S. 564 (1972)
Board of School Commissioners of City of Indianapolis v. Jacobs, 420 U.S. 128 (1975)
Brown v. Oklahoma, 408 U.S. 914 (1972)
Coates v. Cincinnati, 402 U.S. 611 (1971)
Cohen v. California, 403 U.S. 15 (1971)
Cole v. Richardson, 405 U.S. 676 (1972)
Connell v. Higginbotham, 403 U.S. 207 (1971)
Cowgill v. California, 396 U.S. 371 (1971)
Doran v. Salem Inn, Inc., 422 U.S. 922 (1975)
Dyson v. Stein, 401 U.S. 200 (1971)
Eisenstadt v. Baird, 405 U.S. 438 (1972)
Erznoznik v. City of Jacksonville, 422 U.S. 205 (1974)
Flower v. United States, 407 U.S. 197 (1972)
Gertz v. Robert Welch, Inc. 418 U.S. 323 (1974)
Ginzburg v. Goldwater, 396 U.S. 1049 (1970)
Gooding v. Wilson, 405 U.S. 518 (1972)
Grayned v. City of Rockford, 408 U.S. 104 (1972)
Greenbelt Cooperative Publishing Assoc. v. Bresler, 398 U.S. 6 (1970)
Hamling v. United States, 418 U.S. 87 (1974)
Healy v. James, 408 U.S. 169 (1972)
Heller v. New York, 413 U.S. 483 (1973)
Hess v. Indiana, 414 U.S. 105 (1973)
In re Stolar, 401 U.S. 23 (1971)
Jenkins v. Georgia, 418 U.S. 153 (1974)
Jenness v. Fortson, 403 U.S. 431 (1971)
Jones v. State Board of Education, 397 U.S. 31 (1970)
Kaplan v. California, 413 U.S. 115 (1973)
Kleindienst v. Mandel, 408 U.S. 753 (1972)
Laird v. Tatum, 408 U.S. 1 (1972)
Law Students Civil Rights Research Council v. Wadmond, 401 U.S. 154 (1971)
Lehman v. City of Shaker Heights, 418 U.S. 913 (1974)
Lewis v. City of New Orleans, 408 U.S. 913 (1972)
Lloyd v. Tanner, 407 U.S. 551 (1972)
Miller v. California, 413 U.S. 15 (1973)
New York Times v. United States, 403 U.S. 713 (1971)
Ocala Star-Banner Co. v. Damron, 401 U.S. 295 (1971)
Organization for a Better Austin v. Keefe, 402 U.S. 415 (1971)
Papish v. Bd. of Curators of University of Missouri, 410 U.S. 667 (1973)

Paris Adult Theatre v. Slaton, 413 U.S. 49 (1973)
Parker v. Levy, 417 U.S. 733 (1974)
Perez v. Ledesma, 401 U.S. 82 (1971)
Plummer v. City of Columbus, 414 U.S. 2 (1973)
Rabe v. Washington, 405 U.S. 313 (1972)
Radich v. New York, 401 U.S. 531 (1971)
Roaden v. Kentucky, 413 U.S. 496 (1973)
Rosenfeld v. New Jersey, 408 U.S. 901 (1972)
Rowan v. United States Post Office Dept., 397 U.S. 728 (1970)
Schacht v. United States, 398 U.S. 58 (1970)
Southeastern Promotions v. Conrad, 420 U.S. 546 (1974)
Spence v. Washington, 418 U.S. 405 (1974)
Time, Inc. v. Pape, 401 U.S. 279 (1971)
United States Civil Service Commission v. National Association of Letter Carriers, 413 U.S. 548 (1973)
United States v. Orito, 413 U.S. 139 (1973)
United States v. Reidel, 402 U.S. 351 (1971)
United States v. 37 Photographs, 402 U.S. 363 (1971)
United States v. 12 200-Ft. Reels of Super 8 mm Film, 413 U.S. 123 (1973)
Younger v. Harris, 401 U.S. 37 (1971)

INDEX